STREET FRENCH 3

To order the accompanying cassette for

STREET FRENCH 3

See the coupon on the last page for details

STREET FRENCH 3

The Best of Naughty French

David Burke

John Wiley & Sons, Inc.

New York • Chichester • Weinheim • Brisbane • Singapore • Toronto

Design and Production: Optima PrePress
Copy Editor: Nicolas Caron
Front Cover Illustration: Ty Semaka
Inside Illustrations: Ty Semaka

ISBN 0-471-13900-9

Printed in the United States of America
10 9 8 7 6 5

This book is dedicated to my "sister," my shining star, my soul mate:
Lee Murphy.

ACKNOWLEDGMENTS

I can't thank Nicholas Caron enough for his invaluable assistance as copy editor of this book and actor in the audiocassette. Once again, he made these phases of production wonderfully enjoyable and effortless.

I'm forever grateful for finding Ty Semaka, a gifted illustrator who never ceases to amaze me with drawings that are infinitely clever, hilarious, and exciting.

I consider myself so very fortunate to have been under the wing of PJ Dempsey, my wonderful senior editor at John Wiley & Sons. There is no way to mention PJ's name without using adjectives like affable, charming, contagiously energetic, and talented. I also want to give a big thank-you to Chris Jackson, assistant editor, and Elaine O'Neal, editorial assistant. They have been unfailingly accessible, friendly, and supportive.

My associate managing editor, Benjamin Hamilton of John Wiley & Sons, deserves a big *"Chapeau!"* for being one of the most helpful, warm, and gracious people I've had the pleasure of working with.

Last, but certainly not least, I owe an enormous debt of gratitude to Gerry Helferich, my publisher. His insight, support, and enthusiasm created the essential foundation behind this series.

CONTENTS

INTRODUCTION

You may be asking yourself, "What purpose could a book about French obscenities possibly serve other than simply to create shock value by listing gratuitous vulgar words and expressions?" There are three simple answers: (1) to avoid embarrassment; (2) to understand fully a conversation between native speakers; and (3) survival.

Although many teachers prefer not to acknowledge this fact, obscenities are a living part of everyday French. They are used in movies, television and radio shows, news broadcasts, books, newspapers, magazines, etc.

Those who are not completely familiar with the French language often find themselves in awkward or embarrassing situations by using a word in such a way as to create a double meaning or a sexual innuendo. When I was a student living in Paris, an American girl accidently informed the entire classroom that her mother always has sexual intercourse with her father at the front door upon entering the house:

> En rentrant, mon père aime **baiser** ma mère à la porte.

What she meant to say was:

> En rentrant, mon père **fait un baiser** à ma mère à la porte."

Not having a firm grasp on popular French obscenities, she was quite unaware that she had just made a serious yet entertaining *faux pas*, since *"baiser"* can be used as a noun as well as a verb. As a noun, it simply means "a kiss." However, as a verb it takes on the slang meaning of "to fornicate."

STREET FRENCH 3 is the first step-by-step approach of its kind which explores the most common expletives and obscenities used in France. This knowledge is an essential tool in self-defense for nonnative speakers as well as an entertaining guide for native speakers who may not be aware of how colorful the French language truly is.

STREET FRENCH 3 is a self-teaching guide made up of ten chapters, each divided into three primary parts:

■ DIALOGUE

Twenty to thirty popular French terms and idioms are presented as they may be heard in an actual conversation. A translation of the dialogue in standard English is always given on the opposite page, followed by an important phonetic version of the dialogue as it would actually be spoken by a French native. This page will prove vital to any nonnative, since the French tend to rely heavily on contractions, reductions, and other shortcuts in pronunciation.

■ VOCABULARY

This section spotlights all of the slang terms that were used in the dialogue and offers:

1. An example of usage for each entry.
2. The same example rewritten as it may *actually* be spoken by a native speaker. Here you will encounter two symbols:
   (1) ＿＿ an underline indicating:
      a. where a contraction/reduction would be commonly made when spoken; or
      b. where a personal pronoun has been added.
         SEE: *STREET FRENCH 1, Popular Usage of Objective Case Personal Pronouns & Ça, p. 102.*
      (2) ~ a squiggle indicating where *ne* has been dropped.
3. An English translation of the example.
4. In addition, synonyms, antonyms, variations, or special notes are offered to give you a complete sense of the word or expression.

■ A CLOSER LOOK SECTION

This section introduces common idioms and slang pertaining to a specific category such as *obscene name-calling, body parts in slang, etc.*

Whether you're a native of France or a visitor, **STREET FRENCH 3** will prove to be an essential yet hilarious guide to the darker and more *colorful* side of one of the world's most romantic languages.

David Burke
Author

Legend

verb

a term or expression opposite in meaning of the main entry in boldface

boldface words in parentheses are used before the main entry — they appear after the main entry for alphabetization purposes only i.e. *to bet booted.*

literal translation

a common variation of the main entry in boldface

noun

additional information about the main entry in boldface

reserved note (black on white) - useful information about the entry directly above

adjective

expression

a term or expression equivalent in meaning to the main entry in boldface

useful information about the main entry

bend (to) *v.* to be flexible.
ANTONYM: **give an inch (not to)** *exp.* (usually used in the negative) to be very inflexible.

booted (to get) *exp.* to get fired · **(lit.):** to get kicked out by someone in uniform (who typically wears boots).
VARIATION: **get the boot (to)** *exp.*

poll *n.* the place where voting takes place (usually in the plural: *polls).*
ALSO: **straw poll** *n.* a random sampling of opinion.
NOTE: This comes from drawing straws which is used to insure that participants are chosen at random.

dysfunctional *adj.* ineffective.

get to the bottom of something (to) *exp.* to identify something.
SYNONYM: **zero in on something (to)** *exp.*

gubernatorial race *exp.* a contest for the election of governor.
NOTE: **gubernatorial** *adj.* having to do with a governor.

LEÇON UNE - Euphemisms & Dating Terms

Il m'a posé un lapin!

(trans.): He stood me up!
(lit.): He put me a rabbit!

Leçon Une

Josette: Figures-toi qu'il m'a **posé un lapin**! **Zut alors**! Encore un **crétin** qui m'a **fait marcher**.

Cécile: Les hommes, *c'est* [1] tous des **tombeurs** qui sont **portés sur la chose**. Ils voient passer une **nana bien roulée** et *se mettent à* [2] **flirter** en se disant que c'est un **paillasson** ou bien une **pucelle**. Mais dès qu'ils pensent que tu veux **leur mettre le grappin dessus**, ils te **plaquent**.

Josette: Remarque, il n'y a pas que les hommes. Ma sœur est aussi comme ça. La semaine dernière, elle a eu un **rencart** avec un **vieux bonze** qui **a le démon de midi**. A mon avis, il doit aimer **les prendre au berceau** parce que ma sœur *fait* [3] seize ans **à tout casser**! De toute façon, cela a été le **coup de foudre**. Ils se **faisaient du pied** au restaurant, **se bécotaient** au parc, et **se faisaient des mamours** au cinéma. Ils étaient **mordus** l'un de l'autre. Mais hier, elle l'a plaqué parce qu'il est devenu trop sérieux!

Cécile: Mais pourquoi l'amour est-il si douleureux *des fois*? [4] Bon, le prochain *mec* [5] qui se met à flirter avec moi, je vais lui dire de **fiche le camp** et d'aller s'acheter un **journal de cul**!

2

Lesson One

Translation in English

He stood
me up!

Josette: Can you imagine he **stood me up**! **Darn**! Yet another **jerk** who **led me on**.

Cécile: Men. *They're* all **playboys** who are **obsessed with sex**. They see a **hot chick** walk by and they *start* **flirting**, figuring that she's either an **easy lay** or a **virgin**. But as soon as they think you want to **put the bite on them**, they **drop you**.

Josette: Listen, it's not just guys. My sister is like that, too. Last week, she had a **date** with an **old goat** who's **getting horny in midlife**. If you ask me, he must like **robbing the cradle** because my sister *looks like* she's sixteen years old **at the outside**! In any case, it was **love at first sight**. They'd **play footsie** at the restaurant, **make out** in the park, and **grope each other** at the movies. They were **totally in love** with each other. But yesterday, she jilted him because he got too serious!

Cécile: Why is love so painful *sometimes*? Well, the next *guy* who starts flirting with me, I'm going to tell him to **beat it** and go buy himself a **dirty magazine**!

Leçon Une 🔊

Dialogue in slang as it would be spoken

Y m'a posé un lapin!

Josette: Figures-toi qu'y m'a **posé un lapin**! **Zut alors**! Encore un **crétin** qui m'a **fait marcher**.

Cécile: Les hommes, *c'est* tous des **tombeurs** qui sont **portés sur la chose**. Y voient passer une **nana bien roulée** et s'*mettent à flirter* en s'disant que c't'un **paillasson** ou bien une **pucelle**. Mais dès qu'y pensent que tu veux **leur mett' le grappin d'ssus**, y t'**plaquent**.

Josette: Remarque, y a pas qu'les hommes. Ma sœur, elle est aussi comme ça. La s'maine dernière, elle a eu un **rencart** avec un **vieux bonze** qui **a l'démon d'midi**. A mon avis, y doit aimer **les prendr'au berceau** pasque ma sœur, è *fait* seize ans **à tout casser**! De toute façon, cela a été le **coup d'foudre**. Y s'**faisaient du pied** au resto, **s'bécotaient** au parc, et **s'faisaient des mamours** au ciné. Y z'étaient **mordus** l'un d'l'autre. Mais hier, è l'a plaqué pasqu'il est dev'nu trop sérieux!

Cécile: Mais pourquoi l'amour est-il si douleureux *des fois*? Bon, le prochain *mec* qui se met à flirter avec moi, je vais lui dire de **fiche le camp** et d'aller s'ach'ter un **journal de cul**!

4

Vocabulary

```
┌─────────────────────────────────────────────────────────────────────┐
│                 FOOTNOTES FROM THE DIALOGUE                           │
```

(1) _c'est_:

You'll notice that the singular form of the verb _être_ was used in the phrase: _Les hommes, c'**est** tous des tombeurs_, even though the object _(tombeurs)_ is indeed plural. This is a very common construction in spoken French.

(2) _mettre à (se)_:

To begin, to start: _Quand elle m'a vu, elle **s'est mise à** pleurer;_ When she saw me, she started crying.

(3) _faire_:

When the verb _faire_ (literally "to make" or "to do") is used in reference to age, the connotation becomes "to appear," "to look": _Ta mère **fait** très jeune!;_ Your mother looks very young!

(4) _des fois_:

On occasion, sometimes • (lit.): some times.

(5) _mec_:

The masculine noun _mec_ is one of the most popular French slang words for "guy" or "dude."

à tout casser _adv._ at the most, at the outside • (lit.): to break everything.

   example: Sa mère doit avoir trente ans **à tout casser**!

   translation: His mother must be thirty years old **at the outside**!

   as spoken: Sa mère, <u>è</u> doit avoir trente ans **à tout casser**!

   ALSO: **à tout casser** _adv._ total, complete.

   example: Eric est un idiot **à tout casser**!

   translation: Eric is a **total** idiot!

   as spoken: Eric, <u>c't'</u>un idiot **à tout casser**!

bécoter (se) *v.* to kiss, "to neck" • (lit.): to "beak" (since this comes from the masculine noun *bec* meaning "the beak of a bird").

> example: J'ai vu Henri et Madeleine **se bécoter** derrière la maison!
>
> translation: I saw Henri and Madeleine **making out** behind the house!
>
> as spoken: J'ai vu Henri et Madeleine **s'bécoter** derrière la maison!

>> **NOTE:** **bécot** *m.* a kiss.
>>
>> **SYNONYM -1:** **bisou** *m.*
>>
>> **SYNONYM -2:** **bise** *f.*

bien roulée (être) *adj. (said of a woman)* to be voluptuous, to have a great body • (lit.): to be well-rounded.

> example: Elle est **bien roulée** pour son âge!
>
> translation: She's got a **great figure** for her age!
>
> as spoken: [no change]

> **SYNONYM:** **bien balancée (être)** *adj.* • (lit.): to be well-balanced.

coup de foudre *m.* love at first sight • (lit.): thunder clap.

> example: Quand j'ai vu ta maman pour la première fois, c'était le **coup de foudre**!
>
> translation: When I saw your mother for the first time, it was **love at first sight**!
>
> as spoken: Quand j'ai vu ta maman pour la première fois, c'était l'**coup d'foudre**!

crétin *m.* jerk • (lit.): cretin.

> example: Ce **crétin** de Robert m'a demandé de sortir avec lui demain soir.
>
> translation: That **jerk** Robert asked me to go out with him tomorrow night.
>
> as spoken: Ce **crétin** d'Robert, y m'a d'mandé d'sortir avec lui d'main soir.

démon de midi (avoir le) *exp.* to have a midlife crisis, to be a dirty old(er) man or woman • (lit.): to have the devil strike at high noon (i.e. in the middle of one's life).

> example: A l'âge de cinquante ans, M. DuBois sort tous les soirs avec différentes nanas. Je suppose qu'il **a le démon de midi**.
>
> translation: At age fifty, Mr. DuBois goes out every night with all sorts of girls. I guess he **has the midlife hornies**!
>
> as spoken: A l'âge de cinquante ans, M. DuBois, y̲ sort tous les soirs avec différentes nanas. Je suppose qu'il **a l̲'démon d̲'midi**.

faire des mamours à quelqu'un *exp.* to be kissy-kissy with someone, to be all lovey-dovey with someone, to caress someone.

> example: Ils **se font des mamours** en public. Ça m'énerve, ça!
>
> translation: They're **all touchy-feely with each other** in public. I can't stand that!
>
> as spoken: Y̲ **s̲'font des mamours** en public. Ça m'énerve, ça!

> **SYNONYM -1:**   **faire des papouilles à quelqu'un** *exp.* to touch someone all over • (lit.): to make sexual touches to someone.

> **SYNONYM -2:**   **peloter** *v.* to grope, to neck • (lit.): to ball up together like a ball of wool.

> > **NOTE:**   **pelotage** *m.* groping, necking.
>
> example: On a fait une partie de **pelotage** pendant trois heures hier soir!
>
> translation: We engaged in a **makeout session** for three hours last night!
>
> as spoken: On a fait une partie d̲'**pelotage** pendant trois heures hier soir!

faire marcher quelqu'un *exp.* to lead someone on • (lit.): to make someone walk.

> example: Tu me **fais marcher** depuis deux mois et hier j'ai appris que tu es marié!
>
> translation: You've been **leading me on** for two months and yesterday I found out that you're married!
>
> as spoken: Tu m'**fais marcher** depuis deux mois et hier j'ai appris qu't'es marié!

fiche le camp *exp.* to leave, "to beat it" • (lit.): to make the camp.

> example: Tu m'énerves! **Fiche le camp**!
>
> translation: You're bugging me! **Beat it**!
>
> as spoken: [no change]
>
> **VARIATION:** **foutre le camp** *exp.* (a stronger variation of: *fiche le camp*).

flirter *v.* (*Americanism*) to flirt.

> example: Georges a **flirté** avec moi toute la soirée.
>
> translation: George **flirted** with me all night.
>
> as spoken: Georges, il a **flirté** avec moi toute la soirée.

journal de cul *m.* a dirty magazine • (lit.): a newspaper of butt.

> example: Je crois que mon frère cache des **journaux de cul** sous son matelas.
>
> translation: I think my brother hides **dirty magazines** under his mattress.
>
> as spoken: J'crois qu'mon frère, y cache des **journaux d'cul** sous son mat'las.
>
> **NOTE:** It is important to note that although the term *cul* literally means "ass," it does not carry the same degree of vulgarity as it does in English, and is therefore used much for frequently.

mettre le grappin sur quelqu'un *exp.* to put the bite on someone • (lit.): to put the grab on someone.

> example: Quand Marc a vu passer Josette, il s'est tellement amouraché d'elle qu'il lui a **mis le grappin dessus** tout de suite!

> translation: When Mark saw Josette pass by, he was so infatuated with her that he **put the bite on her** right away!

> as spoken: Quand Marc, <u>il</u> a vu passer Josette, <u>y</u> s'ést tellement amouraché d'elle qu'<u>y</u> lui a **mis <u>l'</u>grappin <u>d'</u>ssus** tout <u>d'</u>suite!

> **NOTE:** **amouracher de quelqu'un (s')** *exp.* to be infatuated with someone (from the noun *amour* meaning "love").

mordu(e) de quelqu'un (être) *adj.* to have a crush on someone • (lit.): to be bitten by someone.

> example: Tu as vu la nouvelle étudiante dans notre cours de biologie? Je suis **mordu d'elle**!

> translation: Did you see the new student in our biology class? I have such a **crush on her**!

> as spoken: <u>T'</u>as vu la nouvelle étudiante dans no<u>t'</u> cours de bio~? <u>J'</u>suis **mordu d'elle**!

paillasson *m.* an easy lay • (lit.): a doormat.

> example: Tu es sorti avec Margot? On dit que c'est un **paillasson**, celle-là!

> translation: You went out with Margot? They they she's a real **easy lay**!

> as spoken: <u>T'</u>es sorti avec Margot? On dit <u>qu'c't'</u>un **paillasson**, celle-là!

> **SYNONYM:** **cuisse légère (avoir la)** *exp.* said of someone who is an easy lay • (lit.): to have a light thigh (since they're always up in the air).

pied (faire du) *exp.* to play footsie • (lit.): to make (with the) foot.

　　　　example:　Le dîner d'affaires était horrible! Quand nous étions tous
　　　　　　　　　　à table, le client a commencé a me **faire du pied**!

　　　translation:　The business dinner was horrible! When we were all at
　　　　　　　　　　the table, the client started **playing footsie** with me!

　　　as spoken:　Le dîner d'affaires, <u>il</u> était horrible! Quand nous étions
　　　　　　　　　　tous à table, le client, <u>il</u> a commencé a m'**faire du pied**!

plaquer *v.* to jilt, to dump • (lit.): [none].

　　　　example:　Après onze ans de mariage, Laurent a **plaqué** sa
　　　　　　　　　　femme.

　　　translation:　After eleven years of marriage, Laurent **dumped** his wife.

　　　as spoken:　Après onze ans <u>d'</u>mariage, Laurent, <u>il</u> a **plaqué** sa
　　　　　　　　　　femme.

> **VARIATION:**　**plaquouser** *v.*

> **SYNONYM:**　**laisser choir** *exp.* • (lit.): to let (someone) drop.

porté(e) sur la chose (être) *exp.* to be obsessed with sex • (lit.): to
be carried on the thing.

　　　　example:　Tous ces journaux de cul sont à toi? Mais tu es **porté
　　　　　　　　　　sur la chose** ou quoi?!

　　　translation:　All these dirty magazines are yours? Do you have **sex
　　　　　　　　　　on the brain** or what?!

　　　as spoken:　Tous ces journaux <u>d'</u>cul, <u>y</u> sont à toi? Mais <u>t'</u>es **porté
　　　　　　　　　　sur la chose** ou quoi?!

poser un lapin à quelqu'un *exp.* to stand someone up (on a date
or meeting) • (lit.): to pose a rabbit to someone.

　　　　example:　Ça fait une heure que je l'attends. Il m'a **posé un lapin**
　　　　　　　　　　pour la dernière fois!

　　　translation:　I've been waiting for him for an hour. He's **stood me
　　　　　　　　　　up** for the last time!

　　　as spoken:　Ça fait une heure <u>qu'j'</u>l'attends. <u>Y</u> m'a **posé un lapin**
　　　　　　　　　　pour la dernière fois!

prendre au berceau (les) *exp.* to rob the cradle • (lit.): to take them from the cradle.

> example: Hier soir j'ai vu Jean-Claude avec une très jeune fille. Evidemment il aime **les prendre au berceau**!

> translation: Last night I saw Jean-Claude with a very young girl. Evidently he likes **to rob the cradle**!

> as spoken: Hier soir j'ai vu Jean-Claude avec une très jeune fille. Evidemment il aime **les prendr'au berceau**!

puceau/pucelle *n.* virgin.

> example: A l'âge de trente ans, Jeanne est toujours **pucelle**.

> translation: At thirty years of age, Jeanne is still a **virgin**.

> as spoken: A l'âge de trente ans, Jeanne, <u>elle</u> est toujours **pucelle**.

rencart *m.* (from *rendez-vous*) date.

> example: Je dois me dépêcher. J'ai un **rencart** avec Maurice ce soir!

> translation: I have to hurry. I have a **date** with Maurice tonight!

> as spoken: <u>J'</u>dois <u>m'</u>dépêcher. J'ai un **rencart** avec Maurice ce soir!

> **NOTE -1:** Also spelled: *rencard*.

> **NOTE -2:** **rencarter** *v.* to have a date with someone.

tombeur *m.* a womanizer, seducer, "Don Juan" • (lit.): a faller (i.e. girls fall before him or under his charm).

> example: Eric va se marier?! Mais c'est un sacré **tombeur**, celui-là! Il ne sera jamais content avec une seule fille dans sa vie.

> translation: Eric is getting married?! But the guy's a real **womanizer**! He'll never be happy with just one girl in his life.

> as spoken: Eric, <u>y</u> va <u>s'</u>marier?! Mais <u>c't'</u>un sacré **tombeur**, <u>cui</u>-là! <u>Y</u> ~ <u>s'</u>ra jamais content avec une seule fille dans sa vie.

> **SYNONYM:** **dragueur** *m.*

> > **NOTE:** **draguer** *v.* to cruise (for guys or girls), to flirt.

vieux bonze *m.* old man, an "old fart" • (lit.): old buddhist monk.

> example: Carole est très jeune et très jolie. Je ne sais pas pourquoi elle sort avec un **vieux bonze** comme celui-là.

> translation: Carole is very young and very pretty. I don't know why she goes out with an **old fart** like him.

> as spoken: Carole, <u>elle</u> est très jeune et très jolie. <u>C'hais</u> pas pourquoi <u>è</u> sort avec un **vieux bonze** comme <u>ç'ui-là</u>.

Zut alors! *interj.* Darn!

> example: **Zut alors**! J'ai laissé mes clés au restaurant!

> translation: **Darn**! I left my keys at the restaurant!

> as spoken: **Zut alors**! J'ai laissé mes clés au <u>resto</u>!

> **NOTE:** *Zut* may also be used all by itself. However, *alors* is commonly used for extra emphasis.

A CLOSER LOOK:
Slang Relating to Euphemisms, Dating, Relationships & the Sexes

Since the French are known for being the consummate romantics, it seems only logical to begin by presenting some of the most common terms used in courting. Once you have been armed with the following arsenal of expressions and slang terms, you will surely be ready to *draguer* ("to pick up potential dates")!

Aimer Quelqu'un
(to have a crush on someone)

air pour quelqu'un (l'avoir en l') *exp.* (said of a man) to get an erection over someone • (lit.): to have it in the air for someone.

amouracher de quelqu'un (s') *v.* to have a crush on someone, to be infatuated with someone (from *amour* meaning "love").

NOTE: This comes from the masculine noun *amour* meaning "love."

bander pour quelqu'un
v. (said of a man) to get an erection over someone
• (lit.): to tighten for someone.

bonne (avoir quelqu'un à la) *exp.* • (lit.): to have someone in good (standing).

chipé(e) pour quelqu'un (être) *adj.* to be infatuated with someone.

chouette (avoir quelqu'un à la) *exp.* to think someone is nice.

coiffer de quelqu'un (se) *exp. (outdated but used in jest)* • (lit.): to style one's hair with someone.

craquer pour quelqu'un to like someone.
NOTE: **craquant(e) (être)** *adj.* to be seductive, cute, adorable.

croquer pour quelqu'un (en) *exp.* to crunch some for someone.

enticher de quelqu'un (s') *v.* to have a light crush on someone.

mordu(e) de quelqu'un (être) *exp.* to have a big crush on someone • (lit.): to be bitten by someone.
NOTE: **mordu(e)** *n.* fanatic (*un mordu de tennis:* a tennis buff).

peau (avoir quelqu'un dans la) *exp.* to have a strong sexual attraction to someone • (lit.): to have someone in the skin.

pépin pour quelqu'un (avoir un/le) *exp.* to have a crush on someone • (lit.): to have a/the apple pip for someone (from the expression *être le pépin de ses yeux* meaning "to be the apple [pip] of one's eye").

pincer pour quelqu'un (en) *exp.* to have a crush on someone • (lit.): to pinch some for someone.

raffoler de quelqu'un *v.* to be crazy about someone.
NOTE: This comes from the adjective *fou/folle* meaning "crazy."

tenir pour quelqu'un (en) *exp.* to have a crush on someone • (lit.): to have some of it (affection) for someone.

touch à quelqu'un (faire une) *exp.* to seduce

someone, to make a good impression on someone • (lit.): to make a touch (to someone).

toquade pour quelqu'un (avoir une) *exp.* to have a strong crush on someone.

toqué(e) de quelqu'un (être) *exp.* a variation of: *toquade pour quelqu'un (avoir une).*

Battre (se)
(to fight)

accrochage *m.* **1.** a fight or quarrel • **2.** a traffic accident.

accrocher (s') *v.*
NOTE: **accrochage** *m.* a quarrel.

amocher (s') *v.* to beat each other up, to mess each other up physically • (lit.): to make each other look ugly.
NOTE: **moche** *adj. (very popular)* ugly.

asticotage *m.* a quarrel • (lit.): a "maggot"-ing.

attrapade *f.* a quarrel • (lit.): a "catching."

attrapage *m.* a quarrel • (lit.): a "catching."

badaboum *m.* a big fight.

bagarrer (se) *v.*
NOTE: **bagarre** *f.* a fight.

baroud *m.* a big fight.
VARIATION -1: **barouffe** *m.* (also spelled: *barouf*).
VARIATION -2: **baroufle** *m.* a quarrel.

baston *f.* a big fight.
NOTE: This is from the verb *bâtonner* meaning "to hit with a stick (a *bâton*), to flog, to cane."

bigorner (se) .
NOTE: **bigorne** *f.* a big fight.

bisbille *f.* a quarrel.

bouffer le nez (se) *exp.* to yell at each other • (lit.): to eat each other's nose (said of two people who are yelling inches away from each other).

NOTE: In this expression, any slang synonym for *nez*, meaning "nose," could be used in its place such as: *pif, blair, tarrin, etc.*

chambard *m.* a big fight.

chambardement *m.* a big fight.

cogne *f.* a big fight • (lit.): from the verb *cogner* meaning "to hit" or "to clobber."

corrida *f.* a big fight.

crêper la tignasse (se) *exp.* said of two women in a physical fight where each woman is pulling the other's hair, to cat fight • (lit.): to crimp each other's hair.

NOTE -1: **tignasse** *f.* hair.

NOTE -2: In this expression, any slang synonyms for the slang word *tignasse*, meaning "hair," could be used in its place such as: **tifs** *m.pl.*, **douilles** *f.pl.*, **crayons** *m.pl.*, etc.

NOTE -3 **crêpage de tignasse** *m.* a hair-pulling fight • (lit.): a crimping of the hair.

crêper le chignon (se) *exp.* • (lit.): said of two women in a physical fight where each

woman is pulling the other's hair • (lit.): to crimp each other's hair buns.

NOTE: **crêpage de chignons** *m.* a physical fight between two women (who look as though they are messing each other's hair) • (lit.): a crimping of hair buns.

crocheter (se) *v.* • (lit.): to hook into each other.

NOTE: **crochetage** *m.* a big fight.

échanger des politesses *exp.* an ironic expression literally meaning "to exchange polite words."

engueulade *f.* a quarrel.

NOTE: **engueuler (s')** *v.* to yell and scream and each other.

escagasser *v.* (*used in southern France*).

expliquer (s') *v.* • (lit.): to explain oneself.

VARIATION: **s'expliquer dehors** *exp.* to fight outside, to step outside • (lit.): to explain oneself outside.

flanquer sur la gueule (se) *exp.* to hit each other in the face or mouth • (lit.): to throw oneself at each other's face or mouth.

VARIATION: flanquer des coups, des gnons (se) *exp.* to punch each other
• (lit.): to throw hits at each other.

NOTE -1: flanquer *v.* to throw, to give.

NOTE -2: gueule *f.* derogatory for "mouth" or "face" since its literal translation is "the mouth of an animal."

flanquer une peignée (se) *exp.* said of two women in a physical fight, consequently ruining each other's hairdo • (lit.): to give each other a combing.

NOTE -1: flanquer *v.* to throw, to give.

VARIATION: peigner (se) *v.* to comb each other's hair.

foutre sur la gueule (se) *exp.* a stronger variation of: *flanquer sur la gueule (se)*.

foutre une peignée (se) *exp.* a stronger variation of: *flanquer une peignée (se)*.

frotter (se) *v.* • (lit.): to rub each other.

grabuge *m.* a big fight.

prise de bec *f.* a quarrel
• (lit.): taking of the beak.

NOTE: bec *m.* mouth
• (lit.): beak (of a bird).

prise de gueule *f.* a quarrel
• (lit.): taking of the mouth.

NOTE: gueule *f.* derogatory for "mouth" or "face" since its literal translation is "the mouth of an animal."

riffer (se) *v.* to quarrel.

NOTE -1: rif *m.* a big fight.

NOTE -2: rififi *m.* a big fight.

rixe *f.* a fight.

savon *m.* a quarrel • (lit.): soap.

NOTE: passer un savon (se faire) *exp.* to get yelled at.

secouer la poêle à marrons *exp.* • (lit.): to shake the roasted chestnut pan.

NOTE: marron *m.* blackeye
• (lit.): chestnut.

sonnage *m.* a big fight
• (lit.): that which makes the bells ring (from the verb *sonner* meaning "to ring.")

tabac *m.* a quarrel
• (lit.): tobacco.

tapage *m.* a loud quarrel
• (lit.): loud noise.

> **ALSO:** **tapage nocturne** *m.* late-night noise, noise in the middle of the night.

torchée *f.* a quarrel • (lit.): a wiping.

> **ALSO:** **flanquer une torchée (se faire)** *exp.* to get beaten up.

torcher (se) *v.* to quarrel
• (lit.): to wipe each other (out).

> **ALSO:** **torcher le cul à quelqu'un** *exp.* to beat someone up • *Je vais te torcher le cul!*; I gonna pulverise you!; (lit.): I'm going to wipe your ass!

> **NOTE:** **torchée** *f.* a large fight or quarrel.

Belle Fille
(pretty girl)

beau châssis (avoir un) *exp.* said of a girl with an exceptionally beautiful body • (lit.): to have a handsome chassis.

beau linge *m.* high-class woman, a woman of style and sophistication • (lit.): nice linen.

beau (petit) lot *m.* • said of a woman who has a beautiful face and body • (lit.): nice (little) package.

belle mécanique *f.* • said of a woman with a beautiful body (lit.): nice mechanics.

bien balancée (être) *exp.* said of a woman with a beautiful body, to be put together well • (lit.): to be nicely balanced or thrown together.

bien roulée (être) *exp.* said of a woman with a beautiful body, to be put together well • (lit.): to be rolled together well.

loute *f.* a pretty woman or girl, a foxy woman or girl.

prix de Diane *m.*

> **NOTE:** The *prix de Diane* is a famous horse race in Paris.

Caresser
(to fondle)

chatouilles (faire des) *f.pl.*
> **NOTE:** From the verb
> *chatouiller* meaning "to tickle."

mamours (faire des) *m.pl.*
to kiss and fondle.

papouilles (faire des) *f.pl.*
to fondle sexually.

patouilles (faire des) *f.pl.*
> **NOTE:** From the feminine
> plural noun "pattes" (literally
> meaning "paws") used to
> mean "hands" in French slang.

pattes d'araignée (faire des) *f.pl.* to do light touching
with the tips of the fingers
• (lit.): to make spider feet.

pelotage *m.* heavy petting.

peloter *v.* to pet heavily.

toucher (se) *v.* to touch
one's (or each other's) genitals
• (lit.): to touch oneself or
each other.

Embrasser
(to kiss)

bécoter *v.*
> **NOTE:** **bécot** *m.* a kiss.

bise à quelqu'un (faire une) *exp.* • (lit.): to give
someone a little kiss.

bécot à quelqu'un (faire un) *exp.* • (lit.): to give
someone a little kiss (generally
on the cheek).

bec à quelqu'un (faire un) *exp.* • (lit.): to give
someone a beak.
> **NOTE:** The masculine noun
> *bec*, literally meaning "beak of
> a bird," is commonly used in
> French slang to mean
> "mouth."

bisou à quelqu'un (faire un) *exp.* • (lit.): to give
someone a little kiss.

fourrer la langue à quelqu'un *exp.* to give someone a "French" kiss • (lit.): to stuff one's tongue to someone.

galoche à quelqu'un (faire une) *exp.* to give someone a "French" kiss • (lit.): to make a boot to someone.

lécher (se) *v.* to kiss each other deeply, to "suck face," to "French" kiss • (lit.): to lick each other.

lécher la gueule (se) *exp.* to "suck face" • (lit.): to lick each other's mouth/face.
NOTE: When the feminine noun *gueule,* literally meaning "the mouth of an animal," is used in reference to a person, its connotation is "mouth" or "face," depending on the context.

rouler une galoche *exp.* to "French" kiss • (lit.): to roll a shoe.

rouler un paleau *exp.* to "French" kiss.

rouler une escalope *exp.* to "French" kiss • (lit.): to roll a thin slice of meat.

rouler un patin *exp.* to "French" kiss • (lit.): to roll a skate.

rouler des saucisses *exp.* (*said of two people kissing*) to "French" kiss • (lit.): to roll sausages (referring to the look of the tongue).

sucer la poire (se) *exp.* to "suck face" • (lit.): to suck each other's pear.
NOTE: **poire** *f.* face • (lit.): pear.

Euphémismes
(euphemisms)

caca *m.* (child language) •
1. excrement, "poo-poo" •
2. gross, filthy • (lit.): caca.

example (1): Attention de ne pas marcher dans le **caca**! Il y a des chiens dans ce quartier.

as spoken: Attention d'ne pas marcher dans l'**caca**! ~ Y a des chiens dans c'quartier.

translation: Be careful not to step in the **poo-poo**! There are dogs in this neighborhood.

example (2): Ne te mets pas ça dans la bouche! C'est du **caca**!

as spoken: ~ Te mets pas ça dans la bouche! C'est du **caca**!

translation: Don't put that in your mouth! It's **filthy**!

NOTE: **caca (faire)** *exp.* (*child language*) to go poo-poo.

example: Tu as **fait caca** avant d'aller au lit?

as spoken: T'as **fait caca** avant d'aller au lit?

translation: Did you **go poo-poo** before going to bed?

flûte *interj.* darn.

example: **Flûte**! J'ai perdu mes clés!

as spoken: [no change]

translation: **Darn**! I lost my keys

grosse commission (faire sa) *exp.* to go poo-poo, to go number two
• (lit.): to do one's big portion.

example: Attention! Le chien a **fait sa grosse commission** sur le pas de la porte!

translation: Watch out! The dog **pooped** on the doorstep!

as spoken: Attention! Le chien, il a **fait sa grosse commission** sur le pas d'la porte!

SEE: **petite commission (faire sa)**, *p. 21*.

mince *interj.* wow.

example: **Mince** alors! Je n'ai jamais rien vu de pareil!

as spoken: **Mince** alors! J'ai jamais rien vu d'pareil!

translation: **Wow**! I've never seen anything like it!

nom de deux *interj.* my gosh.

example: **Nom de deux**! Je ne sais pas comment il a pu faire ça!

as spoken: **Nom de deux**! J'sais pas comment il a pu faire ça!

translation: **My gosh**! I don't know how he did managed to do that!

NOTE: This is a euphemism for *nom de Dieu* meaning "my God" or literally, "(in the) name of God."

petit oiseau *m.* (*child language*) penis, "pee-pee"
• (lit.): little bird.

example: Le bébé passe des heures à tripoter son **petit oiseau**.

translation: The baby spends hours playing with his **pee-pee**.

as spoken: Le bébé, y passe des heures à tripoter son **p'tit oiseau**.

SYNONYM -1: **sifflet** *m.*
• (lit.): whistle.

SYNONYM -2: **zizi** *m.*

petite commission (faire sa) *exp.* to go pee-pee, to go number one • (lit.): to do one's little portion.

example: N'oublie pas de **faire ta petite commission** avant de quitter la maison.

translation: Don't forget to **go number one** before you leave the house.

as spoken: ~ Oublie pas d'**faire ta p'tite commission** avant d'quitter la maison.

SEE: **grosse commission (faire sa)**, *p. 20.*

pipi (faire) *exp.* to go pee-pee.

example: Le chat a **fait pipi** sur le tapis.

as spoken: Le chat, il a **fait pipi** sur l'tapis.

translation: The cat **went pee-pee** on the carpet.

ALSO: **pipi de chat** *m.* poor quality wine or beer
• (lit.): cat pee-pee.

popo *m.* excrement • (lit.): caca.

example: Le chien n'a pas la permission d'entrer dans la maison. La dernière fois, il a fait **popo** dans le salon.

translation: The dog isn't allowed to come into the house. The last time, he **pooped** in the living room.

as spoken: Le chien, il a pas la permission d'entrer dans la maison. La dernière fois, il a fait **popo** dans l'salon.

sacristi *interj. (a common interjection used in comic books)* Holy cow!

example: **Sacristi**! Le loup nous poursuit!

as spoken: **Sacristi**! Le loup, y nous poursuit!

translation: **Holy cow**! The wolf is after us!

SYNONYM -1: **saperlipopette** *interj.*

SYNONYM -2: **saperlotte** *interj.*

SYNONYM -3: **sapristi** *interj.*

Femme/Fille
(woman/girl)

boude *m.* a shorted version of *boudin,* meaning "blood sausage," used to describe a fat woman.

boudin *m.* a fat woman
• (lit.): blood sausage.

bougresse *f. (old-fashioned yet used ironically)* country woman.

carrossée (être bien) to have a beautiful body.
    SEE: carrosserie, *(next entry).*

carrosserie *f.* body (used as: *Quelle carrosserie!;* What a beautiful body!) • (lit.): body of a car.

chipie *f.* a shrew, often used in reference to an ill-tempered little girl.

créature *f.* • (lit.): creature.

donzelle *f.*

fatma *f. (from Arabic)* commonly used to mean "wife" as well.

fatmuche *f.* a slang variation of: *fatma.*
    SEE: fatma, *(previous entry).*

femelle *f.* • (lit.): female.

fendue *f. (very derogatory)*
• (lit.): slit.

frangine *f.* • (lit.): sister.
    NOTE: This is a popular slang term for "sister" or "girl."

garce *f.* bitch.

génisse *f.*

gonzesse *f. (very popular)* girl, "chick."

grognasse *f.* girlfriend
• (lit.): groaner.

harpie *f.* shrew.

lamfé *f.*
    NOTE: This is a *largonji* transformation of the feminine noun *femme* meaning "woman."
    SEE: *Street French 2 - Largonji, p. 216.*

lièvre *m.* • (lit.): hare.

mémé *f.* grandma.

meuf f. (very popular).
   NOTE: This is a verlan transformation of the feminine noun femme meaning "woman."
   SEE: Street French 2 - Verlan, p. 187.

moukère f. (from Arabic).

nana f. (extremely popular) woman, girl, "chick."

nénesse f.

nénette f.

paillasse f. • (lit.): straw matress.

paillasson m. • (lit.): door mat.

peau (de vache) f. bitch
   • (lit.): (cow) skin.

pépée f.

pétasse f. (derogatory).

pouffiasse f. (derogatory).

poule f. woman or prostitute
   • (lit.): a hen.

poulette f. • (lit.): a young hen.

pouliche f. • (lit.): a young hen.

poupée f. • (lit.): a doll.

rombière f. a fat woman.

souris f. • (lit.): mouse.

typesse f.
   NOTE: **type** m. guy, "dude."

vache f. • (lit.): cow.

Homme
(man)

bougre m. (pejorative)
   • (lit.): country man.

client m. • (lit.): client.

coco m.

frangin m.
   NOTE -1: This is a popular slang term for "brother" or "man."

   NOTE -2: **frangine** f. sister.

gars m. (very popular) guy, "dude."

gugusse m. idiot.

gus m. (very popular).

guss(e) m.

Jules m. guy, boyfriend, "dude."
NOTE: **Julie** f. woman or girl, "chick."

Julot m. guy, "dude."
NOTE: This is a slang variation of: **Jules**.

loulou m.

loustic m.

mec m. (one of the most popular slang words for "guy").

mecqueton m. (also spelled "mecton").
NOTE: This is a slang variation of: **mec**.

numéro m. • (lit.): number.

oiseau m. • (lit.): bird.

paroissien m.
• (lit.): Parishioner.

piaf m. a small man
• (lit.): Parisian sparrow.

pierrot m.

pistolet m. • (lit.): pistol.

tartempion m. also used to mean "so-and-so" or "what's-his-name."

type m. (very popular) guy, "dude."

zèbre m. guy, "dude."
ALSO: **drôle de zèbre** m. weirdo.

zig m. (also spelled "zigue") guy, "dude."

zigomar(d) m.
NOTE: This is a slang variation of: **zig**.

zigoteau m.
NOTE: This is a slang variation of: **zig**.

zigoto m.
NOTE: This is a slang variation of: **zig**.

zouave m. • (lit.): a type of soldier (known for being very tough) in the Napoleonic army.

More Dating Slang

(encore des mots au sujet de l'amour)

baiser en levrette *exp.* to make love doggy-style
• (lit.): to fuck like a greyhound.

baisodrome *m. (any place where sex takes place such as the bedroom, brothel, etc.)* "fuckotorium".
NOTE: This comes from the slang verb *baiser* meaning "to fuck."

ballet bleu *m.* orgy involving young boys under legal age
• (lit.): blue ballet.

ballet rose *m.* orgy involving young girls under legal age
• (lit.): pink ballet.

capote anglaise *m.* condom, "rubber" • (lit.): an English bonnet.

cloque (être en) *exp.* to be knocked up.
SEE: **encloquer**, *p. 25.*

cocu (être) *adj.* to be cuckold.
SEE: **cocufier**, *(next entry).*

cocufier *v.* to be unfaithful to (one's husband).
SEE: **cocu (être)**, *(previous entry).*

dépuceler *v.* to deflower.
NOTE: **puceau / pucelle** *n.* virgin.

encloquer *v.* to knock up.

histoires paillardes *f.pl.* dirty jokes.
SYNONYM -1: **histoires salées** *f.pl.*
• (lit.): salted stories.
SYNONYM -2: **histoires de cul** *f.pl.*
• (lit.): ass stories.
SYNONYM -3: **gauloiseries** *f.pl.*
• (lit.): Gaulish stories.

mains baladeuses (avoir les) *exp.* to have roving hands • (lit.): [same].

partouse *f.* orgy.

partouse à la bague *f.* daisy chain • (lit.): anus game.
NOTE: **partouse** *f.* a slang variant of *partie* meaning "game."

partouse carrée *f.* wife swapping • (lit.): square game or four-person game.

NOTE: **partouse** *f.* a slang variant of: *partie* meaning "game."

partouser *v.* to participate in orgies.

partouzard(e) *n.* one who likes orgies.

poil (être à) *exp.* to be naked
• (lit.): to be to the hair.

ravages (faire des) *exp.* to break hearts • (lit.): to devestate, to wreck havoc.

rentrer la bite sous le bras *exp.* to come home without having scored a date
• (lit.): to come home with the "dick" under one's arm.

NOTE: **bite** *f.* penis
• (lit.): bitt or bollard (on a ship).

soixante-neuf (faire le) *exp.* to sixty-nine (involving two partners who have positioned their bodies to be able to engage in mutual oral sex).

LEÇON DEUX - Nonvulgar Insults & Putdowns

Il me casse les pieds, celui-là!

(trans.): That guy drives me crazy!
(lit.): That guy breaks my feet!

Leçon Deux

Dialogue in Slang

Véronique: Tiens! Voilà, cet **avorton** de Robert. J'ai l'impression qu'il te suit partout.

Michelle: Oh, **ta gueule**, Véro! Tu sais, personne ne peut le **piffrer** au *boulot* [1] non plus parce que c'est un **faillot**. Si jamais tu arrives en retard, il te dénonce au patron, le **fumier**. C'est un *sacré* [2] **lèche-bottes**, lui. En plus, c'est un **je m'en foutiste** de premier ordre. Il **jacasse** au téléphone toute la journée. C'est une **faignasse**, celui-là.

Véronique: Je ne sortirais jamais avec un **patapouf** pareil. Tu n'as pas vu sa **grosse brioche**? En plus, il est **moche**, a la **casquette en peau de fesses**, et il **cocotte**! Il **tue les mouches à quinze pas**. Et quant à sa personalité, il est **rasoir** et **crâneur**!

Michelle: Oh, il me **casse les pieds**, celui-là!

Translation in English

That guy drives me crazy!

Véronique: Hey! There's that **runt** Robert. I get the feeling that he follows you around everywhere.

Michelle: Oh, **shut up**, Véro! You know, no one can **stand** him at *work* either because he's a **brown-noser**. If you ever arrive late, he reports you to the boss, the **jerk**. He's a *real* **kiss-ass**, that guy. Not only that, he's **doesn't give a damn about anything** big time. He **blabs** on the phone all day. The guy's really **lazy**.

Véronique: I'd never go out with a **lazy fat slob** like that. Didn't you see his **fat gut**? Besides, he's **ugly**, **bald**, and **stinks**! His breath could **kill flies fifteen feet away**. And as for his personality, he's **dull** and a **showoff**!

Michelle: Oh, that guy **drives me crazy**!

Dialogue in slang as it would be spoken

Y m'casse les pieds, çui-là!

Véronique: Tiens! V'là, c't'**avorton** de Robert. J'ai l'impression qu'y t'suit partout.

Michelle: Oh, **ta gueule**, Véro! Tu sais, personne peut l'**piffrer** au *boulot* non plus pasque c't'un **faillot**. Si jamais t'arrives en r'tard, y t'dénonce au patron, l'**fumier**. C't'un *sacré* **lèche-bottes**, lui. En plus, c't'un **j'm'en foutiste** de premier ordre. Y **jacasse** au téléphone toute la journée. C't'une **faignasse**, çui-là.

Véronique: J'sortirais jamais avec un **patapouf** pareil. T'as pas vu sa **grosse brioche**? En plus, il est **moche**, a la **casquette en peau d'fesses**, et y **cocotte**! Y **tue les mouches à quinze pas**. Et quant à sa personalité, il est **rasoir** et **crâneur**!

Michelle: Oh, y m'**casse les pieds**, çui-là!

Vocabulary

FOOTNOTES FROM THE DIALOGUE

(1) _boulot_:

  _m._ One of the most popular slang terms for "work" used by everyone.

(2) _sacré(e)_:

  adj. a real, a blessed • _C'est un **sacré** menteur!;_ He's/She's a blessed liar!

---

avorton _m. (applies to a man)_ runt • (lit.): leftover from an _avortement_ meaning "abortion."

> example: Georges m'a dit qu'il veut devenir mannequin! Mais il rêve, ce petit **avorton**!

> translation: George told me that he wants to become a model! That little **runt** is dreaming!

> as spoken: Georges, y̲ m'a dit qu'y̲ veut dev̲'nir mann̲'quin! Mais y̲ rêve, ce p̲'tit **avorton**!

casquette en peau de fesses (avoir la) _exp._ to be totally bald
• (lit.): to have a cap made out of butt skin.

> example: Ça fait dix ans que je n'ai pas vu Guillaume. Il a toujours eu de beaux cheveux, lui. C'est pour ça que j'étais stupéfait de voir qu'il a une **casquette en peau de fesses** maintenant!

> translation: It's been ten years since I've seen Guillaume. He's always had such beautiful hair. That's why I was shocked to see that he's **totally bald** now!

> as spoken: Ça fait dix ans qu̲'j'ai pas vu Guillaume. Il a toujours eu d̲'beaux ch̲'veux, lui. C'est pour ça qu̲'j'étais stupéfait d̲'voir qu'il a une **casquette en peau d̲'fesses** maintenant!

casser les pieds à quelqu'un *exp.* to bug the daylights out of someone • (lit.): to break someone's feet.

> example: Tu commences à **me casser les pieds** avec tes questions interminables!
>
> translation: You're starting **to bug the daylights out of me** with your interminable questions!
>
> as spoken: Tu commences à **m'casser les pieds** avec tes questions interminables!
>
> **NOTE -1:** This expression is a mild version of the popular expression, *casser les couilles à quelqu'un* meaning "to piss someone off" or literally "to break someone's balls." This expression is also commonly shortened to: *Tu me les casses!* where *"les"* replaces *"couilles."*
>
> **NOTE -2:** **casse-pieds** *m.* an annoying person • (lit.): foot-breaker.
>
> > **NOTE:** This is a mild version of the popular slang term, *casse-couilles* meaning "a pain-in-the-ass" or literally a "ball-breaker."

cocotter *v.* to have an overpowering odor.

> example: Ça **cocotte** dans cette parfumerie!
>
> translation: It **stinks** in this perfume shop!
>
> as spoken: Ça **cocotte** dans c'te parfum'rie!
>
> **SYNONYM:** **schlinguer** *v.*

crâneur, euse *n.* show-off.

> example: Sophie parle toujours de sa fortune. C'est une vraie **crâneuse**, celle-là.
>
> translation: Sophie always talks about her fortune. That girl's a real **show-off**.
>
> as spoken: Sophie, è parle toujours d'sa fortune. C't'une vraie **crâneuse**, celle-là.
>
> **NOTE:** **crâner** *v.* to show off.
>
> **SYNONYM:** **frimeur, euse** *n.*
>
> > **NOTE:** **frimer** *v.* to show off.

faillot *m.* brown-noser, one who sucks up • (lit.): bean.

> example: Georges est un sacré **faillot**. C'est pour ça que le patron lui donne toujours des augmentations.

> translation: George is a real **brown-noser**. That's why the boss always gives him raises.

> as spoken: C't'un sacré **faillot**, Georges. C'est pour ça que l'patron, y lui donne toujours des augmentations.

feignasse *f.* a lazy person, a lazy bum.

> example: Tu vas demander à Léon de te donner un coup de main? Bonne chance! C'est une **feignasse** de premier ordre!

> translation: You're going to ask Leon to give you a hand? Good luck! He's a big-time **lazy bum**!

> as spoken: Tu vas d'mander à Léon de te donner un coup d'main? Bonne chance! C't'une **feignasse** de premier ordre!

> **NOTE -1:** This comes from the noun *feignant(e)* meaning "lazy."

> **NOTE -2:** Also spelled: **faignasse**.

fumier *m.* a disparaging remark applied to either a man or a woman • (lit.): manure.

> example: Il a volé ma voiture, le **fumier**!

> translation: That **bastard** stole my car!

> as spoken: [no change]

grosse brioche *f.* fat stomach, paunch, gut • (lit.): fat brioche.

> example: Tu veux encore une tranche de tarte? Attention. Tu ne veux pas avoir une **grosse brioche** comme celle de Marcel!

> translation: You want another piece of pie? Be careful. You don't want to get a **gut** like Marcel's!

> as spoken: Tu veux encore une tranche de tarte? Attention. Tu ~ veux pas avoir une **grosse brioche** comme celle de Marcel!

jacasser *v.* to talk a lot, to blab.

> example: Henri a **jacassé** pendant toute une heure de ses vacances.
>
> translation: Henry **went on and on** for an entire hour about his vacation.
>
> as spoken: Henri, il a **jacassé** pendant toute une heure d'ses vacances.

je-m'en-foutiste *n.* one who is apathetic and disinterested, one who doesn't give a damn.

> example: Cette compagnie est pleine de **je-m'en-foutistes**.
>
> translation: This company is full of **apathetic people**.
>
> as spoken: Cette compagnie, elle est pleine de **j'm'en-foutistes**.
>
> **SEE:** **je-m'en-foutisme**, *p. 202.*

lèche-bottes *m. (applies to either a man or a woman)* someone who flatters a boss in order to get in his/her good graces; "ass kisser" • (lit.): boot-licker.

> example: Laurent est un vrai **lèche-bottes**. C'est pour ça que le patron l'adore!
>
> translation: Laurent is a real **butt kisser**. That's why the boss loves him.
>
> as spoken: Laurent, c't'un vrai **lèche-bottes**. C'est pour ça qu'le patron, y l'adore!
>
> **NOTE -1:** **lèche-bottes (faire du)** *exp. (figurative)* to kiss someone's butt.
>
> **NOTE -2:** The stronger form of *lèche-bottes* is *lèche-cul* meaning "ass-licker."

moche *adj.* ugly.

> example: Hélène était très **moche** quand elle était petite. Maintenant, elle est devenue une très belle fille.
>
> translation: Helen was very **ugly** when she was little. Now she's become a beautiful girl.

as spoken: Hélène, <u>elle</u> était très **moche** quand elle était <u>p</u>'tite. Maintenant, elle est <u>d</u>'venue une très belle fille.

patapouf m. *(applies to either a man or a woman)* fatso, tub of lard.

example: Je dois me mettre au régime après mes vacances. Sinon, je vais devenir un gros **patapouf**.

translation: I have to put myself on a diet after my vacation. Otherwise, I'm going to become a **tub of lard.**

as spoken: <u>J</u>'dois <u>m</u>'mett<u>r</u>'au régime après mes vacances. Sinon, <u>j</u>'vais de<u>v</u>'nir un gros **patapouf**.

piffrer quelqu'un (ne pas pouvoir) *exp.* to be unable to stand someone • (lit.): to be unable to smell someone (from the slang word *pif* meaning "nose" or "schnoz").

example: Tu as invité Marie à la soirée? Mais je **ne peux pas la piffrer**, celle-là!

translation: You invited Marie to the party? But I **can't stand her**!

as spoken: <u>T</u>'as invité Marie à la soirée? Mais <u>j</u>'**peux pas la piffrer**, celle-là!

SYNONYM: **blairer quelqu'un (ne pas pouvoir)** *exp.* (from the slang word *blair* also meaning "nose" or "schnoz").

rasoir (être) *adj.* to be boring • (lit.): to be rasor.

example: Mon nouveau professeur de biologie est tout à fait **rasoir**. J'ai du mal à rester éveillé dans sa classe.

translation: My new biology teacher is totally **boring**. I have trouble staying awake in his class.

as spoken: Mon nouveau prof~ de bio~, <u>il</u> est tout à fait **rasoir**. J'ai du mal à rester éveillé dans sa classe.

ta gueule *exp.* shut up • (lit.): your mouth.

example: **Ta gueule**! Tu commences à m'énerver!

translation: **Shut up**! You're starting to annoy me!

as spoken: [no change]

tuer les mouches à quinze pas *exp.* said of someone who has bad breath • (lit.): to kill flies fifteen feet away.

example:	Oh, ce chien! Il **tue les mouches à quinze pas**, lui!
translation:	Oh, this dog! He has **horrible breath**!
as spoken:	Oh, c'chien! Y **tue les mouches à quinze pas**, lui!

A CLOSER LOOK:
Nonvulgar Insults & Putdowns
(insultes douces)

Learning popular insults can prove to be extremely handy for those little annoying moments when you need to spout off a good retort as well as being able to recognize when you have been insulted by someone. This following list is sure to get you ready for just about any situation.

bouboule *n. (applies to a man)* fatso.

example: Ce **bouboule**-là a marché sur mon pied!

translation: That **fatso** stepped on my foot!

as spoken: C'**bouboule**-là, il a marché sur mon pied!

boude *m. (applies only to a woman)* variation of: *boudin.*

boudin *m.* ugly and fat woman
• (lit.): blood sausage.

casse-pieds *m. (applies to a man and woman as well as to things)* pain in the neck
• (lit.): foot-breaker.

example: Quel **casse-pieds**! Il ne me laisse jamais tranquille!

translation: What a **pain in the neck**! He never leaves me alone!

as spoken: Quel **casse-pieds**!
Y m'laisse jamais tranquille!

**NOTE: casser les pieds à
quelqu'un** *exp.* to bug the
living daylights out of someone
• (lit.): to break someone's feet.

charognard *m. (applies only to
a man)* bastard • (lit.): carrion
feeder, vulture.

charogne *f. (applies to either a
man or a woman)* variation of:
charognard • (lit.): rotting
carcass, carrion.

écraser *v.* to shut up • (lit.): to
crush.

example: **Ecrase**! Tu parles
trop, toi!

translation: **Put a sock in it**!
You talk too much!

as spoken: [no change]

NOTE: This term is not vulgar
but it is rather harsh and should
be used with caution.

ferme la *interj.* shut up
• (lit.): shut it.

example: Oh, **ferme la**! Tu
racontes des bêtises!

translation: Oh, **shut up**!
You're talking nonsense!

as spoken: [no change]

NOTE: In this interjection, *la*
represents *la bouche* meaning
"the mouth."

VARIATION: La ferme!
interj. Shut up!

NOTE: This is a shortened
version of: *Que tu la ferme!*
meaning "May you shut it!"

fumiste *m. (applies to either a
man or a woman)* lazy
individual, one who doesn't
want to work • (lit.): one who
works with manure.

example: Marcel, tu es un
fumiste. Tu as encore échoué
à l'examen.

translation: Marcel, you're a
lazy bum. You failed the test
again.

as spoken: Marcel, t'es un
fumiste. T'as encore échoué à
l'exam~.

garce *f. (applies only to a woman)*
bitch.

grognasse *f.* bitchy woman.
NOTE: grogner *v.* to groan.

gros lard (être un) *exp.*
*(applies to either a man or a
woman)* to be a fatso • (lit.): to
be a big piece of lard.

example: Si tu continues à
manger comme ça, tu vas
devenir un **gros lard**.

translation: If you keep eating
like that, you're going to
become a **fat pig**.

as spoken: Si tu continues à manger comme ça, tu vas dev'nir un **gros lard**.

> **SYNONYM: gras double (être un)** exp. *(applies to either a man or a woman)* • (lit.): to be a piece of tripe (or "guts").

mon œil! *interj.* my foot! *(in response to a ridiculous comment)* • (lit.): my eye.

> **NOTE:** This is a mild version of: *mon cul!*

> **SEE: mon cul!**, *p. 65.*

ordure *f.* a disparaging remark applied to either a man or a woman • (lit.): trash.

peau de vache *f.* a disparaging remark applied primarily to a woman but may also be used in reference to a man • (lit.): cow skin.

porc *m.* one who overeats, an "oinker" • (lit.): pig.

> example: Le frère de mon mari est un vrai **porc**. Chaque fois qu'il vient chez nous, il mange sans arrêt!

translation: My husband's brother is a real **pig**. Every time he comes to our house, he eats nonstop!

as spoken: Le frère d'mon mari, c't'un vrai **porc**. Chaque fois qu'y vient chez nous, y mange sans arrêt!

> **NOTE:** The invented feminine version of *porc* (*porquesse*) may also be used in reference to an overweight woman.

pourriture *f.* a disparaging remark applied primarily to a man but can also be used in reference to a woman • (lit.): rotting trash.

raclure *f.* a disparaging remark applied to a man • (lit.): scrapings.

> **ALSO: raclure de bidet** *f.* • (lit.): bidet scrapings.

rombière *f.* *(applies only to a woman)* fat woman.

vache *m.* a disparaging remark applied primarily to a woman but may be used in reference to a man • (lit.): cow.

Chauve
(bald)

alfa sur les hauts plateaux (ne plus avoir d') *exp.* • (lit.): not to have any more alfalfa on the high plateaus.

bille de billard (avoir une) *exp.* • (lit.): to have a billiard ball (for a head).

boule de billard bien cirée (avoir la) *exp.*
• (lit.): to have the well-waxed billiard.

caillou déplumé (avoir le) *exp.* • (lit.): to have the plucked pebble.

> **NOTE:** **caillou** *m.* head, "noggin" • (lit.): pebble.

casquette en peau de fesses (avoir la) *exp.*
• (lit.): to have the cap made of butt skin.

> **NOTE:** **casquette** *f.* head, "noggin" • (lit.): helmet.

chauve comme un genou (être) *exp.* • (lit.): to be as bald as a knee.

cresson sur la cafetière (ne plus avoir de) *exp.*
• (lit.): to no longer have watercress on the coffeepot.

> **NOTE:** **cafetière** *f.* head, "noggin" • (lit.): coffeepot.

cresson sur la fontaine (ne plus avoir de) *exp.*
• (lit.): to no longer have watercress on the fountain.

> **NOTE:** **fontaine** *f.* head, "noggin" • (lit.): fountain.

cresson sur la truffe (ne plus avoir de) *exp.*
• (lit.): to no longer have watercress on the truffle.

> **NOTE:** **truffle** *f.* head, "noggin" • (lit.): truffle.

cresson sur le caillou (ne plus avoir de) *exp.*
• (lit.): to no longer have watercress on the stone.

> **NOTE:** **caillou** *m.* head, "noggin" • (lit.): stone.

gazon sur la platebande (ne plus avoir de) *exp.*
• (lit.): to no longer have lawn on the flowerbed.

> **NOTE:** **platebande** *f.* head, "noggin" • (lit.): flowerbed.

gazon sur la prairie (ne plus avoir de) *exp.*
- (lit.): not to have any more grass on the prairie.

gazon sur la terrasse (ne plus avoir de) *exp.*
- (lit.): not to have any more grass on the terrace.

melon déplumé (avoir le) *exp.* • (lit.): to have the plucked melon.

mouchodrome (avoir un) *exp.* • (lit.): to have a fly landing pad.

nib de tifs (avoir) *exp.*
- (lit.): not to have any hair.

 `NOTE -1:` **nib de** *adj.* no more, none • Also seen as: *nib de nib:* nothing at all, zilch.

 `NOTE -2:` **tifs** *m.pl.* hair.

perruque en peau de fesses (avoir une) *exp.*
- (lit.): to have a wig that looks like one's rear end.

poil sur le caillou (ne pas avoir un) *exp.* • (lit.): not to have a hair on the pebble.

 `NOTE:` **caillou** *m.* head
- (lit.): pebble.

tête nickelée (avoir la) *exp.* • (lit.): to have a nickel-plated head.

vélodrome à mouches (avoir un) *exp.* • (lit.): to have a velodrome (which is very smooth-looking) for flies.

Idiot
(idiot)

abruti(e) *n.* idiot.

 `NOTE:` **abrutir** *v.* to make stupid, to drive crazy.

andouille *f. (applies to either a man or a woman)* nerd
- (lit.): sausage.

animal *m. (applies only to a man)*
- (lit.): animal.

araignée dans le plafond (avoir une) *exp. (applies to either a man or a woman)* to have bats in the belfry • (lit.): to have a spider in the ceiling.

NOTE: **plafond** m. head
• (lit.): ceiling.

ballot m. (applies to either a man or a woman) stupid or awkward person • (lit.): bundle.

barjot • (applies to either a man or a woman) • **1.** m. idiot • **2.** adj. crazy.

NOTE: This is a verlan transformation of jobard. Between the two words, barjot is actually the most popular.

SEE: **jobard**, p. 44.

battre la breloque exp. (applies to either a man or a woman) to be off one's rocker; to function badly, to beat the drum.

bécasse f. stupid woman or girl.

bêta m. (applies primarily to a man but may be used in reference to a woman) silly or stupid person.

NOTE -1: This comes from the adjective bête meaning "stupid.

NOTE -2: This is usually seen as gros bêta and is used by children.

bêtasse f. stupid woman or girl.

NOTE: This comes from the adjective bête meaning "stupid."

bête à bouffer du foin (être) exp. (applies to either a man or a woman) to be as stupid as a cow • (lit.): to be stupid enough to eat hay.

bête comme ses pieds (être) exp. (applies to either a man or a woman) to be as dumb as an ox • (lit.): to be as stupid as one's feet.

bourrique f. (applies to either a man or a woman) jackass, stubborn individual • (lit.): (jack)ass.

braque m. (applies to either a man or a woman) harebrained individual • (lit.): hound.

buse f. (applies to either a man or a woman) extremely stupid person • (lit.): buzzard.

SEE: **triple buse**, p. 46.

case en moins (avoir une) exp. not to be cooking on all four burners • (lit.): to be missing a division of the brain.

cave m. (applies only to a man) gullible person, sucker.

chabraque m. (applies only to a man).

chauve souris au plafond (avoir une) *exp. (applies to either a man or a woman)* to have bats in the belfry • (lit.): to have a bat in the ceiling.

cinglé(e) (être) *adj.* to be nuts, cracked.

comprenette dure (avoir la) *exp. (applies to either a man or a woman)* to be dense, thick skulled.

> **NOTE:** This comes from the verb *comprendre* meaning "to understand."

corniaud(e) • **1.** *adj.* jerky • **2.** *n.* jerk, fool • (lit.): crossbred dog.

cornichon *m. (applies only to a man)* • (lit.): pickle.

couche (en avoir une) *exp. (applies to either a man or a woman)* to be stupid • (lit.): to have a coat (of paint, etc.) on it (the brain).

> **VARIATION:** **tenir une couche (en)** *exp.*

cruche *f. (applies only to a woman)* a real idiot, an awkward fool • (lit.): pitcher.

cruchon *m. (applies only to a woman)* a real idiot • (lit.): a small pitcher.

débile (être) *adj. (applies to either a man or a woman)* to be moronic.

déménager *v. (applies to either a man or a woman)* to go crazy, to go out of one's mind • (lit.): to move out (of one's senses).

déplafonné(e) (être) *adj. (applies to either a man or a woman)* to be nuts • (lit.): to be "unroofed."

derrière la porte [le jour de la distribution] (ne pas être) *exp. (applies to either a man or a woman)* said of a stupid person, not to be in line the day brains were handed out • (lit.): not to be behind the door (the day of distribution).

détraqué(e) (être) *adj.* said of anything that is not normal (such as one's health, one's mental state, machinery, etc.) • (lit.): to be off track.

dinde *f.* stupid woman or girl • (lit.): turkey.

dingo • **1.** *m.* idiot • **2.** *adj. (applies to either a man or a woman)* crazy.

écervelé(e) • **1.** *n.* scatterbrain • **2.** *adj.* scatterbrained • (lit.): to be "unbrained."

enflé(e) m. *(applies to either a man or a woman)* fat-head
• (lit.): swollen (one).

enflure m. *(applies to either a man or a woman)* fat-head
• (lit.): swelling.

étourdi(e) (être) adj. to be scatterbrained.

évaporé(e) (être) • **1.** n. to be an irresponsible and scatterbrained person • **2.** adj. to be irresponsible, flightly, scatterbrained • (lit.): to be evaporated.

fada adj. *(Southern French — applies to either a man or a woman)* crazy, cracked.

farfelu m. *(applies to either a man or a woman)* a total nutcase.

fêlé(e) (être) adj. • (lit.): to be nuts, cracked.

fêlure (avoir une) f. • *(applies to either a man or a woman)* (lit.): to have a crack.

foldingue adj. *(applies only to a woman)* crazy, nuts.

follette adj. *(applies only to a woman)* crazy.

follingue adj. *(applies only to a woman)* crazy, nuts.

fou-fou/fofolle adj. a little crazy, eccentric.

> **NOTE -1:** This comes from the adjectives *fou* and *folle* meaning "crazy."

> **NOTE -2:** When *fofolle* is applied to a man, its connotation is "effeminate" or "queeny."

fou/folle à lier (être) exp. to be crazy enough to commit • (lit.): to be crazy enough to tie up.

givré(e) (être) adj. crazy • (lit.): to be frosted over.

gobeur m. *(applies to either a man or a woman)* gullible person, sucker.

> **NOTE:** **gober** v. to eat, gobble up.

> **ALSO:** **gobe-tout** m. one who believes everything he/she hears, sucker.

godiche (être) adj. *(applies only to a woman)* to be awkward and clumsy.

gogo m. *(applies to either a man or a woman)* a person easily fooled, sucker.

grain (avoir un) *exp. (applies to either a man or a woman)* to be nuts, touched in the head • (lit.): to have a grain (in the brain).

hurluberlu *m. (applies to either a man or a woman)* scatterbrain.

inventé la poudre (ne pas avoir) *exp.* said of an idiot • (lit.): not to have invented powder.

inventé le fil à couper le beurre (ne pas avoir) *exp. (applies to either a man or a woman)* said of an idiot • (lit.): not to have invented the wire to cut butter.

jobard *m. (applies only to a man)* idiot, sucker.

louf (être) *adj. (applies to either a man or a woman)* to be nuts.
NOTE: This is a largonji transformation of: *fou* • *SEE: — Street French 2, Largoni, P. 216.*

lourdeau *m. (applies only to a man)* a thickheaded individual, slow.
NOTE: This is from the adjective *lourd(e)* meaning "heavy."

maboul(e) (être) *adj. (applies to either a man or a woman)* crazy, mad.

manquer une case *exp. (applies to either a man or a woman)* • (lit.): to be missing a division in the brain.
SEE: **case en moins (avoir une)**, *p. 41.*

marteau (être) *adj. (applies to either a man or a woman)* to be nuts, cracked • (lit.): to be hammer.

nouille *f. (applies to either a man or a woman)* nerd • (lit.): noodle.

onduler de la toiture *exp. (applies to either a man or a woman)* humorous for "to have a screw loose" • (lit.): to have a buckling roof.

patate *f. (applies to either a man or a woman)* • **1.** idiot • **2.** awkward • (lit.): potato.
ALSO: **patate** *f.* large nose.

perdre la boule *exp. (applies to either a man or a woman)* to lose one's mind • (lit.): to lose the ball.

perdre la boussole *exp. (applies to either a man or a woman)* to lose one's mind • (lit.): to lose the compass.

perdre le nord (ne pas) *exp.* *(applies to either a man or a woman)* to be rational, to know where one is going • (lit.): not to lose the north (point on the compass).

NOTE: This expression is usually used in the negative: *Tu ne perds pas le nord, toi!;* You've got that right!

pigeon *m.* *(applies to either a man or a woman)* gullible person, sucker • (lit.): pigeon

piqué(e) (être) *adj.* to be nuts, cracked, touched in the head • (lit.): to be stung.

plat de nouilles *m.* *(applies to either a man or a woman)* airhead, noodle brain • (lit.): plate of noodles.

plomb dans la cervelle (ne pas avoir de) *exp.* *(applies to either a man or a woman)* said of an idiot, not to be cooking on all four burners • (lit.): not to have any lead in the brain.

schnock *m.* *(applies only to a man)* imbecile, jerk

VARIATION: **duchenock** *m.*

NOTE: **vieux schnock** *m.* an old a senile man.

siphonné(e) (être) *adj.* to be nuts, crazy • (lit.): siphoned (of all intelligence).

sonné(e) (être) *adj.* to be nuts, a "ding-a-ling" • (lit.): to be rung.

souche *f.* *(applies to either a man or a woman)* silly person, dumbell • (lit.): stump (of a tree).

tapé(e) (être) *adj.* • (lit.): to be touched (in the head).

tarte • **1.** *f.* a vulgar and dumb woman • **2.** *adj.* vulgar and dumb (said of a woman).

tenir une dose (en) *exp.* *(applies to either a man or a woman)* to be hopelessly dumb • (lit.): to hold a dose of it (stupidity).

tête de linotte *f.* *(applies only to a woman)* scatterbrain • (lit.): birdhead.

tête de nœud *f.* *(applies to either a man or a woman)* scatterbrain • (lit.): head of knots.

tête dure (avoir la) *exp.* *(applies to either a man or a woman)* to be thick-skulled, dense; stubborn • (lit.): to have a hard head.

timbre fêlé *m.* crackpot, idiot • (lit.): cracked bell.

timbré(e) (être) *adj.* to be nuts, a "ding-a-ling" • (lit.): to be rung.

tordu(e) (être) *adj.* to be crazy, cracked, bizarre • (lit.): to be twisted.

tranche (en avoir une) *exp.* *(applies to either a man or a woman)* • (lit.): to have a slice of it (craziness).

travailler de la casquette *exp. (applies to either a man or a woman)* to be crazy • (lit.): to ferment from the cap.

> **NOTE -1:** In this expression, the verb *travailler* (literally meaning "to work") is used to mean "to ferment" as in wine.

> **NOTE -2:** **casquette** *f.* head • (lit.): cap • *Quand je bois trop, j'ai mal à la casquette;* When I drink too much, I get a headache.

travailler du chapeau *exp.* *(applies to either a man or a woman)* to be crazy • (lit.): to work from the hat.

> **NOTE -1:** In this expression, the verb *travailler* is used to mean "to ferment" as in wine.

travailler du chou *exp.* *(applies to either a man or a woman)* to be crazy • (lit.): to work from the cabbage.

> **NOTE -1:** In this expression, the verb *travailler* is used to mean "to ferment" as in wine.

> **NOTE -2:** **chou** *m.* head • (lit.): cabbage.

triple buse *m. (applies to either a man or a woman)* an extremely stupid person • (lit.): triple idiot.

> **NOTE:** **buse** *m.* buzzard.

veau *m. (applies to either a man or a woman)* a docile and stupid person • (lit.): veal.

> **VARIATION:** **tête de veau** *f.*

tombé(e) sur le crâne (être) *exp.* to be crazy • (lit.): to have fallen on one's skull.

toqué(e) (être) *adj.* to be crazy, cracked.

> **ALSO:** **toqué(e) de quelqu'un (être)** *exp.* to have a crush on someone.

zinzin (être) *adj. (applies to either a man or a woman)* to be nuts.

Ugly Person
(personne laide)

gueule à coucher dehors (avoir une) f. • (lit.): to have a face that should sleep outside.

> **NOTE:** The feminine noun *gueule*, literally meaning the "mouth of an animal," is commonly used in a derogatory fashion to mean "face" or "head."

gueule de raie f. • (lit.): to have a face like a vagina.

> **NOTE:** **raie** f. vagina • (lit.): line.

hideur f. • (lit.): hideousness.

mochard m. one who is *moche* ("ugly").

moche adj. (extremely popular) ugly.

mocheté f. ugliness (from the slang adjective *moche* meaning ugly).

mochetingue m. a slang variant of: *mocheté*.

mocheton m. a slang variant of: *mocheté*.

pas jojo adj. from *joli(e)* meaning "pretty."

sale gueule (avoir une) f. to be ugly • (lit.): to have a dirty face.

Ugly Woman or Girl
(femme laide)

bique f. • (lit.): nanny-goat.

boude m. a slang variation of: *boudin*.

> **SEE:** (next entry).

boudin m. (very popular) an ugly and (usually fat) woman • (lit.): blood sausage.

chèvre f. • (lit.): goat or nanny-goat.

grognasse *f.* • (lit.): a slang variant of the verb *grogner* meaning "to grunt."

guenon *f.* • (lit.): female monkey.

guenuche *f.* a slang variant of *guenon* meaning "a female monkey."

mémée *f.* • (lit.): granny.

mocheté *f.* • (lit.): ugliness (from the slang noun *moche* meaning "ugly").

prix à réclamer *m. (ironic)* • (lit.): a prize to claim.

remède d'amour *m.* • (lit.): a remedy for love.

rombière *f.* old hag.

saucisson *m.* • (lit.): (large dry) sausage.

tarderie *f.*

tardingue *f.* a slang variant of: *tarderie.*

tartavelle *f.* from the slang adjective *tarte* meaning "ugly."

vache *f.* • (lit.): cow.

Ne Pas Pouvoir Supporter Quelqu'un
(to be unable to stand someone)

blair (avoir quelqu'un dans le) *exp.* • (lit.): to have someone in the nose.

> **NOTE:** **blair** *m.* nose, "schnoz."

blairer quelqu'un (ne pas pouvoir) *v.* • (lit.): to be unable to smell someone (since even the mere smell of the person would be too much to bear).

> **NOTE:** This verb comes from the masculine slang term *blair* meaning "nose" or "schnoz."

bonne (ne pas avoir quelqu'un à la) *exp.* • (lit.): not to be in good (standing) with someone.

caille (avoir quelqu'un à la) *exp.* • (lit.): to make someone's blood curdle (since *caille* comes from the verb *cailler* meaning "to curdle").

cul (avoir quelqu'un dans le) *exp.* • (lit.): to have someone in the ass.

encadrer quelqu'un (ne pas pouvoir) *v.* • (lit.): to be unable to frame someone.

encaisser quelqu'un (ne pas pouvoir) *v.* • (lit.): to be unable to cash in someone.

gerber quelqu'un (ne pas pouvoir) *v.* • (lit.): to be unable to vomit someone.

gober quelqu'un (ne pas pouvoir) *v.* • (lit.): to be unable to swallow or gulp down someone.

nez (avoir quelqu'un dans le) *exp.* • (lit.): to have someone in the nose.

piffrer quelqu'un (ne pas pouvoir) *v.* • (lit.): to be unable to smell someone (since even the mere smell of the person would be too much to bear).
NOTE: This verb comes from the masculine slang term *pif* meaning "nose" or "schnoz."

renifler quelqu'un (ne pas pouvoir) *v.* • (lit.): to be unable to sniff someone (since even the mere smell of the person would be too much to bear).

sentir quelqu'un (ne pas pouvoir) *v.* • (lit.): to be unable to smell someone (since the mere smell of the person would be too much to bear).

voir quelqu'un en peinture (ne pas pouvoir) *exp.* • (lit.): to be unable to see someone in a painting (since ever the mere sight of the person would be too much to bear).

Peureux
(scardey-cat)

baisse-froc *m.* • (lit.): pants lowerer.
NOTE: **froc** *m.* (a pair of) pants.

chiasseur, euse *n.* one who is scared shitless • (lit.): shitter.
NOTE: **chiasse (avoir la)** *exp.* to have diarrhea.

déballonné(e) *n.* one who loses courage.

NOTE: This noun comes from verb *ballonner* meaning "to be bloated like a balloon due to gas." Therefore, *débalonné(e)* could be losely translated as "deflated of all gas."

dégonflard(e) *n.* • (lit.): one who is deflated of one's courage.

NOTE: **dégonfler (se)** *v.* to lose one's courage • (lit.): to deflate.

dégonflé(e) *n.* a variation of: *dégonflard(e)*.

dégonfleur, euse *n.* a variation of: *dégonfleur, euse*.

foireux, euse *n.* one who is scared shitless • (lit.): shitter (from intense fear).

NOTE: **foire (avoir la)** *exp.* • **foirade (avoir la)** *exp.* • **foirer** *v.* to have diarrhea.

froussard(e) *n.*

NOTE: **frousse (avoir la)** *exp.* to be scared, to have the creeps.

grelotteur, euse *n.*
• (lit.): shaker.

NOTE -1: **grelots (avoir les)** *exp.* to have the shakes (due to fear).

NOTE -2: **grelotter** *v.*
• (lit.): to shake.

péteux, euse *n.* • (lit.): farter.

NOTE: This comes from the verb *péter* meaning "to fart." Therefore, *péteux, euse* could be translated as "one who farts (due to intense fear causing a loss of control").

pétochard(e) *n.* • (lit.): farter.

NOTE: This is a variation of: *péteux, euse*.

poule mouillée *f.* • (lit.): wet hen.

trouillard(e) *n.* *(very popular)*.

NOTE: **trouille (avoir la)** *exp.* to have intense fear.

Vieux Gronchon / Vieille Gronchonne
(old fart)

baderne (vieille) *f.* old lady
• (lit.): old horse.

bique (vieille) *f.* old lady
• (lit.): old nanny-goat.

bonze (vieux) *m.* • (lit.): old Buddhist monk.

croulant (vieux) *m.*
• (lit.): old "fall-apart" from the verb *s'écrouler* meaning "to collapse."

croûton (vieux) *m.*
• (lit.): old crust.

fossile (vieux) *m.* • (lit.): old fossil.
> **NOTE:** **fossiliser (se)** *v.* to get old • (lit.): to fossilize.

mémé (vieille) *f.* • (lit.): old granny.

noix (vieille) *f.* • (lit.): old (wal)nut.

pépé (vieux) *m.* • (lit.): old grandpa.

rombière (vieille) *f.*
• (lit.): old overbearing woman.

schnock (vieux) *m.*
• (lit.): [no literal translation].

taupe (vieille) *f.* someone who can't see • (lit.): old mole.

toupie (vieille) *f.* • (lit.): old (spinning) top.

vestige (vieux) *m.* • (lit.): old ruin.

vioc *m.* (also spelled: *vioque*).
> **NOTE:** **vioquer** *v.* to get old.

LEÇON TROIS - Vulgar Insults & Name-Calling

Elle doit avoir ses anglais!

(trans.): *She must be on the rag!*
(lit.): *She must be having her English!*

Leçon Trois

Jean:	Oh, **putain** de **bordel** de **merde**! Vous êtes complètement **jetée** ou quoi?
Mimi:	Et vous **foutiez** quoi derrière le volant, **pauvre con**?! Vous avec de la **merde dans les yeux**?
Marc:	Quelle **connasse**! Elle doit **avoir ses anglais**, le **boudin**.
Mimi:	**Espèce d'ordure**! Je vous ai **demandé l'heure**? Je **ne peux pas renifler** des **couillons** comme vous! J'**en ai ras le cul** des **conducteurs du dimanche** comme vous. **Retournez dans votre banlieue de merde**!
Marc:	Qu'elle **boucle son égout**, celle-là. *Non, mais des fois* (1)!
Jean:	Faut pas **déconner**, non?! Mais regardez ce que vous avez fait à ma *tire* (2)! Sale **bourge**! **Mal baisée**!
Mimi:	Je **m'en branle** de votre tire. D'ailleurs, ça **ne vaut pas un pet de lapin**, cette **saloperie**-là.
Jean:	Oh, la vieille **garce**! Elle me bousille ma voiture et en plus elle me **casse les couilles**!

Lesson Three

Translation in English

She must be on the rag!

Jean: Oh, **holy shit**! Are you totally **nuts** or what?

Mimi: And what **the fuck were you doing** behind the wheel, **you pathetic jerk**?! Do you have **shit in your eyes**?

Marc: What a **fucking bitch**! She must **be on the rag**, the **fat blimp**.

Mimi: **You piece of filth**! Was I **talking to you**? I **can't stand assholes** like you! I've **had it up to here** with **Sunday drivers** like you. **Go back to the shitty suburb where you come from**!

Marc: I wish she'd just **shut her face**. *Man, oh man!*

Jean: **Have you lost it**, or what?! I mean, look what you've done to my *car*! **Yuppie scum**! **You bad fuck**!

Mimi: I don't **give a damn** about your car. Besides, it's **not worth a dime**, that **piece of shit** you have there.

Jean: Oh, the old **bitch**! First, she wrecks my car and then she **pisses me off** more!

Dialogue in slang as it would be spoken

È doit avoir ses anglais!

Jean: Oh, **putain** d'**bordel** d'**merde**! Vous êtes complètement **shtée** ou quoi?

Mimi: Et vous **foutiez** quoi derrière l'volant, **pauv' con**?! Vous avez d'la **merde dans les yeux**?

Marc: Quelle **connasse**! È doit **avoir ses anglais**, l'**boudin**.

Mimi: **Espèce d'ordure**! J'vous ai **d'mandé l'heure**? J'**peux pas renifler** des **couillons** comme vous! J'**en ai ras l'cul** des **conducteurs du dimanche** comme vous. **Retournez dans vot' banlieue d'merde**!

Marc: Qu'è **boucle son égout**, celle-là. *Non, mais des fois!*

Jean: Faut pas **déconner**, non?! Mais r'gardez c'que vous avez fait à ma *tire*! Sale **bourge**! **Mal baisée**!

Mimi: J'**m'en branle** d'vot' *tire*. D'ailleurs, ça **vaut pas un pet d'lapin**, c'te **saloperie**-là.

Jean: Oh, la vieille **garce**! È m'bousille ma voiture et en plus è m'**casse les couilles**!

Vocabulary

FOOTNOTES FROM THE DIALOGUE

(1) _Non, mais des fois!_:

A popular expression used to signify annoyance, "Man alive!"

(2) _tire_:

f. car • (lit.): puller.

---

anglais (avoir ses) _exp._ to be on one's period, to be "on the rag" • (lit.): to have one's English.

> example: Geneviève ne peut pas nager aujourd'hui parce qu'elle **a ses anglais**.

> translation: Geneviève can't go swimming today because she's **on the rag**.

> as spoken: Geneviève, è̠ ~ peut pas nager aujourd'hui <u>pasqu</u>'elle **a ses anglais**.

bordel _interj._ an interjection used in anger or disbelief; "holy shit" • (lit.): brothel.

> example: Oh, **bordel**! J'ai brûlé le dîner!

> translation: Oh, **holy shit**! I burned the dinner!

> as spoken: Oh, **bordel**! J'ai brûlé <u>l'</u>dîner!

boucler son égout _exp._ to shut one's mouth • (lit.): to shut one's sewer.

> example: Si tu vas continuer à me critiquer, tu peux **boucler ton égout**.

> translation: If you're going to keep on criticizing me, you can **shut your trap**.

> as spoken: Si tu vas continuer à <u>m'</u>critiquer, tu peux **boucler ton égout**.

boudin *m.* ugly and fat woman • (lit.): blood sausage.

> example: Sophie m'a dit qu'elle veut devenir mannequin. A mon avis, ça ne se réalisera jamais. C'est un **boudin**, celle-là!

> translation: Sophie told me she wants to become a model. In my opinion, it'll never happen. She's a **fat pig**!

> as spoken: Sophie, <u>è</u> m'a dit qu'<u>è</u> veut dev'<u>n</u>ir mann'quin. A mon avis, ça ~ <u>s</u>'réalis'<u>r</u>a jamais. <u>C't'un</u> **boudin**, celle-là!

bourge *m.* a shortened version of the term "bourgeois(e)," yuppie scum.

> example: Laisse-moi tranquille, sale **bourge**!

> translation: Leave me alone, you **yuppie scum**!

> as spoken: [no change]

> **NOTE:** Since France is rather class conscious, insulting a person's status in society or telling a person that he/she comes from a lower class is considered very offensive.

branler (s'en) *v.* *(very popular)* not to give a damn • (lit.): to shake oneself of it.

> example: Je **m'en branle** de ce que tu penses!

> translation: I don't **give a damn** what you think!

> as spoken: J'**m'en branle** de <u>c</u>'que tu penses!

> **NOTE:** **branler (se)** *v.* to masturbate • (lit.): to shake oneself.

casser les couilles à quelqu'un *exp.* to annoy someone greatly, to bug the shit out of someone • (lit.): to break someone's testicles or "balls."

> example: J'espère que tu n'as pas invité Claude à nous rejoindre. Il **me casse les couilles**, celui-là!

> translation: I hope you didn't invite Claude to join us. He **bugs the shit out of me**!

> as spoken: J'espère <u>qu't</u>'as pas invité Claude à nous <u>r</u>'joindre. <u>Y</u> **m'casse les couilles**, çui-là!

NOTE: This expression can also be softened by replacing *les couilles* with *les: Il me les casse, lui!;* • (lit.): He breaks mine!

conducteur du dimanche *m.* Sunday driver • (lit.): same.

example: Oh, ce **conducteur du dimanche** conduit trop lentement!

translation: Oh, this **Sunday driver** is driving too slowly!

as spoken: Oh, c'**conducteur du dimanche**, y conduit trop lent~!

NOTE: You may have noticed that in the previous *as spoken* paragraph, *lentement* was changed to *lent*. It is very common in French to change adverbs to adjectives.

connasse *f.* a very derogatory term for an annoying woman, " fucking bitch."

example: Tu ne vas pas croire ce que cette **connasse** de Marie m'a fait hier soir.

translation: You're not going to believe what that **cunt** Marie did to me last night.

as spoken: Tu ~ vas pas croire c'que cette **connasse** de Marie m'a fait hier soir.

NOTE: This comes from the masculine noun *con* originally meaning "cunt."

SEE: The Many Uses of "Con," *p. 180.*

couillon *m.* jerk.

example: Quel **couillon**, ce mec!

translation: What a **jerk** this guy is!

as spoken: Quel **couillon**, c'mec!

NOTE -1: This comes from the feminine plural noun *couilles* literally meaning "testicles" or "balls."

NOTE -2: **mec** *m. (extremely popular)* guy, "dude."

déconner *v.* to act like a jerk, to lose it.

> example: Arrête de **déconner**! Tu racontes des bêtises!
>
> translation: Stop **acting like a jerk**! You're talking nonsense!
>
> as spoken: [no change]
>
> **NOTE:** This comes from the masculine noun *con*, literally meaning "cunt," which is commonly used to be mean "idiot" or "jerk."
>
> **SEE:** The Many Uses of "Con," *p. 180.*

espèce d'ordure *f.* lowlife scum • (lit.): species of trash.

> example: **Espèce d'ordure**! Tu as ruiné mon tricot!
>
> translation: **You lowlife scum**! You ruined my sweater!
>
> as spoken: **Espèce d'ordure**! <u>T'</u>as ruiné mon tricot!

foutre *v.* to make, to do • (lit.): originally this meant "to fuck."

> example: Qu'est-ce que vous **foutez**, vous deux? Arrêtez ça tout de suite!
>
> translation: What **the hell are you two doing**? Stop that right now!
>
> as spoken: Vous **foutez** quoi, vous deux? Arrêtez ça tout <u>d'</u>suite!
>
> **SEE:** The Many Uses of "Foutre", *p. 195.*

garce *f.* bitch.

> example: Tu as rencontré la nouvelle voisine? C'est une vieille **garce**. Elle m'a dénoncé à la police pour avoir joué du piano à 8 heures du soir parce que ça l'a dérangé!
>
> translation: Did you meet the new neighbor? She's an old **bitch**. She reported me to the police for playing the piano at 8 o'clock at night because it disturbed her!
>
> as spoken: <u>T'</u>as rencontré la nouvelle voisine? <u>C't'</u>une vieille **garce**. <u>È</u> m'a dénoncé à la police pour avoir joué du piano à 8 heures du soir <u>pasque</u> ça l'a dérangé!

Je vous ai/t'ai demandé l'heure? *exp.* a contemptuous
statement meaning "Was I talking to you?" • (lit.): I asked you the time?

>   example: **Je t'ai demandé l'heure**? Ta gueule!

>   translation: **Was I talking to you?** Shut up!

>   as spoken: **J't'ai d'mandé l'heure**? Ta gueule!

jeté(e) (être) *adj.* to be crazy, to be "cracked" • (lit.): to be thrown.

>   example: Ça sent le gaz ici. Oh hé! Mais ne craque pas cette
>   allumette! Tu es **jeté** ou quoi?!

>   translation: It smells like gas here. Hey! Don't strike that match!
>   What are you, **nuts**?!

>   as spoken: Ça sent l'gaz ici. Oh hé! Mais ~ craque pas c't'allumette!
>   T'es **sh'té** ou quoi?!

mal baisée *f.* an extremely vulgar insult for a woman implying that she is
extremely frigid and sexually undesirable • (lit.): bad fuck.

>   example: **Mal baisée**! J'en ai ras le bol de vos insultes!

>   translation: **You pathetic fuck**! I've had it with your insults!

>   as spoken: **Mal baisée**! J'en ai ras l'bol de vos insultes!

>   **NOTE:** **ras le bol (en avoir)** *exp.* (*very mild*) to have had it,
>   to be fed up • (lit.): to have had it to the brim of the bowl.

merde *f.* shit • (lit.): same.

>   example: **Merde**! J'ai raté mon bus!

>   translation: **Shit**! I missed my bus!

>   as spoken: [no change]

>   **SEE:** The Many Uses of "Merde," *p. 149*.

merde dans les yeux (avoir de la) *exp.* an insulting expression
meaning "to be blind as a bat" • (lit.): to have shit in the eyes.

>   example: Hé! Vous venez de me bousculer. Mais vous **avez de
>   la merde dans les yeux**?

>   translation: Hey! You just bumped me. What, do you **have shit
>   in your eyes**?

as spoken: Hé! Vous <u>v</u>'nez <u>d</u>'me bousculer, Mais vous **avez d'**la merde dans les yeux?

pauvre con *m.* a popular expression meaning "poor jerk" or "poor fucker."

example: Ah, le **pauvre con**. Il a perdu sa maison dans une grande incendie.

translation: Oh, the **poor fucker**. He lost his home in a big fire.

as spoken: Ah, l'**pauv'** con. Il a perdu sa maison dans une grande incendie.

putain *f.* used as an interjection to denote surprise or anger • (lit.): whore.

example: Oh, **putain**! Elle est jolie, cette nana!

translation: Oh, **holy shit**! That girl is beautiful!

as spoken: Oh, **putain**! Elle est jolie, <u>c</u>'te nana!

NOTE: **nana** *f. (extremely popular)* girl, "chick."

ras le cul (en avoir) *exp.* a harsh expression meaning "to be fed up" • (lit.): to have had it up to one's ass.

example: Maurice, il a encore menti? Oh, j'**en ai ras le cul**!

translation: Maurice lied again? Oh, I've **had it**!

as spoken: Maurice, <u>il</u> a encore menti? Oh, j'**en ai ras l'cul**!

renifler quelqu'un (ne pas pouvoir) *v.* to be unable to stand someone • (lit.): to be unable to sniff someone (since the mere smell of the person would be too much to bear).

example: Je ne vais pas inviter Suzanne à ma soirée. Je **ne peux pas la renifler**.

translation: I'm not going to invite Suzanne to my party. I **can't stand her**.

as spoken: <u>J</u>'vais pas inviter Suzanne à ma soirée. J'**peux pas la renifler**.

Retournez dans votre banlieue de merde! *exp.* an insulting
meaning "Get the fuck out of here!" • (lit.): Go back to your suburb.

> example: Arrêtez de gueuler et **retournez dans votre banlieue de merde**!

> translation: Stop screaming and **get the fuck out of here**!

> as spoken: Arrêtez d'gueuler et **retournez dans vot' banlieue d'merde**!

saloperie *f.* • **1.** said of something nasty done to someone • **2.** piece of junk.

> example (1): Je ne parle plus à Richard. Il m'a fait une **saloperie**.

> translation: I'm not speaking to Richard anymore. He did **something really nasty** to me.

> as spoken: J'parle <u>pu</u> à Richard. <u>Y</u> m'a fait une **salop'rie**.

> example (2): Tu as vu la robe qu'elle porte, Nancy? Elle a payé deux cent dollars cette **saloperie**!

> translation: Did you see the dress Nancy's wearing? She paid two hundred dollars for that **piece of junk**!

> as spoken: <u>T'</u>as vu la robe qu'<u>è</u> porte, Nancy? Elle a payé deux cent dollars <u>c'</u>te **salop'rie**!

valoir un pet de lapin (ne pas) *exp.* not to be worth a red cent
• (lit.): not to be worth a rabbit's fart.

> example: Tu as vu le collier que Nicole a porté à la soirée? Elle se vantait que son mari l'a payé une fortune mais ça sautait aux yeux que ça **ne valait pas un pet de lapin**!

> translation: Did you the see that necklace Nicole wore to the party? She was bragging that her husband paid a fortune for it but it was obvious that it wasn't **worth shit**.

> as spoken: <u>T'</u>as vu <u>l'</u>collier qu'Nicole a porté à la soirée? <u>È s'</u>vantait qu'son mari, <u>y</u> l'a payé une fortune mais ça sautait aux yeux qu'ça ~ **valait pas un pet d'lapin**!

> **NOTE:** **sauter aux yeux** *exp.* to be obvious • (lit.): to jump to the eyes.

A CLOSER LOOK (1):
Vulgar Insults & Name-Calling

Certainly, one of the best ways to learn offensive name-calling is to hop in a cab in Paris, sit back, and just listen. Within minutes, you will have heard some of the most "earthy" words and imaginative expressions soar out of the cabby's mouth.

Whenever I go back to Paris to visit my family, I am always fortunate enough to be the passenger in a car whose driver surely gives name-calling lessons to the cabbies; a driver who makes even the most foulmouthed trucker cringe with fear — my Aunt Mimi. Since I've gotten into the habit of carrying a pen and paper with me whenever I go driving with her, over the years I've managed to pick up some very colorful and commonly used terms guaranteed to make any visitor fit right in.

casse-couilles m. (applies to a man and woman as well as to things) pain in the ass • (lit.): testicles breaker.

example: Quel **casse-couilles**! Il n'arrête pas de m'énerver!

as spoken: Quel **casse-couilles**! Il ~ arrête pas d'm'énerver!

translation: What a **pain in the ass**! He doesn't stop bugging me!

VARIATION -1:
casse-burnes m. (applies to a man and woman as well as to things) pain in the ass • (lit.): oil can ("testicles") breaker.

VARIATION -2:
casse-noisettes m. (applies to a man and woman as well as to things) pain in the ass • (lit.): nutcracker.

con • **1.** m. (applies only to a man) bastard (very popular) • **2.** adj. stupid, silly • (lit.): cunt.
NOTE: The feminine variation of: con is conne.

con(n)ard m. variation of: con.
SEE: **con**, p. 180.

con(n)arde f. variation of: conne.
SEE: **con**, p. 180.

con(n)asse f. bitchy • (lit.): cunt.
SEE: **con**, p. 180.

conne f. (applies only to a woman) bitch.
SEE: **con**, p. 180.

conneau m. (applies only to a man) a variation of: con.

couillon • *(as a noun, it applies only to a man)* **1.** *m.* idiot • **2.** *adj.* stupid.

example (1): Le patron ne va pas me permettre de prendre mes vacances la semaine prochaine. Il dit que j'ai trop de travail à faire. Quel **couillon**!

translation: The boss isn't going to let me take my vacation next week. He says I have too much work to do. What an **idiot**!

as spoken: Le patron, y ~ va pas m'permett' de prend' mes vacances la s'maine prochaine. Y dit qu'j'ai trop d'travail à faire. Quel **couillon**!

example (2): Josette est venue me chercher au mauvais aéroport! Elle est **couillon**, celle-là!

translation: Josette came to pick me up at the wrong airport! She's **stupid**!

as spoken: Josette, elle est v'nue m'chercher au mauvais aéroport! Elle est **couillon**, celle-là!

NOTE -1: This comes from the slang feminine plural noun *couilles* meaning "testicles."

NOTE -2: The term *couillon* is considered somewhat vulgar.

enculé(e) de ta race *exp.* *(extremely vulgar)* fucker • (lit.): fucked of your race.

fils de pute *m.* son of a bitch • (lit.): son of a whore.

VARIATION: **fille de pute** *f.* bitch • (lit.): daughter of a whore.

lèche-cul *m.* *(applies to either a man or a woman)* kiss-ass • (lit.): ass licker.

example: Le patron adore Jean-Claude parce que c'est un **lèche-cul** fini!

translation: The boss loves Jean-Claude because he's a total **kiss-ass**!

as spoken: Le patron, y adore Jean-Claude pasque c't'un **lèche-cul** fini!

NOTE -1: **fini** *adj.* total, complete • (lit.): finished.

NOTE -2: **lèche-cul (faire du)** *exp.* to kiss up, to kiss someone's ass • (lit.): to do butt-licking.

mon cul! *inter.* my ass (in response to a ridiculous comment) • (lit.): my ass.

example: "Guy m'a dit qu'il est millionnaire."
"**Mon cul**! Il travaille nuit et jour pour faire joindre les bouts."

translation: "Guy told me he's a millionaire."
"**My ass**! He works night and day to make ends meet.

as spoken: "Guy, y m'a dit qu'il est millionaire."

"**Mon cul**! Y travaille nuit et jour pour faire join<u>d'</u> les bouts."

VARIATION: **Et mon cul, c'est du poulet?** *exp.* •
(lit.): and my ass is made of chicken?

nique ta mère *exp. (extremely vulgar)* disparaging remark about someone's mother •
(lit.): fuck your mother.

NOTE: This is also the name of a popular rap group in France.

pétasse *f.* a disparaging remark applied only to a woman •
(lit.): fart.

NOTE: This comes from the verb *péter* meaning "to fart."

pouffiasse *f.* fat slob of a woman, whore, "blimp."

salaud *m. (extremely popular; applies only to a man)* bastard.

example: Ce **salaud** de Pierre! Il m'a menti!

translation: Pierre, that **bastard**! He lied to me!

as spoken: Ce **salaud** <u>d</u>'Pierre! Y m'a menti!

SEE: **salope**, *p. 66.*

saligaud *m.* variation of: *salaud.*

saloparde *f.* variation of: *salope.*

salopard *m.* variation of: *salaud.*

salope *f. (extremely popular)* bitch.

example: Cette **salope** de Marie. Elle a volé mon petit ami!

translation: Marie, that **bitch**. She stole my boyfriend!

as spoken: <u>C</u>'te **salope** de Marie. Elle a volé mon <u>p</u>'tit ami!

SEE: **salaud**, *p. 66.*

NOTE: The term *salope* also has the connotation of "a sexually promiscuous woman."

ta grand-mère fait du vélo sans selle *exp.* disparaging remark about someone's grandmother •
(lit.): your grandmother rides a bike without a seat (and therefore rides on the end of the rod).

ta gueule *interj.* shut up •
(lit.): your mouth.

example: **Ta gueule**! Arrête de parler de Robert comme ça!

translation: **Shut up**! Stop talking about Robert like that!

as spoken: [no change]

NOTE: When the feminine noun *gueule*, literally meaning "the mouth of an animal," is used in reference to a person, its connotation is derogatory for "mouth" or "face," depending on the context.

ta mère a le dos chaud *exp.* disparaging remark about someone's mother • (lit.): your mother has a hot back.

trou du cul *m.* (*applies to a man or woman*) • (lit.): asshole.

A CLOSER LOOK (2):
Offensive Name-Calling for a Man

Once you've learned the following useful words for driving the street of Paris, you'll be ready to create some of your own personalized insults. Following this list is a Name-Calling "Buffet." Simply choose an item from each column to form a series of handy phrases to draw upon for those unexpected traffic emergencies.

bordille *f.* bastard, piece of junk.

bourdille *f.* a variation of: *bordille.*

charognard *m.* bastard.

con *m.* bastard.

con(n)ard *m.* a variation of: *con.*

conneau *m.* a variation of: *con.*

couillon *m.* idiot.

NOTE: This comes from the feminine noun *couilles* meaning "testicles" or "balls."

fils de pute *m.* son of a bitch • (lit.): son of a whore.

fumier *m.* bastard, "piece of shit" • (lit.): manure.

ordure *f.* bastard • (lit.): trash.

peau de vache *f.* bastard • (lit.): cow skin.

pourriture *f.* bastard • (lit.): rotting trash.

raclure *f.* bastard • (lit.): scrapings.
> **NOTE:** **raclure de bidet** *f.* • (lit.): bidet scrapings.

salaud *m.* (*very popular*) bastard.

saligaud *m.* a variation of: *salaud.*

salopard *m.* variation of: *salaud.*

troufignon *m.* variation of: *trou du cul* meaning "asshole."

troufignard *m.* variation of: *trou du cul* meaning "asshole."

trouduc *m.* abbreviation of: *trou du cul* meaning "asshole."

trou du cul *m.* asshole.

vache *f.* bastard • (lit.): cow.

NAME-CALLING "BUFFET" FOR A MAN		
		bordille *f.*
		bourdille *f.*
		charognard *m.*
		charogne *f.*
		con *m.*
	sale (dirty)	**con(n)ard** *m.*
		conneau *m.*
		couillon *m.*
espèce de ("you...")	**grand(e)** (big)	**fils de pute** *m.*
		fumier *m.*
		ordure *f.*
putain de ("you fucking...")	**gros(se)** (fat)	**peau de vache** *f.*
		pourriture *f.*
		raclure *f.*
	vieux, vieille (old)	**salaud** *m.*
		saligaud *m.*
		salopard *m.*
		trou du cul *m.*
		trouduc *m.*
		troufignard *m.*
		troufignon *m.*
		vache *f.*

A CLOSER LOOK (3):
Offensive Name-Calling for a Woman

boude *m.* variation of: *boudin.*

boudin *m.* ugly and fat woman
 • (lit.): blood sausage.

con(n)arde *f.* variation of: *connasse.*

con(n)asse *f.* bitch • (lit.): cunt.

copaille *f.* bitch.

fumelle *f.* broad.

gale *f.* bitch • (lit.): mange.

garce *f.* bitch.

grognasse *f.* bitchy woman.
 NOTE: **grogner** *v.* to groan.

limace *f.* bitch • (lit.): slug.

mistonne *f.* bitch.

ordure *f.* bitch • (lit.): trash

peau de vache *f.* bitch •
 (lit.): cow skin.

pétasse *f.* fart.

pouffiasse *f.* fat slob of a
 woman, "blimp."

pourriture *f.* bitch •
 (lit.): rotting trash.

raclure *f.* bitch • (lit.): scrapings.
 ALSO: **raclure de bidet** *f.*
 bidet scrapings.

rombière *f.* bitch, overbearing
 woman.

salope *f.* (*very popular*) bitch.

saloparde *v.* variation of: *salope.*

tarderie *f.* old hag.

tartavelle *f.* ugly woman.

truie *f.* old bitch • (lit.): sow.

vache *f.* bitch • (lit.): cow.

vieille peau *f.* old hag •
 (lit.): old skin.

NAME-CALLING "BUFFET" FOR A WOMAN		
espèce de ("you...") **putain de** ("you fucking...")	**sale** (dirty) **grand(e)** (big) **gros(se)** (fat) **vieux, vieille** (old)	**boude** *f.* **boudin** *m.* **con(n)arde** *f.* **con(n)asse** *f.* **copaille** *f.* **fumelle** *f.* **garce** *f.* **gale** *f.* **grognasse** *f.* **limace** *f.* **mistonne** *f.* **ordure** *f.* **peau de vache** *f.* **pétasse** *f.* **pouffiasse** *f.* **pourriture** *f.* **raclure** *f.* **rombière** *f.* **saloparde** *f.* **salope** *f.* **tarderie** *f.* **tartavelle** *f.* **truie** *f.* **vache** *f.*

Quelle tignasse!

(trans.): What a mop of hair!
(lit.): [same]

Leçon Four

Anne: Nancy! Merci tellement de nous avoir invités. On s'amuse super bien!

(Puis, à voix basse…)

Ce qu'on **se fait chier** dans ce **trou**.

Luc: Et la **bouffe**, elle est **gerbos**! J'ai failli **dégueuler mes tripes** quand j'ai goûté la **barbaque**!

Anne: Je n'aurais pas dû **me morfaler** comme ça, mais j'avais tellement **la dalle**.

Luc: Tu arrives à croire comment elle **caquette** sans arrêt, Nancy? C'est une vraie **mitrailleuse**, celle-là. Tiens! Tu as **mâté** *un peu* (1) les **écrases-merde** de l'**andouille** qui vient d'entrer? Ils sont **crados**!

Anne: Je le connais, lui. Ce n'est pas ce qu'on appelle **propre-sur-soi**. C'est normal qu'il **schlingue** parce qu'il ne **se décrotte** jamais! Et sa **tignasse**…n'en parlons même pas!

Luc: Au moins, ce n'est pas un **abruti** comme celui à côté de cette **pouffiasse**-là.

Anne: C'est Henri Durelle, ça. Quel **phénomène**, lui. On travaille ensemble. Le patron l'aime beaucoup parce que c'est un *beau* (2) **lèche-cul**. Oh, il **me casse les oreilles**. Une fois il m'a dit qu'il a mis une **pouliche en cloque** mais à mon avis, ce ne sont que des **couillonnades** pour faire macho.

Translation in English

What a mop!

Anne: Nancy! Thank you so much for inviting us. We're having such a wonderful time!

(Then, in a low voice…)

Am I ever **bored shitless** in this **joint**.

Luc: And the **food** is **gross**! I almost **barfed my guts out** when I tasted the **meat**!

Anne: I shouldn't have **pigged out** like that, but I was really **hungry**.

Luc: Can you believe how Nancy **blabs** nonstop? She's a real **blabbermouth**. Hey! Did you **get a load of** the **big ugly shoes** on the **nerd** that just walked in? They're **filthy**!

Anne: I know him. He's not what you'd call **squeaky-clean**. Of course he **stinks** because he never **cleans himself**! And his **hair**…let's not even go there!

Luc: At least he's not an **idiot** like the guy next to that **fat woman** over there.

Anne: That's Henri Durelle. What a **character** that guy is. We work together. The boss really likes him because he's a *total* **kiss-ass**. Oh, the way he **talks my ear off**. Once he told me he got a **girl knocked up**, but in my opinion that's just a bunch of **bullshit** to make himself out to be macho.

Dialogue in slang as it would be spoken

Quelle Tignasse!

Anne: Nancy! Merci tellement d'nous avoir invités. On s'amuse super bien!

(*Puis, à voix basse…*)

C'qu'on **s'fait chier** dans c'**trou**.

Luc: Et la **bouffe**, elle est **gerbos**! J'ai failli **dégueuler mes tripes** quand j'ai goûté la **barbaque**!

Anne: J'aurais pas dû **m'morfaler** comme ça, mais j'avais tellement **la dalle**.

Luc: T'arrives à croire comment è **caquette** sans arrêt, Nancy? C't'une vraie **mitrailleuse**, celle-là. Tiens! T'as **mâté** *un peu* les **écrases-merde** d'l'**andouille** qui vient d'entrer? Y sont **crados**!

Anne: Je l'connais, lui. C'est pas c'qu'on appelle **prop'-sur-soi**. C'est normal qu'y **schlingue** pasqu'y **z'décrotte** jamais! Et sa **tignasse**…n'en parlons même pas!

Luc: Au moins, c'est pas un **abruti** comme celui à côté d'c'te **pouffiasse**-là.

Anne: C'est Henri Durelle, ça. Quel **phénomène**, lui. On travaille ensemble. Le patron, y l'aime beaucoup pasque c't'un *beau* **lèche-cul**. Oh, y **m'casse les oreilles**. Une fois y m'a dit qu'il a mis une **pouliche** en **cloque** mais à mon avis, ce sont qu'des **couillonnades** pour faire macho.

Vocabulary

FOOTNOTES FROM THE DIALOGUE

(1) _un peu:_

The is a popular adverbial expression used to add emphasis to the verb it modifies. It could be translated as _"just"_ when used with a verb: _Ecoute **un peu** cette jolie musique!;_ Just listen to this beautiful music!

(2) _beau/belle:_

When used to modify a noun, these adjectives are loosely translated as "one hell of a": _C'est un **beau** menteur, lui!;_ That guy's one hell of a liar!

abruti _m._ idiot, jerk, nerd.

> example: Quel **abruti**! Jean se promène en shorts alors qu'il pleut dehors!

> translation: What a **jerk**! Jean is walking around in shorts and it's raining outside!

> as spoken: Quel **abruti**! Jean, y s'promène en shorts alors qu'y pleut dehors!

> **SYNONYM:** SEE: **andouille**, _(next entry)._

andouille _f._ idiot, jerk, nerd.

> example: Quelle **andouille**, ce Patrice! Au restaurant, il a renversé tout un verre de jus de tomate sur Michelle et elle portait une nouvelle robe blanche!

> translation: What a **nerd** Patrice is. At the restaurant, he spilled an entire glass of tomato juice on Michelle and she was wearing a new white dress!

> as spoken: Quelle **andouille**, c'Patrice! Au resto, il a renversé tout un verre d'jus d'tomate sur Michelle et è portait une nouvelle robe blanche!

barbaque *f.* inferior meat.

> example: Tu as goûté la **barbaque** que Jacqueline a servi hier
> soir? C'était horrible!
>
> translation: Did you taste the **shoe leather** that Jacqueline served
> last night? It was horrible!
>
> as spoken: T'as goûté la **barbaque** qu'elle a servi hier soir,
> Jacqueline? C't'ait horrible!

bouffe *f.* food, "grub," "chow."

> example: J'ai faim. Tu as de la **bouffe** chez toi?
>
> translation: I'm hungry. You got any **chow** at your house?
>
> as spoken: J'ai faim. T'as d'la **bouffe** chez toi?
>
> **NOTE:** **bouffer** *v. (extremely popular)* to eat.

caqueter *v.* to blab on and on • (lit.): to cackle.

> example: Arthur parle sans arrêt. Il a **caqueté** pendant toute une
> heure de la même histoire!
>
> translation: Arthur talks nonstop. He **blabbed on and on** for an
> entire hour about the same story!
>
> as spoken: Arthur, y parle sans arrêt. Il a **caqueté** pendant toute
> une heure d'la même histoire!

casser les oreilles à quelqu'un *exp.* to talk someone's ear off •
(lit.): to break someone's ears.

> example: Voilà Thérèse! Je dois me cacher. Si elle me voit, elle
> va **me casser les oreilles** comme d'habitude!
>
> translation: There's Theresa! I have to hide. If she sees me, she'll
> **talk my ear off** as usual.
>
> as spoken: V'là Thérèse! J'dois m'cacher. Si è m'voit, è va
> **m'casser les oreilles** comme d'habitude!

chier (se faire) *v.* to bug the shit out of someone • (lit.): to make someone shit.

>   example: Je peux supporter Alain pour cinq minutes maximum. Après ça, il commence à **me faire chier**.

>   translation: I can tolerate Alan for five minutes max. After that, he starts **bugging the shit out of me**.

>   as spoken: J'peux supporter Alain pour ci<u>n</u>' minutes maximum. Après ça, <u>y</u> commence à **m'faire chier**.

cloque (être en) *exp.* to be knocked up • (lit.): to be in blister (to look as if one is wrapped up in a big blister).

>   example: Tu as entendu les nouvelles? Irène est **en cloque** et elle n'a que seize ans!

>   translation: Did you hear the news? Irene is **knocked up** and she's only sixteen years old!

>   as spoken: <u>T</u>'as entendu les nouvelles? Irène, <u>elle</u> est **en cloque** et elle ~ a <u>qu</u>'seize ans!

couillonnades *f.pl.* nonsense, "bullshit."

>   example: Ne crois rien à ce qu'il te dit. Tout ce qu'il balance ne sont que des **couillonnades**.

>   translation: Don't believe anything he tells you. Everything that comes out of his mouth is nothing but **bullshit**.

>   as spoken: ~ Crois rien à <u>c</u>'qu'<u>y</u> te dit. Tout <u>c</u>'qu'<u>y</u> balance ~ sont <u>qu</u>'des **couillonnades**.

> **NOTE -1:** **balancer** *v.* to jabber, to chatter on about something • (lit.): to throw.

> **NOTE -2:** The term *couillonnades* comes from the feminine plural noun *couilles* meaning "testicles" or "balls."

crados (être) *adj. (pronounced: "crados" with the "s" articulated)* to be filthy.

>   example: Enlève tes chaussures avant d'entrer. Elles sont **crados**!

>   translation: Take off your shoes before you come in. They're **filthy**!

>   as spoken: Enlève tes chaussures avant d'entrer. <u>È</u> sont **crados**!

dalle (avoir la) *exp. (very mild)* to be hungry.

    example: J'ai **la dalle**, moi. Tu veux aller prendre à manger?

    translation: I'm **hungry**. Do you want to get something to eat?

    as spoken: J'ai **la dalle**, moi. Tu veux aller prendr_à manger?

    SYNONYM: **fringale (avoir la)** *exp. (very mild)*.

décrotter (se) *v.* to clean oneself • (lit.): to "uncrap" oneself.

    example: On doit quitter la maison d'ici cinq minutes! Va **te décrotter** tout de suite!

    translation: We have to leave the house in five minutes! Go **clean yourself up** right now!

    as spoken: On doit quitter la maison d'ici cin' minutes! Va **t'décrotter** tout d'suite!

    NOTE: **crotte** *f.* turd, crap.

dégueuler ses tripes *exp.* to barf one's guts out • (lit.): to "unmouth" one's guts.

    example: Le bateau n'a pas arrêté de balotter de long en large. J'ai **dégueulé mes tripes** pendant tout le voyage.

    translation: The boat didn't stop tossing back and forth. I **barfed my guts out** during the entire trip.

    as spoken: Le bateau, il ~ a pas arrêté d'balotter d'long en large. J'ai **dégueulé mes tripes** pendant tout l'voyage.

    NOTE: **gueule** *f.* derogatory for "mouth" or "face" when applied to a person since its literal translation is "the mouth of an animal."

écrases-merde *f.pl.* shoes, "shit-kickers" • (lit.): shit-smashers.

    example: Mais, tu ne vas pas porter ces **écrases-merde**-là! On va à un restaurant de luxe!

    translation: You're not going to wear those **shit-kickers**! We're going to a fancy restaurant!

    as spoken: Mais, tu ~ vas pas porter ces **écrases-merde**-là! On va à un resto d'luxe!

gerbos (être) *adj.* to be gross • (lit.): to be enough to make one vomit.

> example: Suzanne est cuisinière horrible. Son dîner d'hier était **gerbos**!

> translation: Suzanne is a horrible cook. Her dinner last night was **gross**!

> as spoken: Suzanne, <u>elle</u> est cuisinière horrible. Son dîner d'hier, <u>il</u> était **gerbos**!

> **NOTE:** **gerber** *v.* to throw up, to "barf."

lèche-cul *m.* "kiss-ass" • (lit.): ass-licker.

> example: David a acheté au patron un gros cadeau pour son anniversaire. Quel **lèche-cul**, lui!

> translation: David bought the boss a big present for his birthday. What an **ass-licker**!

> as spoken: David, <u>il</u> a ac<u>h</u>'té au patron un gros cadeau pour son anniversaire. Quel **lèche-cul**, lui!

mâter *v.* to look, to "check out."

> example: Tu as **mâté** la robe qu'elle porte, Sylvie? C'est horrible!

> translation: Did you **get a load of** the dress Sylvie is wearing? It's horrible!

> as spoken: <u>T</u>'as **mâté** la robe qu'<u>è</u> porte, Sylvie? C'est horrible!

> **NOTE -1:** This is a stronger variation of *lèche-bottes* (as seen earlier on page 34).

mitrailleuse *f.* a very talkative woman, blabbermouth • (lit.): machine gun.

> example: Evelyne parle sans arrêt. Quelle **mitrailleuse**, cella-là!

> translation: Evelyn talks nonstop. What a friggin' **blabbermouth**!

> as spoken: Evelyne, <u>è</u> parle sans arrêt. Quelle **mitrailleuse**, cella-là!

morfaler (se) *v.* to pig out.

> example: Je me sens malade. Je **me suis morfalé** trop de desserts!
>
> translation: I feel sick. I **pigged out** on too many desserts.
>
> as spoken: Je m̲'sens malade. Je **m̲'suis morfalé** trop d̲'desserts!

phénomène *m.* a strange person • (lit.): a phenomenon.

> example: Roger, c'est un vrai **phénomène**. Il ne porte que du noir tous les jours.
>
> translation: Roger is a **strange guy**. He dresses in black every day.
>
> as spoken: Roger, c̲'t̲'un vrai **phénomène**. Y̲ porte que du noir tous les jours.

pouffiasse *f.* a fat woman or girl.

> example: Si tu continues à manger comme ça, tu vas devenir **pouffiasse**.
>
> translation: If you keep eating like that, you're going to turn into a **fatso**.
>
> as spoken: Si tu continues à manger comme ça, tu vas dev̲'nir **pouffiasse**.

pouliche *f.* woman, "chick" • (lit.): filly.

> example: Tu connais cette **pouliche**-là? Je la trouve super jolie!
>
> translation: Do you know that **chick**? I think she's totally beautiful!
>
> as spoken: Tu connais c̲'te **pouliche**-là? J̲'la trouve super jolie!

propre-sur-soi (être) *exp.* to be squeaky-clean (said of a person) • (lit.): to be clean on oneself.

> example: Je vois que tu as pris une douche. Voilà ce qui s'appelle **propre-sur-soi**!
>
> translation: I see you took a shower. Now that's what I call **squeaky-clean**!
>
> as spoken: J̲'vois qu̲' t̲'as pris une douche. V̲'là c̲'qui s'appelle **propre-sur-soi**!

schlinguer *v.* to stink.

   example: Je n'aime pas ce fromage parce que ça **schlingue**!

  translation: I don't like this cheese because it **stinks**.

  as spoken: J'aime pas c'fromage pasque ça **schlingue**!

tignasse *f.* hair.

   example: Je vais me faire couper la **tignasse**.

  translation: I'm going to get my **hair** cut.

  as spoken: J'vais m'faire couper la **tignasse**.

  SYNONYM: **tifs** *m.pl.*

trou *m.* place in general, "joint" • (lit.): hole.

   example: Je refuse d'entrer dans ce **trou**. C'est plein de fumeurs!

  translation: I refuse to go into that **joint**. It's full of smokers!

  as spoken: Je r'fuse d'entrer dans c'**trou**. C'est plein d'fumeurs!

A CLOSER LOOK:
Body Parts in Slang

When it comes to inventing colorful slang terms, the French would certainly never be accused of lacking imagination — as demonstrated by the following terms. This list will present you with an array of words and phrases for everything from your feet to the top of your head, with several stops along the way!

Anus
(anus)

boîte à pâté *f.* • (lit.): pâté box.

cul *m.* • (lit.): ass.

 NOTE: The term *cul* is also used to means "buttocks."

entrée de service *f.*
 • (lit.): service entrance.

fion *m.* • (lit.): the finish (of an article).

luc *m.*

> **NOTE:** This is *verlan* for *cul* meaning "ass" — *SEE: Street French 2, Verlan, p. 187.*

œil de bronze *m.*
- (lit.): bronze eye.

œillet *m.* *(extremely popular)*
- (lit.): carnation.

pastille *f.* *(popular)*
- (lit.): lozenge.

pot d'échappement *m.*
- (lit.): exhaust pipe.
> **NOTE:** This can also be shorten to: *pot.*

petit *m.* • (lit.): the little (area).

rondelle *f.* *(popular)*
- (lit.): washer.

rosette *f.* *(popular)* • (lit.): that which is pink.

trou de balle *m.*
- (lit.): gunshot hole.

trou du cul *m.* • (lit.): asshole.

troufignard *m.*
> **NOTE:** A slang variation of: *troufion.*

troufignon *m.*
> **NOTE:** A slang variation of: *troufion.*

troufion *m.* • (lit.): asshole (since *fion* means "anus" in French slang).

turbine à chocolat *f.*
- (lit.): chocolate turbine.

tuyau à gaz *m.* • (lit.): gas pipe.

Clitoris
(clitoris)

berlingot *m.* • (lit.): a type of candy made out of burnt sugar.

bouton d'amour *m.*
- (lit.): love button.

bouton de rose *m.*
- (lit.): rose button.

clicli *m.* a slang abbreviation of: *clitoris.*

cliquette *f.* a slang abbreviation of: *clitoris*.

clito *m.* *(extremely popular)* a slang abbreviation of: *clitoris*.

cliton *m.* a slang abbreviation of: *clitoris*.

framboise *f.* • (lit.): raspberry.

grain de café *m.* • (lit.): coffee bean.

haricot *m.* • (lit.): bean.

noisette *f.* • (lit.): hazelnut.

praline *f.* • (lit.): praline.

Postérieur
(posterior)

arrière-boutique *m.*
 • (lit.): back-shop.

arrière-train *m.*
 • (lit.): caboose.

baba *m.* • (lit.): from baba-au-rhum (due to its round shape, like one's buttocks).

ballon *m.* • (lit.): **1.** balloon • **2.** rubber ball.

bottom *m.* *(Americanism)*.

brioches *f.pl.* • (lit.): brioches (breads).

cadran solaire *m.*
 • (lit.): sundial.

croupe *f.* • (lit.): rump.

croupion *m.* *(also spelled: "croupillon")* • (lit.): rump (of bird).

cul *m.* *(very popular)* • (lit.): ass.

demi-lunes *f.pl.* • (lit.): half moons.

der *m.* • (lit.): abbreviation of *derrière* meaning "backside."

derche *m.*
 NOTE: This is a slang variation of *derrière* meaning "backside."

derge *m.*
 NOTE: This is a slang variation of *derrière* meaning "backside."

derrière *m.* • (lit.): behind.

deux frangines *f.pl.*
- (lit.): two sisters.

faubourg *m.* • (lit.): suburb, outlying part (of town).

fessier *m.* • (lit.): buttock (academic term).

   NOTE: This comes from the feminine noun *fesse* meaning the "cheek of the buttock."

fiacre *m.* • (lit.): cab.

fion *m.* *(extremely popular)*
- (lit.): end or finish (of an article).

luc *m.* *(extremely popular)*
- (lit.): a *verlan* transformation of *cul* meaning "ass."

lune *f.* • (lit.): moon.

médaillon *m.* • (lit.): medallion.

meules *f.pl.* **1.** posterior • **2.** breasts • (lit.): stacks, piles (of hay, etc.).

   NOTE: The difference between definitions **1.** and **2.** simply depends on the context.

pains au lait *m.pl.*
- (lit.): white breads.

panier à crottes *m.*
- (lit.): turd basket.

pétard *m.* • (lit.): farter (from the verb *péter* meaning "to fart."

pont arrière *m.* • (lit.): rear axle.

popotin *m.* *(extremely popular)*
- (lit.): [no literal translation].

postère *m.* an abbreviation of: *postérieur* meaning "posterior, buttocks."

postérieur *m.* • (lit.): posterior.

pot *m.* • (lit.): pot.

pot à crottes *m.* • (lit.): turd pot.

train *m.* • (lit.): train.

   ALSO: **arrière-train** *m.*
- (lit.): caboose.

Pénis
(penis)

andouille à col roulé *f.*
- (lit.): sausage with a rolled-down collar.

anguille de calecif *f.*
- (lit.): underwear eel.
  NOTE: **calecif** *m.* a slang transformation of *caleçon* meaning "underwear."

asperge *f.* • (lit.): asparagus.

baigneur *m.* • (lit.): bather

baïonnette *f.* • (lit.): bayonet.

baisette *f.* • (lit.): little fucker.
  NOTE: This comes from the slang verb *baiser* meaning "to fuck."

balayette *f.* • (lit.): small broom.

baveuse *f.* • (lit.): drooler.

bazar *m.* penis and testicles
- (lit.): bazaar.

béquille *f.* • (lit.): crutch.

berloque *f.* • (lit.): charm, trinket.

bijoux de famille *m.pl.* penis and testicles • (lit.): family jewels.

bite *f.* (*very popular*) • (lit.): bitt, bollard (on a ship).

boudin blanc *m.* • (lit.): white sausage.

bout *m.* • (lit.): end.

braquemard *m.* • (lit.): the pointer.
  NOTE: This comes from the verb *braquer* meaning "to point a gun (at something or someone)."
  VARIATION: **braquemart** *m.*

canne *f.* • (lit.): cane.

carabine *f.* • (lit.): rifle.

Charles-le-Chauve *m.*
- (lit.): Charles the Bald.

chose *f.* • (lit.): thing.

cigare à moustache *m.*
- (lit.): cigar with a moustache.

clarinette *f.* • (lit.): clarinet.

colonne *f.* • (lit.): column.

cornemuse *f.* • (lit.): bagpipe.

cyclope *m.* the "one-eyed monster" • (lit.): cyclops.

dard *m.* • (lit.): prick.

dardillon *m.* • (lit.): small prick.

défonceuse *f.*
 • (lit.): penetrator.

doigt du milieu *m.*
 • (lit.): middle finger.

flageolet *m.* • (lit.): flageolet (which is a type of bean).

flûte *f.* • (lit.): flute.

frétillante *f.* • (lit.): wagger.
 NOTE: This comes from the verb *frétiller* meaning "to wag."

frétillard *m.* • (lit.): wagger
 NOTE: This comes from the verb *frétiller* meaning "to wag."

gaule *f.* penis or erection
 • (lit.): (long, thin) pole, stick.

gland *m.* • (lit.): acorn.
 NOTE: This comes from the masculine noun *gland* meaning "acorn" and has taken the slang connotation of "penis, dick" due to its shape.

goupillon *m.* • (lit.): sprinkler (for holy water).

gourde à poils *f.*
 • (lit.): gourd with hairs.

gourdin *m.* • (lit.): club, bludgeon.

instrument *m.*
 • (lit.): instrument.

jambe du milieu *f.*
 • (lit.): middle leg.

macaroni *m.* • (lit.): macaroni.

machin *m.* • (lit.): thing.

mandrin *m.* • (lit.): bandit, ruffian.

marchandise *f.* penis and testicles • (lit.): merchandise.

marsouin *m.* • (lit.): porpoise.

monté (être bien) *adj.* to be well hung • (lit.): to be well mounted.

morceau *m.* • (lit.): morsel, piece.

nœud *m.* • (lit.): knot.

os à moelle *m.* • (lit.): marrow bone.

outil *m.* • (lit.): tool.

paquet *m.* penis and testicles
 • (lit.): package.

petit frère m. • (lit.): little brother.

pine f. *(extremely popular)*.

pointe f. • (lit.): point.

poireau m. • (lit.): leek.

Popaul m.
> **VARIATION:** **Popol** m.

quéquette f. *(child language)*.

queue f. *(very popular in Belgium)* • (lit.): tail.

quille f. • (lit.): (bowling) pin.

quiquette f.

quiqui m. *(child language)*.

sabre m. • (lit.): saber.

tracassin m. • (lit.): worrier (since the penis has a tendency to get wet when excited, like a person's forehead when worried).

tringle f. • (lit.): rod.

trique f. • (lit.): heavy stick.

troisième jambe f. • (lit.): third leg.

verge f. *(medical term)* • (lit.): rod, wand, cane.

zeb m.

zizi m. *(child language)*.

zob m. *(extremely popular)*.

zobi m.

Seins
(breasts)

amortisseurs m.pl. • (lit.): shock absorbers.

ananas m.pl. • (lit.): pineapples.

avant-postes m.pl. • (lit.): outposts.

avant-scènes f.pl. • (lit.): apron (of stage).

avantages m.pl. • (lit.): advantage.

balcon m. • (lit.): balcony.

ballons *m.pl.* large breasts
• (lit.): balloons.

boîtes à lait *f.pl.* • (lit.): milk
cans.

devanture *f.* • (lit.): front (of
building, etc.).

flotteurs *m.pl.* • (lit.): floaters.

globes *m.pl.* • (lit.): globes,
spheres.

il y a du beau monde *exp.*
said of a woman with large
breasts • (lit.): there are a lot of
people there.

il y a du monde au balcon
exp. said of a woman with large
breasts • (lit.): there are people
on the balcony.

il y a de quoi s'amuser *exp.*
said of a woman with large
breasts • (lit.): there's a lot
to have fun with.

lolos *m.pl.* • (lit.): little milkers.
NOTE: lolo *m.* child's
language for "milk."

mamelles *f.pl.* large breasts
• (lit.): *(anatomy)* mammae.

mappemonde *f.* • (lit.): map of
the world in two hemispheres.

melons *m.pl.* large breasts
• (lit.): melons.

miches *f.pl.* • (lit.): loaves of
bread.

nénés *m.pl.*

nibards *m.pl.*

nichons *m.pl.* *(very popular)*.

oranges *f.pl.* • (lit.): oranges.

pare-chocs *m.pl.*
• (lit.): bumpers.

pelotes *f.pl.* • (lit.): balls (of
wool, string, etc.).

roberts *m.pl.*

tétés *m.pl.*
NOTE: This comes from the
verb *téter* meaning "to suck (a
mother's breast)."

tétons *m.pl.* tits.
NOTE: This comes from the
verb *téter* meaning "to suck (a
mother's breast)."

Testicules
(*testicles*)

balloches *f.pl.* • (lit.): balls.

bibelots *m.pl.* • (lit.): trinkets.

bijoux de famille *m.pl.*
 • (lit.): family jewels.

billes *f.pl.* • (lit.): (small) balls.

bonbons *m.pl.* • (lit.): goodies.

breloques *f.pl.* • (lit.): charms,
 trinkets.

burettes *f.pl.* • (lit.): oilcans.

burnes *f.pl. (extremely popular)*.

couilles *f.pl. (very popular)*.

couillons *m.pl.*
 NOTE: This is a masculine
 variation of the feminine plural
 noun *couilles*.

croquignoles *f.pl.*
 • (lit.): biscuits.

joyeuses *f.pl.* • (lit.): the joyful
 ones, the ones that cause great
 joy.

noisettes *f.pl.* • (lit.): hazelnuts.

noix *f.pl.* • (lit.): nuts.

olives *f.pl.* • (lit.): olives.

pendeloques *f.pl.*
 • (lit.): **1.** pendants • **2.** jewels
 (of drop earring).

pendentifs *m.pl.*
 • (lit.): pendentives, "hangers."

petits oignons *m.pl.*
 • (lit.): little onions.

précieuses *f.pl.* • (lit.): precious
 ones.

rognons *m.pl.* • (lit.): kidneys.

rouleaux *m.pl.* • (lit.): rollers.

roustons *m.pl. (extremely
 popular)*.

valseuses *f.pl.* • (lit.): waltzers.

Vagin
(vagina)

baisoir *m.* • (lit.): place where one has sex such as the bedroom, brothel, etc.
NOTE: This comes from the slang verb *baiser* meaning "to fuck."

barbu *m.* • (lit.): the bearded one.

baveux *m.* • (lit.): drooler.

bénitier *m.* • (lit.): (holy water) basin.

boîte à ouvrage *f.*
• (lit.): work box.

bonbonnière *f.*
• (lit.): sweetmeat box.

bonnet à poils *m.* • (lit.): hair bonnet.

bréviaire d'amour *m.*
• (lit.): breviary of love.

chagatte *f.* • (lit.): cat, "pussy."
NOTE: This is a javanais transformation of the feminine word *chatte* meaning "cat" or "pussy." Javanais is a formula occasionally applied to slang words where the letters "ag" or "av" are added between syllables. Therefore *chat* becomes *chagatte*.

chat *m.* • (lit.): cat, "pussy."

chatte *f. (extremely popular)*
• (lit.): cat, "pussy."

cheminée *f.* • (lit.): chimney.

cicatrice *f.* • (lit.): scar.

con *m.* • (lit.): cunt.

connasse *f.* • (lit.): cunt.

crevasse *f.* • (lit.): crevice.

étau *m.* • (lit.): vise.

fente *f.* • (lit.): crack, crevice, split.

figue *f.* • (lit.): fig.

greffier *m.* • (lit.): cat, scratcher, "pussy."
NOTE: This comes from the verb *griffer* meaning "to scratch."

grippette *f.* • (lit.): pouncer.

NOTE: This comes from the verb *gripper* meaning "to seize, pounce upon."

mille-feuilles *m.pl.*
- (lit.): Napoleon pastry.

mimi *m.* • (lit.): kitty, "pussy."

minet *m.* • (lit.): kitty, "pussy."

minou *m.* • (lit.): kitty, "pussy."

motte *f.* • (lit); mound.

moule *f.* *(extremely popular)*
- (lit.): mussel.

panier *m.* • (lit.): basket.

panier d'amour *m.*
- (lit.): love basket.

pince *f.* • (lit.): holder, gripper.

portail *m.* • (lit.): portal.

tire-lire *f.* • (lit.): piggy bank.

trou *m.* • (lit.): hole.

LEÇON CINQ - Sexual Slang

Il est chaud de la pince, lui!

(trans.): That guy has sex on the brain!
(lit.): He has a hot claw!

Leçon Cinq

Douglas: Il fait beau ce soir. Si on faisait une balade à Pigalle?

Martine: Place Pigalle? Pour quoi faire — regarder les **bisenesseuses** qui **font le tapin**?! *Faut pas exagérer, non* (1)? C'est un quartier pour les **macs** et les **michés**. Ça me **fout** un peu la **trouille**, moi.

Douglas: Oh, c'est instructif, tu sais. La dernière fois que j'y suis passé, tu ne vas pas croire qui j'ai vu. Je suis tombé sur Etienne avec une des **putes** — une **bandeuse** *de première* (2). Je parie qu'elle peut **faire flasher** les mecs *facile* (3).

Martine: Je parie qu'il t'aurait **foutu en l'air** s'il savait que tu l'avais vu!

Douglas: *Comme tu dis* (4). Il était en train de lui **rouler une pelle**! Je ne savais pas qu'il payait pour **s'alléger les bourses**!

Martine: *Bof* (5), ça ne m'étonne pas tellement. Il a toujours été **chaud de la pince**, lui, et un peu **pervers sur les bords**.

Douglas: Mais, je n'avais pas la moindre idée qu'il était **porté sur la bagatelle** à ce point-là! C'est quand-même **craignos**!

Martine: Ah, ouais! J'espère qu'il est prudent, au moins. Avec une nana comme ça qui a **la cuisse légère**, il risque de **ramasser la chtouille** ou le **SIDA** s'il **la trempe** sans **capote**.

Douglas: Non, je suppose qu'il voulait juste **une petite pipe**, c'est tout. C'est bizarre — rien que l'idée d'aller au **boxon**, je me sentirais tellement mal à l'aise que je serais **constipé de l'entre-jambe**.

Lesson Five

Translation in English

That guy has sex on the brain!

Douglas: It's beautiful tonight. What do you say we take a stroll to Pigalle?

Martine: Place Pigalle? What for — to look at the **working girls** who are **hooking**?! *Are you kidding?* That's a neighborhood for **pimps** and **johns**. It all **gives** me the **creeps**.

Douglas: Oh, it's informative! The last time I went by there, you're not going to believe who I saw. I ran into Etienne with one of the **hookers** — *real* **hot stuff**. I bet she can **turn on** guys *easily*.

Martine: I bet he would have **killed you** if he knew you saw him!

Douglas: *You know it.* He was in the middle of **French kissing her**! I didn't know that he pays **to get off**!

Martine: Oh, it doesn't really surprise me. That guy's always had **sex on the brain**, and he's a little **kinky**.

Douglas: But I didn't have the slightest idea that he was **sex crazed** to that degree! It's kind of **scary**!

Martine: *Yeah!* I hope he's careful at least. With a girl like that who **sleeps around**, he's at risk of **catching the clap** or **AIDS** if he **screws** without a **rubber**.

Douglas: No, I figure that he just wanted a quick **blow job**, that's all. It's strange — just the idea of going to a **whorehouse**, I'd be so uptight that I would even be able **to get it up**.

Dialogue in slang as it would be spoken

Il est chaud d'la pince, lui!

Douglas: Y fait beau c'soir. Si on faisait une balade à Pigalle?

Martine: Place Pigalle? Pour quoi faire — regarder les **bisenesseuses** qui **font l'tapin**?! *Faut pas exagérer, non?* C't'un quartier pour les **macs** et les **michés**. Ça m'**fout** un peu la **trouille**, moi.

Douglas: Oh, c'est instructif, tu sais. La dernière fois qu'j'y suis passé, tu vas pas croire qui j'ai vu. J'suis tombé sur Etienne avec une des **putes** — une **bandeuse** *de première.* J'parie qu'è peut **faire flasher** les mecs *facile.*

Martine: J'parie qu'y t'aurait **foutu en l'air** s'y savait qu'tu l'avais vu!

Douglas: *Comme tu dis.* Il était en train d'lui **rouler une pelle**! J'savais pas qu'y payait pour **s'alléger les bourses**!

Martine: *Bof,* ça m'étonne pas tellement. Il a toujours été **chaud d'la pince**, lui, et un peu **pervers sur les bords**.

Douglas: Mais, j'avais pas la moindre idée qu'il était **porté sur la bagatelle** à c'point-là! C'est quand-même **craignos**!

Martine: Ah, ouais! J'espère qu'il est prudent, au moins. Avec une nana comme ça qui a **la cuisse légère**, y risque de **ramasser la chtouille** ou l'**SIDA** s'y **la trempe** sans **capote**.

Douglas: Non, j'suppose qu'y voulait juste **une p'tite pipe**, c'est tout. C'est bizarre — rien qu'l'idée d'aller au **boxon**, j'me sentirais tellement mal à l'aise que je s'rais **constipé d'l'entre-jambe**.

Vocabulary

FOOTNOTES FROM THE DIALOGUE

(1) *Faut pas exagérer, non?*:

This has to be one of the most commonly heard French expressions meaning, "You've got to be kidding!" It is interesting to note that the full expression, *Il ne faut pas exagérer, non?* is rarely used. However, in its shortened form, it is extremely popular and used by everyone.

(2) *de première*:

adj. first-rate, top-notch • *Nancy, c'est une chanteuse **de première***; Nancy is a top-notch singer.

(3) *facile*:

In the opening dialogue, this adjective was actually used as an adverb, a common practice in spoken French. Example: [academic French] *Je l'ai fait facilement*; I did it easily • [spoken French] *Je l'ai fait facile*; I did it easy.

(4) *Comme tu dis*:

exp. You said it! You bet! • (lit.): As you say.

(5) *Bof*:

interj. used to indicate a lack of enthusiasm • *Bof, le film n'était pas vraiment bien*; Well, the film wasn't really that good.

---

alléger les bourses (s') *exp.* to have sex, to "get off" • (lit.): to lighten one's purse.

example: Guillaume **s'allège les bourses** avec les prostituées!

translation: William **gets off** with prostitutes!

as spoken: Guillaume, y **s'allège les bourses** avec les prostituées!

NOTE: **bourses** *f.pl.* testicles • (lit.): purses.

bandeuse *f.* a "hot number," sexy woman • (lit.): one who causes men to *bander* meaning "to have an erection."

> example: Carole est connue pour être une **bandeuse** et couche avec un différent gars chaque nuit!

> translation: Carole is known for being a **nymphomaniac** et goes to bed with a different guy every night!

> as spoken: Carole, <u>elle</u> est connue pour êt<u>r'</u>une **bandeuse** et couche avec un différent gars chaque nuit!

bisenesseuse *f.* a prostitute, "working girl" • (lit.): a "businesswoman."

> example: Ce quartier a beaucoup changé. Maintenant, c'est plein de **bisenesseuses**.

> translation: This neighborhood has changed a lot. Now it's full of **working girls**.

> as spoken: Ce quartier, <u>il</u> a beaucoup changé. Maintenant, c'est plein <u>d'</u>**bisenesseuses**.

boxon *m.* • **1.** whorehouse • **2.** a complete mess, chaos.

> example (1): Je vois toujours des drôles de mecs et des nanas super sexy entrer chez les voisins d'à côté. Je commence à avoir l'impression que leur maison est un **boxon**!

> translation: I always see strange men and sexy girls go into the neighbor's house next door. I'm starting to get the feeling that their home is a **whorehouse**!

> as spoken: <u>J'</u>vois toujours des drôles <u>d'</u>mecs et des nanas super sexy entrer chez les voisins d'à côté. <u>J'</u>commence à avoir l'impression qu<u>'</u>leur maison, <u>c't'</u>un **boxon**!

> example (2): Va ranger ta chambre tout de suite! Quel **boxon**!

> translation: Go clean up your room right now! What a **pigsty**!

> as spoken: Va ranger ta cham<u>b'</u> tout <u>d'</u>suite! Quel **boxon**!

capote *f.* condom, "rubber."

> example: De nos jours, il faut absolument porter une **capote** pour participer dans des rapports sexuels.

> translation: Nowadays, it's absolutely necessary to wear a **rubber** when participating in sexual relations.

> as spoken: De nos jours, ~ faut absolument porter une **capote** pour participer dans des rapports sexuels.

chaud de la pince (être) *exp. (only applies to men)* to be oversexed
  • (lit.): to have a hot claw.

> example: Même à son âge, il est toujours **chaud de la pince**.

> translation: Even at his age, he's still **oversexed**.

> as spoken: Même à son âge, il est toujours **chaud d'la pince**.

constipé de l'entre-jambe (être) *exp.* said of a man who can not "get it up" • (lit.): to be constipated in the "in-between" leg.

> example: Quand j'ai eu ma première rencontre, j'étais tellement nerveux que j'étais **constipé de l'entre-jambe**.

> translation: When I had my first encounter, I was so nervous that I **couldn't get it up**.

> as spoken: Quand j'ai eu ma première rencontre, j'étais tellement nerveux qu'j'étais **constipé d'l'entre-jambe**.

craignos (être) *adj.* to be scary (from the verb *craindre* meaning "to have fear").

> example: Tu as entendu parler de l'avion de ligne qui est tombé du ciel en panne? C'est **craignos**, ça!

> translation: Did you hear about the commercial plane that conked out and crashed? That's **scary**.

> as spoken: T'as entendu parler d'l'avion d'ligne qu'est tombé du ciel en panne? C'est **craignos**, ça!

cuisse légère (avoir la) *exp.* said of a loose girl, "to have light ankles"
  • (lit.): to have the light thigh.

>   example: Tous les gars draguent Véronique parce qu'elle a **la**
>   **cuisse légère**.
>
>   translation: All the guys flirt with Veronica because she **has light**
>   **ankles**.
>
>   as spoken: Tous les gars, y̲ draguent Véronique pasqu̲'elle a **la**
>   **cuisse légère**.
>
> **NOTE:** **draguer** v. *(extremely popular)* to flirt, to cruise (for
> sexual encounters).

en l'air (foutre quelqu'un) *exp.* to kill someone • (lit.): to throw
  someone up in the air.

>   example: Elle a **foutu en l'air** son mari quand elle l'a trouvé au
>   lit avec une autre femme.
>
>   translation: She **wasted** her husband when she found him in bed
>   with another woman.
>
>   as spoken: Elle a **foutu en l'air** son mari quand è̲ l'a trouvé au
>   lit avec une aut̲' femme.

flasher (faire) *v.* to turn on sexually • (lit.): to startle with a flash of light.

>   example: Diane n'est pas très belle mais elle **fait flasher** les
>   mecs sans effort.
>
>   translation: Diane isn't very pretty but she **turns on** guys without
>   any effort.
>
>   as spoken: Diane, e̲l̲l̲e̲ ~ est pas très belle mais è̲ **fait flasher** les
>   mecs sans effort.

foutre *v.* to put • (lit.): to fuck.

>   example: **Fous**-moi ça dehors tout de suite!
>
>   translation: **Put** that outside for me right now!
>
>   as spoken: **Fous**-moi ça dehors tout d̲'suite!

mac m. short for *maquereau* meaning "pimp" • (lit.): mackerel.

> example: Tu as vu comment il est habillé, celui-là. Je parie que c'est un **mac**.

> translation: Did you see how he's dressed? I bet he's a **pimp**.

> as spoken: T'as vu comment il est habillé, çui-lá. J'parie que c't'un **mac**.

> **NOTE:**   **maquerelle** f. Madam (of a brothel).

miché m. prostitute's client, "john."

> example: Afin de combattre le problème de la prostitution dans le quartier, la police a commencé à arrêter tous les **michés**.

> translation: In order to fight the prostitution problem in this neighborhood, the police have started to arrest all the **johns**.

> as spoken: Afin d'combatt' le problème d'la prostitution dans l'quartier, la police, elle a commencé à arrêter tous les **michés**.

pervers sur les bords (être) exp. to be kinky • (lit.): to be perverted around the edges.

> example: Je suis sorti avec Léon hier soir et j'ai découvert qu'il est un peu **pervers sur les bords**.

> translation: I went out with Léon last night and I found out that he's a little **kinky**.

> as spoken: J'suis sorti avec Léon hier soir et j'ai découvert qu'il est un peu **pervers sur les bords**.

pipe f. blow job • (lit.): pipe.

> example: Marcel m'a dit que Lucienne lui a fait une **pipe** dans la voiture!

> translation: Marcel told me that Lucienne gave him a **blow job** in the car!

> as spoken: Marcel, y m'a dit qu'Lucienne, è lui a fait une **pipe** dans la voiture!

> **NOTE:**   **faire une pipe** exp. to give a blow job.

porté(e) sur la bagatelle (être) *exp.* to be oversexed, to have sex on the brain • (lit.): to be carried on the frivolity.

> example: Grégoire sort avec une différente nana chaque soir. Il est vraiment **porté sur la bagatelle**, celui-là.

> translation: Gregory goes out with a different girl every night. He's really **got sex on the brain**.

> as spoken: Grégoire, y sort avec une différente nana chaque soir. Il est vraiment **porté sur la bagatelle**, cui-là.

pute *f.* prostitute, whore.

> example: Edouard a une nouvelle petite amie et tout le monde sait qu'elle est **pute** sauf lui!

> translation: Edward a a new girlfriend and everyone knows she's a **prostitute** except for him!

> as spoken: Edouard, il a une nouvelle p'tite amie et tout l'monde sait qu'elle est **pute** sauf lui!

> **SYNONYM:**   **putain** *f.*

ramasser la chtouille *exp.* to catch a venereal disease, to catch the "clap."

> example: La première fois que j'ai eu des rapports sexuels, j'ai **ramassé la chtouille**.

> translation: The first time I had sex, I **got the clap**.

> as spoken: La première fois qu'j'ai eu des rapports sexuels, j'ai **ramassé la chtouille**.

rouler une pelle *exp.* to deep-kiss with the tongue, to "French" kiss • (lit.): to roll a shovel.

> example: Quand il m'a fait un baiser, il m'a **roulé une pelle**!

> translation: When he kissed me, he **slipped me his tongue**!

> as spoken: Quand y m'a fait un baiser, y m'a **roulé une pelle**!

> **SYNONYM:**   **rouler une escalope** *exp.* • (lit.): to roll a thin slice of meat.

SIDA *m.* an abbreviation for *Syndrome Immuno-Déficitaire Acquis* meaning "AIDS (Acquired Immune Deficiency Syndrome)."

> example: Marie n'est pas du tout prudente. Un de ces jours, elle va sûrement finir par attraper le **SIDA**.

> translation: Marie isn't careful at all. One of these days, she's definitely going to end up catching **AIDS**.

> as spoken: Marie, <u>elle</u> est pas du tout prudente. Un <u>d'</u>ces jours, <u>è</u> va sûrement finir par attraper l'**SIDA**.

tapin (faire le) *exp.* to work the streets (said of a prostitute).

> example: La pauvre. Elle **fait le tapin** pour gagner sa vie.

> translation: The poor thing. She **works the streets** to earn her living.

> as spoken: La pauvre. <u>È</u> **fait l'tapin** pour gagner sa vie.

tremper (la) *exp.* to fornicate • (lit.): to dip it in.

> example: Tu as entendu les nouvelles? Albert **la trempe** avec une nana deux fois plus âgée que lui.

> translation: Did you hear the news? Albert **is having sex** with a woman twice as old as he is.

> as spoken: <u>T'</u>as entendu les nouvelles? Albert, <u>y</u> **la trempe** avec une nana deux fois plus âgée qu'lui.

> **NOTE:** In this expression, *la* represents *la pine* meaning "penis."

trouille (avoir la) *exp.* to be scared to death.

> example: J'ai eu **la trouille** quand j'ai vu le voleur!

> translation: I was **scared to death** when I saw the thief!

> as spoken: J'ai eu **la trouille** quand j'ai vu <u>l'</u>voleur!

A CLOSER LOOK:
Sexual Slang

The French have one of the richest and most innovative collection of slang terms and expressions for anything having to do with sex that I have ever seen. Since the French are so comfortable with the subject of sex, you'll discover that many of the following terms are actually treated with a great deal of humor.

Chambre
(bedroom)

cambuse *f.* • (lit.): storeroom on a ship.

crèche *f.* • (lit.): crib.
> **NOTE:** **crécher** *v.* to live.

gourbi *m.* • (lit.): hut *(from Arabic)*.

guitoune *f.* • (lit.): tent.

piaule *f.* pad, room.

turne *f.* room.
> **NOTE:** **co-turne** *n.* roommate.

Éjaculer / Orgasme (avoir un)
(to ejaculate/to have an orgasm)

balancer (se) *v.* • (lit.): to sway and rock oneself.

balancer la sauce *exp.*
• (lit.): to throw the sauce.

balancer la/sa purée *exp.*
• (lit.): to throw the/one's purée.

cracher son venin *exp.*
• (lit.): to spit one's venom.

décharger *v.* • (lit.): to discharge.

dégorger *v.* • (lit.): to vomit.

égoutter son cyclope *exp.*
• (lit.): to drain one's cyclops.
> **NOTE:** The masculine noun *cyclope* is a popular synonym for "penis" or "one-eyed monster."

envoyer en l'air (s') *exp.*
- (lit.): to throw oneself into the air.

envoyer sa came/ la purée/la sauce/ la semoule *exp.* • (lit.): to send out one's junk/purée/ sauce/cream of wheat.

> **NOTE:** **came** *f.* • **1.** sperm • **2.** junk (in general) • **3.** personal belongings, one's "stuff" • **4.** cocaine.

faire une carte *exp.* to have a wet dream • (lit.): to make a map.

jeter sa purée/son venin *exp.* • (lit.): to throw purée/one's venom.

jouir *v.* (*very popular*) • (lit.): to enjoy.

juter *v.* (*very popular*) • (lit.): to give off juice.

lâcher sa came/ une giclée/son jus/ sa purée/la semoule/ son venin *exp.* • (lit.): to release one's cum/a squirt/ juice/purée/ cream of wheat/ venom.

> **NOTE:** **came** *f.* • **1.** sperm • **2.** junk (in general) • **3.** personal belongings, one's "stuff" • **4.** cocaine.

mettre les doigts de pieds en éventail *exp.* • (lit.): to spread one's toes apart.

> **NOTE:** This expression also means "to relax."

pleurer le cyclope (faire) *exp.* • (lit.): to make the cyclops cry.

> **NOTE:** The masculine noun *cyclope* is a popular synonym for "penis" or "one-eyed monster."

prendre son panard/son pied *exp.* (*extremely popular*) • (lit.): to take one's foot/one's foot.

tirer une giclée *exp.* • (lit.): to pull a squirt.

vider les burettes (se) *exp.* • (lit.): to empty one's testicles.

> **NOTE:** **burettes** *f.pl.* testicles, balls • (lit.): oilcans.

voir les anges *exp.* • (lit.): to see angels.

Enceinte
(pregnant)

arrondir (s') *v.* • (lit.): to make oneself round.

arrondir le devant (se faire) *exp.* • (lit.): to get one's front end rounded.

arrondir le globe (se faire) *exp.* • (lit.): to get one's globe rounded.

attraper le ballon *exp.* • (lit.): to catch the balloon (in one's stomach).

avalé le pépin (avoir) *exp.* • (lit.): to have swallowed the seed.

ballon (avoir le) *exp.* • (lit.): to have the balloon (in one's stomach).

butte (avoir sa) *exp.* • (lit.): to have one's little hill.

cloque (être en) *exp. (very popular)* to be knocked up • (lit.): to be in a big blister.

> **NOTE -1:** **mettre en cloque** *exp.* to knock up.

> **NOTE -2:** **encloquer** *v.* to knock up.

engrossée (être) *adj.* (*pejorative*) to be knocked up

• (lit.): to be fattened up (used for animals).

> **NOTE:** **engrosser** *v.* to knock up.

gondoler de la devanture *exp.* • (lit.): to warp from the display window.

moufflet dans le tiroir (avoir un) *exp.* • (lit.): to have a kid in the drawer.

petit polichinelle dans le tiroir (avoir un) *exp.* • (lit.): to have a little joker in the drawer.

> **NOTE:** A *polichinelle* is the little clown figure often seen in a group of marionettes.

tombée sur un clou rouillé (être) *exp.* • (lit.): to have fallen on a rusty nail (and therefore swollen).

travailler pour Marianne *exp.*

> **NOTE:** *Marianne* is the female incarnation of France and the revolution. Therefore, if you are having a baby, you are said to be producing a new citizen for Marianne and the Republic.

Érection (avoir une)
(to have an erection)

air (l'avoir en l') *exp.*
- (lit.): to have it in the air.

arquer *v.* • (lit.): to bend.

balle dans le canon (avoir une) *exp.* • (lit.): to have a bullet in the cannon.

bandaison (avoir une) *f.*
- (lit.): to have a boner.
  SEE: **bander**, *(next entry)*.

bander *v.* *(extremely popular)* to be erect • (lit.): to tighten or stretch.

bandocher *m.*
  NOTE: This is a slang variation of: *bander*.

bâton (avoir le) *m.* • (lit.): to have the club.

canne (avoir la) *exp.*
- (lit.): to have the cane.

dure (l'avoir) *exp.* • (lit.): to have it hard.

garde-à-vous (être au) *exp.*
- (lit.): (military) to be at attention.

gaule (avoir la) *f.* *(popular)*
- (lit.): to have the pole.

gourdin (avoir le) *m.*
- (lit.): to have the club or bludgeon.

manche (avoir le) *m.*
- (lit.): to have the sleeve.

marquer midi *exp.* • (lit.): to be hitting straight up at noon.

os (avoir l') *m.* • (lit.): to have the bone.

porte-manteau dans le pantalon (avoir un) *exp.*
- (lit.): to have a coat rack in the pants.

raide (l'avoir) *exp.* • (lit.): to have it stiff.

tendre pour *exp.* • (lit.): to tighten for (someone).

tringle (avoir la) *f.* *(popular)*
- (lit.): to have the rod.

trique (avoir la) *f.* *(popular)*
- (lit.): to have the heavy stick.
  SEE: **triqué(e) (être)**, *(next entry)*.

triqué(e) (être) *adj.* • (lit.): to be "sticked."
  SEE: **trique (avoir la)**, *(previous entry)*.

Fellation (faire une)
(to perform fellatio)

brouter la tige *exp.* • (lit.): to graze the stem.

croquer (se faire) *exp.*
• (lit.): to get oneself eaten or munched.

dents (se laver les) *exp.*
• (lit.): to wash one's teeth.

dévorer *v.* • (lit.): to devour.

manger *v.* • (lit.): to eat.

pipe (faire une) *exp.*
(extremely popular) • (lit.): to do a pipe.

pomper *v. (very popular)*
• (lit.): to pump.

pompette *f.* blow job.
NOTE: This is from the verb *pomper* meaning "to pump."

pompier (faire un) *exp.*
• (lit.): to do (like) a fireman and pump (water).

pomplard (faire un) *exp.*
• (lit.): to do (like) a fireman.
NOTE -1: This is a variation of: *faire un pompier.*

NOTE -2: The masculine noun *pomplard* is a slang synonym for *pompier* meaning "fireman."

ronger l'os *exp.* • (lit.): to gnaw at the bone.

souffler dans la canne *exp.*
• (lit.): to blow in the cane.

souffler dans le mirliton *exp.* • (lit.): to blow in the toy flute.

sucer *v. (very popular)* • (lit.): to suck.

tailler une pipe *exp.*
• (lit.): *(very popular)* • (lit.): to trim a pipe.

tailler une plume *exp.*
• (lit.): to trim a pen.

Forniquer
(to fornicate)

aiguiller *v.* to "dick" someone
• (lit.): to give the needle.

NOTE: **aiguille** *f.* penis, dick
• (lit.): needle.

amener le petit au cirque
exp. • (lit.): to take the little one to the circus.

asperger le persil *exp.*
• (lit.): to sprinkle water on the parsley.
  NOTE -1: **asperge** *f.* penis • (lit.): asparagus.
  NOTE -2: **persil** *m.* vagina, pubic hair • (lit.): parsley.

baiser *v.* • (lit.): to fuck.
  NOTE: There is an *enormous* difference between *baiser* the verb and *baiser* the noun. As a noun, *baiser* simply means a "kiss." For example: *Il m'a fait un baiser en rentrant*; He gave me a kiss upon coming home. Mistakenly and dangerously, many Americans use *baiser* as a verb assuming that it means "to kiss" when it actually means "to fuck." Therefore, *Il m'a baisé en rentrant* would be translated as "He fucked me upon coming home."

baisouiller *v.* a slang variation of: *baiser*.

besogner *v.* • (lit.): to work hard.

biter *v.* to "dick" someone.
  NOTE: **bite** *f.* penis, dick.

bourre (aller à la) *exp.*
• (lit.): to screw.

NOTE: **bourre** *f.* lay, screw • *Carole, c'est une bonne bourre!*; Carole is a good lay.

bourrer *v.* (*popular*) • (lit.): to stuff.

bourriquer *v.* to screw like a donkey.
  NOTE: **bourrique** *f.* donkey, she-ass.

caramboler *v.* • (lit.): to push and shove.

caser *v.* • (lit.): to put or stow (something) away.

casser la canne *exp.* • (lit.): to break the cane.
  NOTE: **canne** *f.* penis, dick • (lit.): cane.

chevaucher *v.* • (lit.): to ride horseback.

coucher avec *exp.* (*very popular*) • (lit.): to sleep with.

cracher dans le bénitier
exp. • (lit.): to spit in the holy water basin.
  NOTE: **bénitier** *m.* vagina • (lit.): holy water basin.

défoncer *v.* • (lit.): to break open (a box, etc.).

dérouiller *v.* • (lit.): to rub the rust off (something).

dérouiller à sec *exp.* to dry fuck • (lit.): to rub the rust off (something dry).

dérouiller son petit frère *exp.* • (lit.): to rub the rust off one's little brother.
NOTE: **petit frère** *exp.* penis, dick • (lit.): little brother.

dérouiller Totor *exp.* • (lit.): to rub the rust off Totor.
NOTE: **Totor** *m.* penis, dick.

enfiler (s') *v.* • (lit.): to thread oneself.

enfoncer (se l') *v.* • (lit.): to drive it in.

enjamber *v.* • (lit.): to put in one's "third leg."
NOTE: This comes from the feminine noun *troisième jambe* meaning "third leg" or "penis, dick."

envoyer en l'air (s') *exp.* (*extremely popular*) • (lit.): to send oneself into the air.

faire (le) *exp.* • (lit.): to do it.

faire ça *exp.* • (lit.): to do it.

faire la bête à deux dos *exp.* • (lit.): to make like the beast with two backs (said of two people who are fused together during sex).

faire quelqu'un (se) *v.* (*very popular*) • (lit.): to do someone.

faire un carton *exp.* • (lit.): to do some target practice.

faire une partie d'écarté *exp.*
NOTE: This is a pun based on the expression *faire une partie de cartes* meaning "to play a hand of cards." However, in this expression, the noun *cartes* has been replaced with the adjective *écarté* meaning "spread apart" as with one's legs during sex.

faire une partie de jambes en l'air *exp.* • (lit.): to play a game of "legs in the air."

faire une partie de balayette *exp.* • (lit.): to "play a hand of" small broom.
NOTE: **balayette** *f.* penis, dick • (lit.): small broom.

farcir quelqu'un (se) *v.* • **1.** to fornicate • **2.** to put up with someone (ex: *Je ne peux pas supporter mon nouveau voisin, mais il faut **se le farcir**!*; I can't stand my new neighbor but I have to put up with him! • (lit.): to stuff oneself with someone.

filer un coup d'arbalète
exp. • (lit.): to give (someone) a shot with the crossbow.
> **NOTE:** **arbalète** *f.* penis, dick • (lit.): crossbow.

filer un coup de sabre *exp.*
• (lit.): to give (someone) a shot with the saber.
> **NOTE:** **sabre** *m.* penis, dick • (lit.): saber.

filer un coup de brosse
exp. • (lit.): to give (someone) a shot of the brush.

fourailler *v.* • (lit.): to stuff.
> **NOTE:** This is a variation of the verb *fourrer* meaning "to stuff."

fourrer *v.* • (lit.): to stuff.

frotter *v.* • (lit.): to rub.

limer *v.* • (lit.): to polish.

mettre (le) *exp.* • (lit.): to put it (in).

mouiller le goupillon *exp.*
• (lit.): to wet one's sprinkler.
> **NOTE:** **goupillon** *m.* penis, dick • (lit.): sprinkler (for holy water).

niquer *v. (from Arabic)* • (lit.): to fuck.

**payer un petit coup
(s'en)** *exp.* • (lit.): to treat oneself to a little bit.

piner *v.* • (lit.): to "dick" (someone).
> **NOTE:** This comes from the feminine noun *pine* meaning "penis, dick."

planter *v.* • (lit.): to plant.

pousser sa pointe *exp.*
• (lit.): to push (in) one's point.
> **NOTE:** **pointe** *f.* penis, dick • (lit.): point.

queuter *v. (used in Belgian French)* • (lit.): to "dick" (someone).
> **NOTE:** This comes from the feminine noun *queue* which literally means "tail" but has taken the slang connotation of "penis, dick" particularly in Belgium.

ramoner *v. (humorous)*
• (lit.): to sweep (a chimney).
> **NOTE:** **cheminée** *f.* vagina • (lit.): chimney.

sauter *v. (very popular)*
• (lit.): to jump (one's bones).

taper (se) *v. (very popular)*
• (lit.): to treat oneself.

torpiller *v.* • (lit.): to torpedo (someone).

tremper son baigneur *exp.*
- (lit.): to dip one's bather.

  NOTE: **baigneur** *m.* penis, dick • (lit.): bather.

tremper son biscuit *exp.*
- (lit.): to dip one's biscuit.

tringler *v.* (*very popular*)
- (lit.): to "dick" (someone).

  NOTE: This comes from the feminine noun *tringle* which literally means "rod" but has taken the slang connotation of "penis, dick."

verger *v.* • (lit.): to "dick" (someone).

  NOTE: This comes from the feminine noun *verge*, which literally means "rod, wand, cane," but has taken the slang connotation of "penis, dick."

voir la feuille à l'envers
exp. to have sex under a tree
- (lit.): to see the leaf (or leaves) from underneath.

Lit
(bed)

boîte à puces *f.* • (lit.): flea box.

champ de manœuvre *m.*
- (lit.): parade ground.

dodo *m.* • (lit.):

  NOTE: **dodo (faire)** *exp.* (child language) to go "sleepy-bye."

nid *m.* • (lit.): nest.

paddock *m.* • (lit.): a paddock (a place where horses are kept), horse's stall.

  NOTE: **paddocker (se)** *v.* to go to bed, to hit the hay.

pieu *m.* (*most popular*)
- (lit.): spike.

  NOTE: **pieuter (se)** *v.* to go to bed, to hit the hay.

plumard . (*very popular*)
- (lit.): that which is made of *plumes* or feathers.

  NOTE: **plumarder (se)** *v.* to go to bed, to hit the hay.

plume *m.* • (lit.): feather.

  NOTE: **plumer (se)** *v.* to go to bed, to hit the hay.

Maison de Prostitution
(brothel)

baisodrome m.
- (lit.): "fuckodrome."

NOTE: This comes from the verb *baiser* meaning "to fuck."

boxon m.

NOTE: This comes from the masculine noun *box* meaning "cubicle (in a dormitory)."

casbah m.

NOTE: This comes from Arabic meaning "the Arab city" or "the house."

chabanais m.

clandé m. • (lit.): clandestin.

claque m. • (lit.): opera hat.

NOTE: Also spelled: *clac*.

foutoir m. • **1.** brothel • **2.** a big dirty mess • (lit.): "fuckodrome."

NOTE: This comes from the verb *foutre* meaning "to fuck."

maison d'abattage f.
high-volume house
- (lit.): house of slaughter (referring to a business where the pace is fast and mechanical).

maison de passe f. an official word for "brothel" • (lit.): house of transaction.

pinarium m.

NOTE: This comes from the feminine noun *pine* meaning "penis."

tringlodrome m.

NOTE: This comes from the feminine noun *tringle* which literally means "rod" but has taken the slang connotation of "penis, dick."

volière f. • (lit.): henhouse (since *poule*, literally meaning "hen," is used in French slang to mean "prostitute."

Maladies Vénériennes
(sexual diseases)

SIDA m. (*Syndrome Immuno-Déficitaire Acquis*) AIDS (Acquired Immune Deficiency Syndrome).

Gonorrhée
(gonorrhea)

castapiane *f.*

chaude-lance *f.* • (lit.): hot urine.

> **NOTE -1:** **lance** *f.* • **1.** water • **2.** urine.

> **NOTE -2:** **lancequiner** *v.* • **1.** to rain • **2.** to urinate.

chaude-pince *f.* • (lit.): hot claw.

chaude-pisse *f.* (*very popular*) • (lit.): hot piss.

> **NOTE:** **pisser** *v.* to urinate, to piss.

coulante *f.* • (lit.): dripper (since gonorrhea causes the penis to drip).

Syphilis
(syphilis)

schtouille *f.* (also spelled: *chtouille*).

syph *f.* an abbreviation for: *syphilis*.

syphlotte *f.* a slang variation for: *syphilis*.

vérole *f.* • (lit.): the old-fashioned word for "pox."

Masturbation / Poigne
(masturbation / hand job)

branlée *f.* • (lit.): shaking.

> **NOTE:** **branler (se)** *v.* to masturbate • (lit.): to shake oneself.

branlette *f.* (*popular*) • (lit.): shaking.

> **NOTE:** **branler (se)** *v.* to masturbate • (lit.): to shake oneself.

branlette maison *f.* • (lit.): shaking of the house.

NOTE -1: **branler (se)** *v.* to masturbate • (lit.): to shake oneself.

NOTE -2: This construction, where *maison* is used as an adjective, is commonly seen in restaurants referring to the "house" speciality such as *pâté maison*.

branlure *f.* • (lit.): shaking.

NOTE: **branler (se)** *v.* to masturbate • (lit.): to shake oneself.

paluche *f.* hand job • (lit.): slang for "hand."

pignole *f.*

pogne *f.* hand job • (lit.): slang for "fist."

secouette *f.* • (lit.): shaking.

NOTE: **secouer (se)** *v.* to masturbate • (lit.): to shake oneself.

veuve Poignet *m.*
• (lit.): Widow Wrist.

Masturber (se) [les femmes]
(to masturbate) [women]

NOTE: Some of these terms may be used in reference to a man as well, while others may only be used in reference to a woman.

SEE: Masturbate (to) [men], *p. 116.*

astiquer le bouton (s') *exp.*
• (lit.): to polish one's button.
NOTE: **bouton** *m.* clitoris
• (lit.): button.

branler (se) *v.* • (lit.): to shake oneself.
NOTE: **branlette** *f.* masturbation.

compter les poils (se) *exp.*
• (lit.): to count one's (pubic) hairs.

jouer de la mandoline *exp.*
• (lit.): to play the mandolin.

NOTE: This is based on a famous painting depicting a naked woman playing the mandolin which covers her genitalia.

secouer son grain de café *exp.* • (lit.): to shake one's coffee bean.

soulager (se) *v.* • (lit.): to confort oneself.

toucher (se) *v.* • (lit.): to touch oneself.

Masturber (se) [hommes]
(to masturbate) [men]

NOTE: Some of these terms may be used in reference to a woman as well, while others may only be used in reference to a man.

SEE: Masturbate (to), [women], *p. 115.*

achever à la manivelle (s') *exp.* • (lit.): to reach completion with the hand crank.

agacer le sous-préfet *exp.* • (lit.): to annoy the subprefect.

agiter le poireau (s') *exp.* • (lit.): to agitate the leek.
NOTE: **poireau** *m.* penis, "dick" • (lit.): leek.

allonger (se l') *exp.* • (lit.): to lengthen it.

allonger la couenne (s') *exp.* • (lit.): to lengthen one's foreskin.
NOTE: **couenne** *f.* skin of ham.

allonger le macaroni (s') *exp.* to lengthen one's macaroni.
NOTE: **macaroni** *m.* penis, "dick" • (lit.): macaroni.

amuser tout seul (s') *exp.* • (lit.): to have fun alone.

astiquer (s') *v.* • (lit.): to polish oneself.

astiquer la baguette (s') *exp.* • (lit.): to polish one's baguette.
NOTE: **baguette** *f.* penis, "dick" • (lit.): baguette, long rounded loaf of bread.

battre une (s'en) *exp.* • (lit.): to beat one.

branler (se) *v. (very popular)* • (lit.): to shake oneself.

chatouiller le poireau (se) *exp.* • (lit.): to tickle one's leek.
NOTE: **poireau** *m.* penis, "dick" • (lit.): leek.

cinq contre un (faire) *exp.* • (lit.): to do five against one.

douce (se faire une) *exp.* • (lit.): to do oneself a sweet thing.

écrémer (se faire) *exp.* • (lit.): to make oneself cream.

épouser la veuve Poignet *exp.* • (lit.): to marry the Widow Wrist.

étrangler Popaul *exp.*
- (lit.): to strangle Popaul.

NOTE -1: Also spelled: *Popol.*

NOTE -2: **Popaul/Popol** *m.* penis, "dick."

fréquenter (se) *v.* • (lit.): to frequent oneself.

glouglouter le poireau (se faire) *exp.* • (lit.): to make one's leek gurgle.

NOTE: **poireau** *m.* penis, "dick" • (lit.): leek.

gonfler son andouille *exp.*
- (lit.): to swell one's sausage.

mettre la main à la pâte
exp. (used in the culinary world) to get in there with one's hands
- (lit.): to put the hand to the dough.

mousser le créateur (se faire) *exp.* • (lit.): to make one's creator foam.

palucher (se) *v.* • (lit.): to give oneself a hand job.

NOTE: **paluche** *f.* hand.

pogne (se faire une) *exp.*
- (lit.): to give oneself a hand job.

NOTE: **pogne** *f.* fist, hand.

pogner (se) *v.* • (lit.): to have oneself a hand job.

NOTE: **pogne** *f.* fist, hand.

reluire (se faire) *exp.*
- (lit.): to make oneself glisten.

sauter la cervelle à Charles-le-Chauve (faire) *exp.* • (lit.): to blow out the brains of Charles-the-Bald.

secouer le bonhomme (se) *exp.* • (lit.): to shake one's good-natured man.

soulager (se) *v.* **1.** to masturbate • **2.** to go to the bathroom • (lit.): to relieve oneself.

taper sur l'os (se) *exp.*
- (lit.): to tap on one's bone.

taper sur la colonne (se) *exp.* • (lit.): to tap on one's column.

NOTE: **colonne** *f.* penis, "dick" • (lit.): column.

taper une (s'en) *exp.*
- (lit.): to treat oneself to one.

touche (se faire une) *exp.*
- (lit.): to give oneself a touch.

toucher (se) *v.* • (lit.): to touch oneself.

NOTE: This applies to both male and female and is often used as a polite way to report that a child has started masturbating.

tripoter (se) *v.* • (lit.): to play with oneself.

NOTE: This verb is used the same as *se toucher* but is more familiar.

tutoyer (se) *v.* • (lit.): to be on familiar terms with oneself.

venir aux mains (en) *exp.*
• (lit.): to come to hands.

NOTE: The expression *en venir aux mains* is commonly used to mean "to come to blows." However, since it literally means "to come to hands," it may be used humorously to suggest masturbation.

visiter la veuve et les cinq orphelines *exp.*
• (lit.): to visit the widow and five orphans.

Préservatif
(condom)

capote *f. (very popular)*
• (lit.): bonnet.
　　SYNONYM: **capote anglaise** • (lit.): English bonnet.

chapeau *m.* • (lit.): hat.

imper(méable) à Popol *m.*
• (lit.): Popol's raincoat.
　　NOTE -1: **Popol** *m.* penis.
　　NOTE -2: Also spelled: *Popaul.*

scaphandre de poche *m.*
• (lit.): pocket-size diving suit.

Prostituée
(prostitute)

amazone *f.* • (lit.): high-class prostitute.

bisenesseuse *f.* • (lit.): business woman, working girl.

bourrin *m.* prostitute, loose woman • (lit.): horse or nag.

catin *f.*

cocotte (faire) *f.* • *Le décor chez elle, ça fait cocotte;* Her home looks like a whorehouse.

dossière *f.* • (lit.): a woman who lies on her back often.

NOTE: This comes from the masculine noun *dos* meaning "back."

essoreuse *f.* a prostitute who squeezes her clients dry of all their money • (lit.): spin dryer.

fille de joie *f.* • (lit.): girl of joy (or who spreads joy).

fille *f.* • (lit.): girl.

gagneuse *f.* • (lit.): girl who earns money.

garce *f.* • (lit.): *(derogatory)* bitch.

grue *f.* • (lit.): a crane (since cranes are known for standing on one foot much like a prostitute who waits for a client while leaning back against the wall of a building, one foot on the ground with the other against the wall).

horizontale *f.* • (lit.): a horizontal (because of the position she frequently assumes).
ALSO: **grande horizontale** *f.* a very high-class prostitute.

marcheuse *f.* a girl who walks the streets • (lit.): walker.

pétroleuse *f.* • (lit.): a woman who heats up a man (since *pétrole*, meaning "petroleum").

pouffiasse *f.* low-class prostitute • (lit.): *(derogatory)* woman.

poule *f.* girl • (lit.): hen.

pouliche *f.* young girl • (lit.): young horse.

putain *f.* *(very popular)* whore.

pute *f.* an abbreviation of: *putain.*

raccrocheuse *f.* • (lit.): woman who accosts men.

racoleuse *f.* • (lit.): woman who recruits or solicits men.

sauterelle *f.*
• (lit.): grasshopper.
NOTE: This is actually a play on words since the verb *sauter* (literally meaning "to jump") has the slang meaning of "to jump sexually."

tapin *f.*
NOTE: **faire le tapin** *exp.* to prostitute oneself.

tapineuse *f.*

traînée *f.* slut • (lit.): one who loiters (on the sidewalk, etc.).
NOTE: This comes from the verb *traîner* meaning "to dawdle, to loiter."

travailleuse *f.* • (lit.): working girl.

Règles (avoir ses)
(to menstruate)

affaires (avoir ses) *f.pl.*
- (lit.): to have one's business.

anglais (avoir ses) *f.pl.*
- (lit.): to have one's English.

argagnasses (avoir ses) *f.pl.*

cardinales (avoir ses) *f.pl.*
- (lit.): to have one's cardinals.

coquelicots (avoir ses)
m.pl. • (lit.): to have one's red
poppies.

**drapeau-rouge (avoir
son)** *m.* • (lit.): to have one's
red flag.
- **SEE:** **pavoiser**, *p. 120.*

époques (avoir ses) *exp.*
- (lit.): to have one's epoch or
era.

histoires (avoir ses) *exp.*
- (lit.): to have one's stories.

marquer *v.* • (lit.): to mark.

ours (avoir ses) *m.pl.*
- (lit.): to have one's bears.

pavoiser *v.* • (lit.): to deck
(house, etc.) with flags, in this
case, red flags.
- **SEE:** **drapeau-rouge
(avoir son)**, *p. 120.*

ramiaous (avoir ses) *m.pl.*

recevoir sa famille *exp.*
- (lit.): to receive one's family.

recevoir ses cousins *exp.*
- (lit.): to receive one's cousins.

**repeindre sa grille en
rouge** *exp.* • (lit.): to repaint
one's grill red.

rue barrée (avoir sa) *f.*
- (lit.): to have one's street
closed • *Rue barrée;* No
thoroughfare.

sauce-tomate (avoir sa) *f.*
- (lit.): to have one's tomato
sauce.

tomates (avoir ses) *f.pl.*
- (lit.): to have one's tomatoes.

trucs (avoir ses) *m.pl.*
- (lit.): to have one's things.

visite (avoir de la) *f.*
- (lit.): to have visitors.

Sodomiser
(to sodomize)

casser le pot *exp.* • (lit.): to break the pot.

> **NOTE:** **pot** *m.* buttocks • (lit.): pot.

défoncer la pastille *exp.*
• (lit.): to smash through the lozenge.

> **NOTE:** **pastille** *f.* anus • (lit.): lozenge.

emmancher *v.*

empaffer *v.*

empaler *v.* • (lit.): to impale.

empapaouter *v.*

empétarder *v.* • (lit.): to receive something through the back.

> **NOTE:** This is an "antonym" of the verb *pétarader* meaning "to backfire."

enculer *v.*

> **NOTE -1:** This comes from the masculine noun *cul* meaning "ass."

> **NOTE -2:** This verb originally meant "to sodomize" and is now mainly used to mean "to fornicate."

enfoirer *v.* • (lit.): to "enter something into one's anus."

> **NOTE:** This is an "antonym" of the verb *foirer* meaning "to have diarrhea."

englander *v.* • (lit.): to insert the acorn (which looks like the head of a penis).

> **NOTE:** This comes from the masculine noun *gland* meaning "acorn" and has taken the slang connotation of "penis, dick" due to its shape.

entuber *v.* • (lit.): to put one's "tube" into something.

jouer au bilboquet ensemble *exp.*

> **NOTE:** *Bilboquet* is a child's game in which the player holds a long wooden peg which has a string attached to it. At the end of the string is a ball with a hole. The object is to swing the ball up then down onto the peg using only one hand.

péter la rondelle *exp.*
• (lit.): to explode the ring.

> **NOTE:** **rondelle** *f.* anus • (lit.): ring, small round disc.

troncher *v.* • **1.** to sodomize • **2.** to fornicate.

> **NOTE:** This comes from the feminine noun *tronche* meaning "log."

Soliciter
(to hustle)

arpenter le bitume *exp.*
- (lit.): to survey the asphalt.

asperges (aller aux) *exp.* to go to (find) some penis
- (lit.): to go to the asparagus.
  NOTE: **asperge** *f.* penis
- (lit.): asparagus.

bitume (faire le) *m.*
- (lit.): to do the asphalt.

business (faire le) *m.*
- (lit.): to do the business.

chasser le mâle *exp.* • (lit.): to hunt the male (species).

défendre (se) *v.* to make a living • (lit.): to defend oneself.

dérouiller *v.* to get the first client of the day • (lit.): to take the rust off (something).

draguer *v.* • (lit.): to cruise (someone).

emballer *v.* • (lit.): to excite (someone).

grue (faire la) *f.* • (lit.): to do like a crane (since cranes are known for standing on on foot much like a prostitute who waits for a client while leaning back against the wall of a building, one foot on the ground with the other against the wall).

levage (faire un) *m.*
- (lit.): to make a pickup.

lever un client *exp.* • (lit.): to pick up a client.

macadam (faire le) *exp.* (*very popular*) • (lit.): to do the macadam or sidewalk.

pavé (faire le) *m.* • (lit.): to do the pavement.

quart (faire le) *m.* • (lit.): to keep watch.

raccroc (faire le) *m.*
  SEE: **raccrocher**, (*next entry*).

raccrocher *v.* • (lit.): to accost (men).
  SEE: **raccroc (faire le)**, (*previous entry*).

tapin (faire le) *exp.* (*very popular*) to do the street.
  NOTE: **tapineuse** *f.* hooker, prostitute.

tapiner *v.*
  SEE: **tapin (faire le)**, (*previous entry*).

tas (faire le) *m.* • (lit.): to do (a lot of) work.

> **NOTE:** **tas** *m.* work • (lit.): heap, stack.

trottoir (faire le) *exp.* (*very popular*) • (lit.): to do the sidewalk.

turbin (faire le) *exp.*
• (lit.): to do hard work

> **NOTE:** **turbin** *m.* work, grind.

turbiner *v.*

> **SEE:** **turbin (faire le)**, (*previous entry*).

turf (aller au) *exp.* • (lit.): to go to the turf.

> **SEE:** **turf (faire le)**, (*next entry*).

turf (faire le) *exp.* • (lit.): to do the turf.

turfer *v.*

> **SEE:** **turf (faire le)**, (*previous entry*).

usiner *v.* • (lit.): to work hard (as one would in a *usine* or "factory").

Souteneur
(pimp)

> **NOTE:** Many of the following slang synonyms for "pimp" are, oddly enough, types of fish.

barbeau *m.*

brochet *m.* • (lit.): pike.

hareng *m.* • (lit.): herring.

Jules *m.* (*very popular*) • **1.** pimp • **2.** boyfriend • **3.** dude, guy (ex: *Hé, Jules!*; Hey, my man!) • (lit.): Jules, a man's first name.

Julot *m.* diminutive of: *Jules*.

mac *m.* (*very popular*) abbreviation of: *macquereau*.

maquereau *m.* (*very popular*) • (lit.): mackerel.

marchand de barbaque *m.* pimp, white slaver • (lit.): meat seller.

> **NOTE:** **barbaque** *f.* (low quality) meat.

marchand de bidoche m.
pimp, white slaver • (lit.): meat seller.
> **NOTE:** **bidoche** f. (low quality) meat.

marchand de viande m.
pimp, white slaver • (lit.): meat seller.

marle m. an abbreviation of: marlou.

marlou m.

mec m. • (lit.): guy, dude.

mecton m. • (lit.): little guy.

merlan m. • (lit.): whiting.

proxémac m.
> **NOTE:** This is a slang transformation of the masculine noun proxénète meaning "white slaver."

proxo m. an abbreviation of: proxénète.

Sperme
(sperm)

blanc m. • (lit.): white (stuff).

came f. • (lit.): cum.
> **NOTE:** **came** f. • 1. sperm • 2. junk (in general) • 3. personal belongings, one's "stuff" • 4. cocaine.

foutre m. (very popular).
> **NOTE:** This is from the verb foutre meaning "to fuck."

jus de corps m. • (lit.): body juice.

jus de cyclope m.
• (lit.): cyclops juice.
> **NOTE:** **cyclope** m. penis, "one-eyed bandit"
• (lit.): cyclops.

purée f. • (lit.): purée.

sauce f. • (lit.): sauce.

semoule f. • (lit.): cream of wheat.

venin m. • (lit.): venom.

jus m. • (lit.): juice.

LEÇON SIX - Bodily Functions, Sounds & Smells

Je pense que je vais gerber!

(trans.): I think I'm gonna heave!
(lit.): I think I'm going to sheave (corn, etc.)!

Leçon Six

Paul: Avant qu'on *se tire* (1), il faut que je **fasse pleurer mon colosse**.

Richard: Tu es sûr, parce que ça **pue la merde** dans ces **chiottes**-là! En plus, il n'y a jamais ni savon ni **torche-cul** et on dirait qu'on a **molardé** et **pissé** sur les murs. Que ça me fait **chier** quand on ne nettoie pas! Une fois, j'y suis entré et il y avait un sacré **péteur** dans une des cabines. J'ai eu envie de **gerber**!

Paul: Je crois que je vais attendre de rentrer. Les **étrons** et la **pisse**, *ça ne me dit pas grand' chose* (2).

Translation in English

I think I'm gonna heave!

Paul: Before we *leave*, I need to **take a leak**.

Richard: Are you sure, because it **stinks like shit** in those **bathrooms**! Besides, there's never any soap or **ass-wipe** and it looks like people have **spit** and **pissed** on the walls. It really **bugs the shit out of me** when people aren't clean! Once I went in there and there was this total **farter** in one of the stalls. I felt like I was going **to lose it**!

Paul: I think I'll wait till I get home. **Turds** and **piss** *don't do a lot for me.*

Dialogue in slang as it would be spoken

Je pense que j'vais gerber!

Paul: Avant qu'on *s'tire*, faut qu'j'**fasse pleurer mon colosse**.

Richard: T'es sûr, pasque ça **pue la merde** dans ces **chiottes**-là! En
          plus, y a jamais ni d'savon ni d'**torche-cul** et on dirait qu'on a
          molardé et **pisser** sur les murs. Que ça m'fait **chier** quand
          on nettoie pas! Une fois, j'y suis entré et y'avait un sacré **péteur**
          dans une des cabines. J'ai eu envie d'**gerber**!

Paul: J'crois qu'j'vais attend' de rentrer. Les **étrons** et la **pisse**,
          ça m'dit pas gran' chose.

Vocabulary

FOOTNOTES FROM THE DIALOGUE

(1) _tirer (se):_

    _v._ to leave, to "spit" • (lit.): to pull oneself (away).

(2) _ça ne me dit pas grand' chose:_

    exp. (heard as: _ça m'dit pas grand' chose_) This is a very popular expression meaning "It doesn't do a thing for me," or literally, "It doesn't speak to me." It is interesting to note that although the noun _chose_ is feminine, in this expression it takes on the masculine adjective _grand_ instead of _grande_ as one would assume.

---

chier _v._ to shit, to crap.

        example: Ah, non! Ces oiseaux de malheur ont **chié** sur ma nouvelle voiture!

    translation: Oh, no! These darn birds **crapped** on my new car!

    as spoken: Ah, non! Ces oiseaux d'malheur, y z'ont **chié** sur ma nouvelle voiture!

chiottes _f.pl._ (_extremely popular_) the bathroom, the "shit house."

        example: Je dois aller aux **chiottes** avant de partir.

    translation: I have to go to the **shit house** before we leave.

    as spoken: J'dois aller aux **chiottes** avant d'partir.

étron _m._ turd.

        example: C'est dégoutant! Il y a des **étrons** de chiens sur tout le trottoir!

    translation: This is disgusting! There are dog **turds** all over the sidewalk!

    as spoken: C'est dégoutant! Y a des **étrons** d'chiens sur tout l'trottoir!

gerber *v.* to vomit, to "barf."

> example: Je suis très malade. J'ai **gerbé** toute la matinée.

> translation: I'm very sick. I **barfed** all morning.

> as spoken: J'suis très malade. J'ai **gerbé** toute la matinée.

molarder *v.* to spit, to hock "loogies."

> example: Il est interdit de **molarder** dans le métro.

> translation: It's forbidden to **spit** in the subway.

> as spoken: Il est interdit d'**molarder** dans l'métro.

péteur *m.* one who farts a lot • (lit.): farter (from the verb *péter* meaning "to fart").

> example: Si tu ne manges rien que des fibres, tu vas devenir un **péteur** de premier ordre!

> translation: If you eat nothing but fiber, you're doing to turn into one heck of a **farter**!

> as spoken: Si tu ~ manges rien que des fibres, tu vas dev'nir un **péteur** de premier ordre!

pisse *f.* urine • (lit.): piss.

> example: Tu as un chat? Ça sent la **pisse** dans le salon.

> translation: Do you have a cat? It smells like **piss** in the living room.

> as spoken: T'as un chat? Ça sent la **pisse** dans l'salon.

> **SEE:** **pisser**, *(next entry)*.

pisser *v.* to urinate • (lit.): to piss.

> example: Quand j'ai soulevé le bébé, il a commencé à **pisser**.

> translation: When I lifted the baby, he started **pissing**.

> as spoken: Quand j'ai soul'vé l'bébé, il a commencé à **pisser**.

> **SEE:** **pisse**, *(previous entry)*.

pleurer son colosse (faire) *exp.* to urinate, to take a leak • (lit.): to make one's colossal one cry.

> example: Après tous les verres d'eau que j'ai descendu, je dois **faire pleurer mon colosse**.

> translation: After all the glasses of water I downed, I need to **take a leak**.

> as spoken: Après tous les verres d'eau qu'j'ai descendu, j'dois **faire pleurer mon colosse**.

puer la merde *exp.* • **1.** to stink to high heaven • **2.** to smell fishy (said of something dishonest or shady) (lit.): to stink like shit.

> example (1): Nous sommes près des égouts? Ça **pue la merde** ici.

> translation: Are we near a sewer? It **stinks like shit** here.

> as spoken: On est près des égouts? Ça **pue la merde** ici.

> example (2): C'te voiture t'a coûté un malheureux mille francs?! Ça **pue la merde**. Ça peut être une voiture volée, ça!

> translation: That car cost you a measly one thousand francs?! That **smells fishy**. It could be a stolen car!

> as spoken: Cette voiture, è t'a coûté un malheureux mille francs?! Ça **pue la merde**. Ça peut êtr'une voiture volée, ca!

torche-cul *m.* toilet paper, "ass-wipe" • (lit.): wipe-ass.

> example: La dernière fois que je suis allé faire du camping, j'avais complètement oublié d'apporter le **torche-cul**.

> translation: The last time I went camping, I totally forgot to bring **toilet paper**.

> as spoken: La dernière fois qu'j'suis allé faire du camping, j'avais complètement oublié d'apporter l'**torche-cul**.

> **SYNONYM:** **pécul** *m.* an abbreviation of *papier-cul* meaning "toilet paper" or literally, "ass paper."

A CLOSER LOOK:
Bodily Functions and Sounds

Adults often comment about children's preoccupation with "toilet humor" and talking about bodily functions and sounds. Well, kids, move over and make room for your parents, because the following extensive list was created by grown-ups!

Cabinet (le)
(bathroom)

NOTE: In France, the bathtub and toilet are often in two separate rooms. Therefore, the *salle de bain* (literally: "bathroom") refers to the room containing only the bathtub, and the *cabinet* refers to the room where only the toilet is located.

cabzingue *m.pl.* (short for *cabinet*).

chiards *m.pl.* the shithouse.
   NOTE: This comes from the verb *chier* meaning "to shit."

chiottes *f.pl.* *(extremely popular)* the shithouse.
   NOTE: This comes from the verb *chier* meaning "to shit."

lieux *m.pl.* • (lit.): the places.

ouatères *m.pl.* *(from British-English)* a shorten version of *water-closet* meaning "bathroom."

petit coin *m.* *(child language)*
   • (lit.): the little corner.

pipi-room *m.* *(Americanism)*.

téléphone *m.*
   NOTE: This come from the fact that many public outhouses found on the street are shaped like telephone booths.

vécé *m.* *(extremely popular)*.
   NOTE: This is a doubly shortened version of the masculine noun *water-closet* meaning "bathroom." *Water-closet* is commonly shortened to *W.C.* and further shortened to *V.C.* (pronounced: *vécé*).

Cracher
(to spit)

glaviot *m.* spit wad, loogie.

glavioter *v.* to hawk a loogie.

gluau *m.* spit wad, loogie.

graillon *m.* spit wad, loogie.

graillonner *v.* to cough up phlegm.

huître *f.* spit wad, loogie
 • (lit.): oyster.

molard *m.* spit wad, loogie.

molarder *v.* to spit, to hawk a loogie.

postillon *m.* spit, spittle.
 NOTE: **postillonner** *v.* to spit while one speaks.

Déféquer
(to defecate)

affaires (faire ses) *exp.*
 • (lit.): to do one's business.

aller où le Roi va à pied *exp.* • (lit.): to go where the king goes by foot.

caca (faire) *exp.* • (lit.): to make caca.

chier *v.* • (lit.): to shit.

couler un bronze *exp.*
 • (lit.): to flow out a bronze (thing).

débloquer *v.* • (lit.): to free, to unblock.

déboucher son orchestre *exp.* • (lit.): to uncork one's orchestra (of farting sounds).

débourrer sa pipe *exp.*
 • (lit.): to remove the tobacco from one's pipe.
 NOTE: This expression may also be shorted simply to: *débourrer*.

foirer *v.* • (lit.): to have diarrhea.

grande commission (faire sa) *exp.* • (lit.): to do one's big job.
 SEE: **aller faire sa petite commission**, *p. 137.*

grands besoins (faire ses) *exp.* • (lit.): to do one's big needs.

gros (faire son) *exp.* • (lit.): to do one's fat (job).

mouler un bronze *exp.*
• (lit.): to mold a bronze (thing).

planter une borne *exp.*
• (lit.): to plant a milestone.

poser sa pêche *exp.* • (lit.): to deposit one's peach.

poser un colombin *exp.*
• (lit.): to deposit pigeon manure.

poser un rondin *exp.*
• (lit.): to set down a log.

poser une prune *exp.*
• (lit.): to deposit a plum.

poser une prune *exp.*
• (lit.): to set down a plum.

poser une sentinelle *exp.*
• (lit.): to set down a sentinel.

pousser le bouchon *exp.*
• (lit.): to push the cork.

Diarrhea
(diarhée)

chiasse (avoir la) *f.*
• (lit.): to have the shits.
NOTE: This comes from the verb *chier* meaning "to shit."

courante (avoir la) *f.*
• (lit.): to have the runs.

foirade (avoir la) *f.*

NOTE: This comes from the crude verb *foirer* meaning "to have diarrhea."

VARIATION: **foire (avoir la)** *f.* • (lit.): to have diarrhea.

Étron
(turd)

borne *f.* • (lit.): milestone.

boudin *m.* • (lit.): blood sausage.

bouse *f.* • *bouse de vache;* cow patty.

bronze *m.* • (lit.): a bronze (one).

caca *m.* • (lit.): caca.

colombin *m.* • (lit.): pigeon manure.

merde *f.* • (lit.): shit.

orphelin *m.* • (lit.): orphan.

pêche *f.* • (lit.): peach.

prune *f.* • (lit.): plum.

rondin *m.* • (lit.): log.

Mauvaise Haleine (avoir une)
(to have bad breath)

plomber du goulot *exp.*
• (lit.): to fall like lead from the bottleneck.

puer du bec *exp.* • (lit.): to stink from the mouth.
NOTE: **bec** *m.* mouth
• (lit.): beak of a bird.

repousser du goulot *exp.*
• (lit.): to repel from the bottleneck.

NOTE: **goulot** *m.* neck
• (lit.): bottleneck.

taper du saladier *exp.*
• (lit.): to knock from the salad bowl.
NOTE: **saladier** *m.* head
• (lit.): salad bowl.

tuer les mouches à quinze pas *exp.* • (lit.): to kill flies fifteen feet away.

Péter
(to fart)

déchirer la toile *exp.*
• (lit.): to rip the linen.

détacher une pastille *exp.*
• (lit.): to detach a lozenge.
SEE: **pastille**, p. 136.

flouser *v.*

flousse *m.* fart.

fusante *f.* • (lit.): that which bursts out (like *une fusée* meaning "a rocket").

fuser *v.* • (lit.): to burst out.
> **NOTE:** **fusée** *f.* rocket.

lâcher les gaz *exp.* • (lit.): to release gases.

lâcher un[e] (en) *exp.*
• (lit.): to let one go.

lâcher une louise *exp.*
• (lit.): to release a louise.
> **SEE:** **louise**, *p. 136.*

lâcher une perle *exp.*
• (lit.): to release a pearl.
> **SEE:** **perle**, *p. 136.*

lâcher une perlouse *exp.*
variation of: *lâcher une perle.*

louise *f.* fart.

pastille *f.* fart • (lit.): lozenge.
> **SEE:** **détacher une pastille**, *p. 135.*

perle *f.* fart • (lit.): pearl.

perlouse *f.* slang variation of: *perle.*

pet mouillé (faire un) *exp.* to wet fart • (lit.): [same].

vesse *f.* silent fart, S.B.D. (silent but deadly).

vesser *v.* to fart silently.

Puer
(to stink)

boucaner *v.* • (lit.): to cure or smoke-dry meat.

cocoter *v.*

fouetter *v.* • (lit.): to whip.

puer *v.* • (lit.): to stink.

refouler *v.* • (lit.): to push back.

rougnotter *v.*

schlingotter *v.*

schlinguer *v.*

sentir le fauve *exp.* • (lit.): to smell like wild animal.

taper *v.* • (lit.): to hit.

Roter
(to burp)

renvoi (faire un) *exp.*
> **NOTE:** This comes from the verb *renvoyer* meaning "to send back" or in this case "to send back up."

rot (faire un) *exp.* • (lit.): to make a burp.

Uriner
(to urinate)

aller faire sa petite commission *exp.* • (lit.): to go do one's little job.
> **SEE:** **grande commission (faire sa)**, *p. 133*.

arroser les marguerites *exp.* • (lit.): to go water the daisies.

égoutter (se l') *exp.* • (lit.): to drain it.

égoutter Popol *exp.* • (lit.): to drain Popol.
> **NOTE -1:** **Popol** *m.* penis, dick.
> **NOTE -2:** Also spelled: *Popaul.*

égoutter sa sardine *exp.* • (lit.): to drain one's sardine.

égoutter son colosse *exp.* • (lit.): to drain one's giant.

égoutter son cyclope *exp.* • (lit.): to drain one's cyclops.

faire pipi *exp.* • (lit.): to go pee-pee.

faire pleurer le costaud *exp.* • (lit.): to make the hefty one cry.

faire pleurer le petit Jésus *exp.* • (lit.): to make little Jesus cry.

faire sa goutte *exp.* • (lit.): to do one's drop.

faire une vidange (se) *exp.* • (lit.): to do an emptying of oneself.

glisser un fil *exp.* • (lit.): to slip (out) a thread (of urine).

jeter de la lance *exp.*
- (lit.): to throw out urine.

NOTE: **lance** *f.* • **1.** urine • **2.** water.

SEE: **lancequiner**, *p. 138.*

lâcher l'écluse *exp.* • (lit.): to release the floodgate.

lâcher les vannes *exp.*
- (lit.): to release the floodgates.

lâcher un fil *exp.* • (lit.): to release a thread (of urine).

lancequiner *v.* **1.** to urinate • **2.** to rain.

SEE: **jeter de la lance**, *p. 138.*

mouiller le mur *exp.*
- (lit.): to wet the wall.

mouiller une ardoise *exp.*
- (lit.): to wet a slate.

ouvrir les écluses *exp.*
- (lit.): to open the floodgates.

pisser *v.* • (lit.): to piss.

pisser son coup *exp.*
- (lit.): to piss one's shot.

tenir l'âne par la queue *exp.* • (lit.): to hold the donkey by the tail.

Urinoir
(public urinal)

ardoises *f.pl.* • (lit.): slates.

lavabe *m.*
NOTE: This is short for *lavabo* meaning "sink."

lav *m.*
NOTE: This is short for *lavabo* meaning "sink."

pissoir *m.*

NOTE: This comes from the verb *pisser* meaning "to piss."

pissotière *f.*

NOTE -1: This comes from the verb *pisser* meaning "to piss."

NOTE -2: Although the *pissotières* no longer exist (due to their horrible smell), the term is still used in jest.

Vomir
(to vomit)

aller au renard *exp.* • (lit.): to
go to the fox.

dégobiller *v.* *(very popular)*.

NOTE: This comes from the
verb *gober* meaning "to gobble
down (food, etc.)."

dégueuler *v.* *(extremely
popular)*.

NOTE: This comes from the
feminine noun *gueule* meaning
"mouth."

évacuer le couloir *exp.*
• (lit.): to evacuate the hall.

gerber *v.* • (lit.): to sheave
(corn, etc.).

gicler *v.* • (lit.): to spray.

rendre son quatre heures
exp. • (lit.): to give back one's
cookies and milk (that which
one eats at *quatre heures*
meaning "four o'clock").

rendre *v.* *(a polite form of
"vomir")* • (lit.): to give back.

LEÇON SEPT - The Many Uses of "Merde"

Il ne se prend pas pour de la petite merde!

(trans.): He thinks his shit doesn't stink!
(lit.): He doesn't take himself for a little shit!

Leçon Sept

David: *On dirait que* [1] tu **l'as à la merde**. **Oui ou merde**?

Nicolas: Mais, oui! Je suis **dans la merde** parce que le patron me dit que je dois bosser ce soir *alors que* [2] je comptais sortir avec une super nana! Oh, il m'**emmerde**, ce petit **merdeux**. Comment est-ce que je vais **me démerder**?

David: **Merde**! C'est **emmerdant**. Quel **merdier**!

Nicolas: Je l'**emmerde**, cet **emmerdeur**! Il me *fout* [3] toujours des **emmerdements**. J'en ai marre de ce patron **merdique**! Il **ne se prend pas pour de la petite merde**, lui. *Ça y est* [4]. Je le quitte! D'ailleurs, je **m'emmerde** à ce boulot!

Lesson Seven

He thinks his shit doesn't stink!

David: You *look like* you're in **a shitty mood. Yes or no**?

Nicolas: I'll say! I'm **in deep shit** because the boss says I have to work tonight *and* I was planning on going out with a great girl! Oh, he **bugs the shit out of me**, the little **shit**. How am I going to **get out of this shit**?

David: **Shit**! It's **really annoying**. What a **mess**!

Nicolas: I **fucking can't stand him**, that **pain in the ass**! He always *gives* me **shit**. I've had it with this **shitty** boss! He **thinks his shit** doesn't stink. *That did it.* I'm quitting! Besides, I'm **bored shitless** at this job!

Dialogue in slang as it would be spoken

Y s'prend pas pour d'la p'tite merde!

David: *On dirait qu'*tu **l'as à la merde**. Oui ou **merde**?

Nicolas: Mais, oui! J'suis **dans la merde** pasque l'patron, y m'dit que j'dois bosser c'soir *alors qu'*j'comptais sortir avec une super nana! Oh, y m'**emmerde**, c'p'tit **merdeux**. Comment j'vais **m'démerder**?

David: **Merde**! C'est **emmerdant**. Quel **merdier**!

Nicolas: J'**l'emmerde**, c't'**emmerdeur**! Y m'*fout* toujours des **emmerdements**. J'en ai marre d'ce patron **merdique**! Y **s'prend pas pour d'la p'tite merde**, lui. Ça y est. J'le quitte! D'ailleurs, j'**m'emmerde** à c'boulot!

Vocabulary

```
┌─────────────────────────────────────────────────────────────┐
│              FOOTNOTES FROM THE DIALOGUE                      │
```

(1) *on dirait que*:

exp. it looks like, it would appear that • (lit.): one would say that.

(2) *alors que*:

conjunction phrase meaning "and" or "when" • *Ma sœur a invité toutes ses amies chez nous ce soir* **alors que** *j'ai un tas de devoirs à faire!;* My sister invited all of her friends to the house when I have all this work to do!

(3) *fout*:

v. (from the verb *foutre*) to give, to put.

SEE: The Many Uses of "Foutre," *p. 195.*

(4) *Ça y est*:

exp. • **1.** That did it! • **2.** There! (used upon completion of something, as a way of saying "There! It's done!").

---

dans la merde (être) *exp.* to be in a bad predicament, to be up shit creek • (lit.): to be in shit.

example: Le patron m'a dit que je suis **dans la merde** si j'arrive encore en retard au boulot.

translation: The boss told me that I'm **up shit creek** if I arrive to work late again.

as spoken: Le patron, y m'a dit qu'j'suis **dans la merde** si j'arrive encore en r'tard au boulot.

démerder (se) *v.* to get out of a fix, to get out of a shitty situation • (lit.): to "unshit" oneself.

example: J'ai promis à Gisèle que j'irais à sa soirée mais je viens de savoir que mon ancien petit ami, que je ne peux pas supporter, va y être aussi! Je ne veux plus y aller! Comment je vais **me démerder**?

translation: I promised Gisèle that I'd go to her party, but I just found out that my old boyfriend, who I can't stand, is going to be there, too! How am I going **to get out of this**?

as spoken: J'ai promis à Gisèle que j'irais à sa soirée mais j'viens d'savoir qu'mon ancien p'tit ami, que j'peux pas supporter, va y êtr'aussi! J'veux pu y aller! Comment j'vais **m'démerder**?

NOTE: When the verb *savoir* is used in the previous manner, its connotation changes from "to know" to "to find out."

emmerdant(e) (être) *adj.* to be annoying as hell.

example: Elle est **emmerdante**, celle-là. Elle me pose des questions sans arrêt.

translation: She's as **annoying as hell**. She asks me questions nonstop.

as spoken: Elle est **emmerdante**, celle-là. È m'pose des questions sans arrêt.

emmerdements *m.pl.* a big problems.

example: J'ai un tas d'**emmerdements** au boulot aujourd'hui. Pour commencer, mon assistant a donné sa démission.

translation: I have a pile of **problems** at work today. For starters, my assistant quit.

as spoken: J'ai un tas d'**emmerdements** au boulot aujourd'hui. Pour commencer, mon assistant, il a donné sa démission.

emmerder (s') *v.* to be bored to death, to be bored shitless.

example: Je **m'emmerde** dans cette classe de philosophie!

translation: I'm **bored shitless** in this philosophy class!

as spoken: J'**m'emmerde** dans c'te classe de philo~!

emmerder quelqu'un *v.* • **1.** to annoy someone, to bug the shit out of someone • **2.** to tell someone to fuck off.

example (1):   Il **m'emmerde** avec toutes ses questions.

translation: He **bugs the shit out of me** with all of his questions.

as spoken: Y **m'emmerde** avec toutes ses questions.

example (2): Voilà Marguerite! Je **l'emmerde**! Elle a couché avec mon petit ami!

translation: There's Marguerite! She can go **fuck off**! She went to bed with my boyfriend!

as spoken: V'là Marguerite! J'**l'emmerde**! Elle a couché avec mon p'tit ami!

emmerdeur, euse *n.* a pain in the ass (said of a person).

example: Quel **emmerdeur**, ce professeur. Il nous a donné un tas de devoirs à faire ce weekend.

translation: What a **pain in the ass** this professor is. He gave us a pile of homework to do over the weekend.

as spoken: Quel **emmerdeur**, c'prof~. Y nous a donné un tas de d'voirs à faire c'weekend.

merde *interj.* shit (used to signify disbelief, surprise, or anger — same as in English) • (lit.): shit.

example: Oh, **merde**! J'ai cassé mes lunettes!

translation: Oh, **shit**! I broke my glasses!

as spoken: [no change]

merde (l'avoir à la) *exp.* to be in a terrible mood • (lit.): to have it (one's personality) like shit.

example: On dirait que tu **l'as à la merde**. Qu'est-ce qu'il y a? Ton interview ne s'est pas bien passé?

translation: You look like you're **in a shitty mood**. What's wrong? Your interview didn't go well?

as spoken: On dirait qu'tu **l'as à la merde**. Qu'est-c'qu'il y a? Ton interview, y ~ s'est pas bien passé?

merdeux, euse *n.* a despicable person, a little "shit" • (lit.): shitty person.

    example: Comment est-ce que tu arrives à supporter ce petit **merdeux** de François? Il est carrément méchant.

    translation: How do you manage to tolerate that little **shit** François? He's plain mean.

    as spoken: Comment t'arrives à supporter c'p'tit **merdeux** d'François? Il est carrément méchant.

merdier *m.* a predicament, a "shitload" of trouble.

    example: Je suis dans un sacré **merdier**. J'ai pris la voiture de mon père sans permission et je l'ai démolie dans un accident!

    translation: I'm in a real **fix**. I took my father's car without permission and I wrecked it in an accident!

    as spoken: J'suis dans un sacré **merdier**. J'ai pris la voiture d'mon père sans permission et j'l'ai démolie dans un accident!

merdique (être) *adj.* shitty.

    example: J'en ai marre de ce boulot **merdique**!

    translation: I'm fed up with this **shitty** job!

    as spoken: J'en ai marre d'ce boulot **merdique**!

oui ou merde *exp.* yes or no • (lit.): yes or shit.

    example: Tu vas me rendre mon argent? Oui ou **merde**.

    translation: Are you going to give me back my money? Yes or **no**.

    as spoken: Tu vas m'rend' mon argent? Oui ou **merde**.

prendre pour de la petite merde (ne pas se) *exp.* to think highly of oneself, to think one's shit doesn't stink • (lit.): not to take oneself for a little shit.

    example: Cécile est très arrogante. Elle **ne se prend pas pour de la petite merde**.

    translation: Cecily is very arrogant. She **thinks her shit doesn't stink**.

as spoken: Cécile est très arrogante. È **s'prend pas pour d'la p'tite merde**.

NOTE: The mild form of this expression is: *prendre pour de la petite bière (ne pas se)* literally meaning "not to take oneself for a little beer."

A CLOSER LOOK:
The Many Uses of "Merde"

A common marketing boo-boo many years ago involved the Chevy Nova. When this car entered the Hispanic market, it was not well received. Why? Because *Nova (no va)* in Spanish means "No go!" Who's going to buy a car that just sits there?!

Well, the Chevy Nova is not alone. The French community was rather surprised when Toyota introduced the *MR2*. Try pronouncing *MR2* in French and you'll be just as surprised as the makers of the car when they discovered that *MR2* becomes *Eh, merde!* which is commonly pronounced as three syllables: *(M-R-2) Eh-mer-de!*

avoir à la merde (l') *exp.* to be in a shitty mood.

example: Qu'est-ce qu'il y a? On dirait que tu **l'as à la merde** aujourd'hui.

translation: What's wrong? You look like you're **in a shitty mood** today.

as spoken: Qu'est-c'qu'y a? On dirait qu'tu **l'as à la merde** aujourd'hui.

avoir de la merde dans les yeux *exp.* to be as blind as a bat, not to pay attention.

example: Tu **as de la merde dans les yeux** ou quoi? Tu ne fais pas attention à la route!

translation: Do you **have shit in your eyes** or what? You're not paying attention to the road!

as spoken: T'as **d'la merde dans les yeux** ou quoi? Tu ~ fais pas attention à la route!

avoir un œil qui dit merde à l'autre *exp.* to be cross-eyed • (lit.): to have an eye that says shit to the other.

example: Je crois qu'il a besoin de porter des lunettes. Il **a un œil qui dit merde à l'autre**.

translation: I think he needs glasses. He's **cross-eyed**.

as spoken: J'crois qu'il a b'soin d'porter des lunettes. Il **a un œil qui dit merde à l'autre**.

dans la merde (être) *exp.* to be up shit creek • (lit.): to be in shit.

example: Si je manque mon avion, je suis **dans la merde**!

translation: If I miss my plane, I'm **up shit creek**!

as spoken: Si j'manque mon avion, j'suis **dans la merde**!

dans le merdier (être) *exp.* to be up shit creek • (lit.): to be in the craphouse.

example: Si mon père découvre ce que j'ai fait à sa voiture, je serai **dans le merdier**!

translation: If my father finds out what I did to his car, I'm **up shit creek**!

as spoken: Si mon père, y découv' c'que j'ai fait à sa voiture, je s'rai **dans l'merdier**!

démerdard(e) *n.* • **1.** a shrewd and crafty individual (who can get out of shit) • **2.** lawyer.

example (1): Georges est un beau **démerdard**. Il peut se tirer d'une mauvaise situation sans problème.

translation: George is a real **shrewd and crafty guy**. He can get himself out of a bad situation without any problem.

as spoken: Georges, c't'un beau **démerdard**. Y peut s'tirer d'une mauvaise situation sans problème.

NOTE: The adjectives *beau* and *belle* are commonly used in everyday French to mean "a real."

example (2): Thierry s'est fait arrêter par la police hier soir! J'espère qu'il a trouvé un bon **démerdard**.

translation: Thierry got arrested by the police last night. I hope he found a good **lawyer.**

as spoken: Thierry, y s'est fait arrêter par la police hier soir! J'espère qu'il a trouvé un bon **démerdard**.

démerder (se) *v.* • **1.** to get out of a fix • • (lit.): to pull oneself out of shit **2.** to get by •

to stay out of shit **3.** to hurry •
(lit); to get the shit out.

example (1): Quelle situation
difficile! Je ne sais pas **me
démerder**!

translation: What a difficult
situation! I don't know how **to
dig myself out**!

as spoken: Quelle situation
difficile! J'sais pas
m'démerder!

example (2): J'ai trop de choses
à faire. Je ne peux pas **me
démerder** tout seul.

translation: I have too much to
do. I can't **get through this**
alone.

as spoken: J'ai trop d'choses à
faire. J'peux pas **m'démerder**
tout seul.

example (3): **Démerde-toi**!
Nous sommes en retard!

translation: **Hurry**! We're late!

as spoken: **Démerde-toi**! On
est en r'tard!

démerdeur m./**démerdeuse**
f. one who always manages to
land on his/her feet • (lit.): one
who can always get out of
(deep) shit.

example: Ne t'inquiète pas pour
lui. C'est un sacré **démerdeur**.

translation: Don't worry about
him. He's a real **survivor**.

as spoken: T'inquiète pas pour
lui. C't'un sacré **démerdeur**.

écrase-merdes m.pl. shoes,
shit kickers • (lit.): shit-smashers.

example: Tu ne peux pas porter
des **écrase-merdes** comme
ça avec ta nouvelle robe!

translation: You can't wear **shit
kickers** like that with your
new dress.

as spoken: Tu ~ peux pas porter
des **écrase-merdes** comme
ça avec ta nouvelle robe!

emmerdant(e) (être) adj. •
1. to be annoying, to be a pain
in the ass • **2.** to be boring.

example (1): Oh, ces nouveaux
voisins sont **emmerdants**. Il
font du bruit toute la nuit!

translation: Oh, these new
neighbors are **pains in the
ass**. They make noise all night!

as spoken: Oh, ces nouveaux
voisins, y sont **emmerdants**.
Y font du bruit toute la nuit!

example (2): Hier Robert m'a
invité à dîner chez lui. Quelle
soirée **emmerdante**!

translation: Yesterday Robert
invited me to have dinner at his
house. What a **boring** night!

as spoken: Hier Robert, y m'a
invité à dîner chez lui. Quelle
soirée **emmerdante**!

emmerdé(e) (être) *adj.* to be worried and anxious.

example: Mais tu as l'air **emmerdé**. Qu'est-ce qu'il y a?

translation: You look really **worried**. What's wrong?

as spoken: Mais t'as l'air **emmerdé**. Qu'est-c'qu'y a?

emmerdements *m.pl.* real problems.

example: Depuis qu'il a quitté son boulot, Jean n'a que des **emmerdements** financiers.

translation: Ever since Jean quit his job, he's had nothing but financial **troubles**.

as spoken: Depuis qu'il a quitté son boulot, Jean, il ~ a qu'des **emmerdements** financiers.

emmerder (s') *v.* to be bored shitless.

example: Je **m'emmerde** chez eux!

translation: I'm **bored shitless** at their house.

as spoken: J'**m'emmerde** chez eux!

emmerder *v.* to bug the shit out of someone.

example: Le patron commence à m'**emmerder**. Il me donne trop de responsabilités.

translation: The boss is starting to **bug the shit out me**. He's giving too many responsibilities.

as spoken: Le patron, y commence à m'**emmerder**. Y m'donne trop d'responsabilités.

emmerdeur *m.* / **emmerdeuse** *f.* an annoying person, a pain in the ass.

example: C'est un vrai **emmerdeur**. Il me pose des questions sans arrêt!

translation: He's a real **pain in the ass**. He asks me questions nonstop.

as spoken: C't'un vrai **emmerdeur**. Y m'pose des questions sans arrêt!

et merde! *exp.* "What the hell!"

example: **Et merde**! Je vais prendre un dessert.

translation: **What the hell**! I'm going to get a dessert.

as spoken: **Et merde**! J'vais prend' un dessert.

VARIATION: Et puis merde! *exp.*

faire le merdeux/la merdeuse *exp.* to have a high opinion of oneself, to think one's shit doesn't stink.

example: Après son augmentation, Cécile **fait la merdeuse**.

translation: After her promotion, Cecily **thinks her shit doesn't stink**.

as spoken: Après son augmentation, Cécile, **è fait la merdeuse**.

il y a de la merde au bout du bâton exp. the shit is going to hit the fan • (lit.): there is shit at the end of the stick.

example: Je ne m'en mêlerais pas si j'étais à ta place. **Il y a de la merde au bout du bâton**.

translation: I wouldn't get involved if I were in your place. **The shit's gonna hit the fan**.

as spoken: **J'**m'en mêl'rais pas si j'étais à ta place. **Y a d'la merde au bout du bâton**.

Je l'emmerde exp. To hell with him/her!

example: Je me suis disputé avec Henri pour la dernière fois. **Je l'emmerde**!

translation: I fought with Henry for the last time. **Screw him**!

as spoken: Je **m'**suis disputé avec Henri pour la dernière fois. **J'l'emmerde**!

laisser tomber quelqu'un comme une merde exp. to drop someone like a bad habit.

example: Richard et moi, nous étions de bons amis mais récemment, il m'a **laissé tomber comme une merde**.

translation: Richard and I were good friends but recently he **dropped me like a bad habit**.

as spoken: Richard et moi, on était d'bons amis mais récemment, y m'a **laissé tomber comme une merde**.

VARIATION: laisser tomber quelqu'un comme de la merde exp.

merde! interj. good luck! break a leg!

example: Il est temps que tu montes sur la scène. Ton public t'attend. **Merde!**

translation: It's time for you to get on stage. Your public awaits you. **Break a leg!**

as spoken: Il est temps qu'tu montes sur la scène. Ton public, y t'attend. **Merde!**

merde (être de la) exp. •
1. to be nonsense, bullshit •
2. junk • (lit.): to be (a bunch of) shit.

example (1): François t'a dit qu'il est président d'une grande compagnie?! C'est de la **merde**, ça!

translation: François told you he's president of a big company?! That's a bunch of **bullshit**!

as spoken: François, y t'a dit qu'il est président d'une grande compagnie?! C'est d'la **merde**, ça!

example (2): Ne me dis pas que tu vas acheter ce truc. C'est **de la merde**, ça!

translation: Don't tell me you're going to buy that thing. It's **a bunch of shit**!

as spoken: ~ Me dis pas qu'tu vas ach'ter c'truc. C'est **d'la merde**, ça!

merde alors! *interj.* oh, shit!

example: **Merde alors**! J'ai enfermé mes clés dans la voiture!

translation: **Holy shit**! I locked my keys inside the car!

as spoken: [no change]

merde pour *exp.* to hell with.

example: **Merde** pour ce boulot!

translation: **To hell with** this job!

as spoken: **Merde** pour c'boulot!

NOTE: **boulot** *m.* *(extremely popular)* job, work.

Merde! *interj.* • **1.** Damn! • **2.** Wow! • (lit.): Shit!

example (1): **Merde!** J'ai perdu mon portefeuille!

translation: **Shit!** I lost my wallet!

as spoken: [no change]

example (2): **Merde!** Ta nouvelle robe est très belle!

translation: **Shit!** Your new dress is really pretty!

as spoken: **Merde!** Ta nouvelle robe, elle est très belle!

VARIATION -1: **Merde et contre-merde!** *interj.* • (lit.): Shit and double shit!

VARIATION -2: **Et puis merde!** *interj.*

VARIATION -3: **Merde de merde!** *interj.*

VARIATION -4: **Mille merdes!** *interj.*

merder (se) *v.* to fail or botch something.

example: Je me suis **merdé** à l'examen!

translation: I **botched** the test!

as spoken: Je m'suis **merdé** à l'exam~!

merder *v.* to fail miserably.

example: J'ai complètement **merdé à** l'examen.

translation: I totaly **blew** the test.

as spoken: J'ai complètement **merdé à** l'exam~.

merdique (être) *adj.* • **1.** to be difficult, to be a real bitch (said of a situation or problem) • **2.** to be for the birds, for shit.

example (1): Je n'arrive pas à résoudre ce problème. C'est complètement **merdique**.

translation: I can't seem to solve this problem. It's a real **bitch**.

as spoken: J'arrive pas à résoud' ce problème. C'est complètement **merdique**.

example (2): Cette pièce de théâtre est complètement **merdique**.

translation: This play is really **shitty**.

as spoken: C'te pièce de théâtre, elle est complètement **merdique**.

merdouille *f.* shit.

example: Attention! Tu as failli marcher dans la **merdouille**!

translation: Watch out! You almost walked in some **shit**!

as spoken: Attention! T'as failli marcher dans la **merdouille**!

merdouiller *v.* to flounder.

example: Ça ne m'étonnerait pas si Georges trouvait un nouveau boulot. Il ne fait que **merdouiller** ici.

translation: It wouldn't surprise me if George found a new job. He does nothing but **flounder** here.

as spoken: Ça ~ m'étonn'rait pas si Georges trouvait un nouveau boulot. Y fait que **merdouiller** ici.

mouche à merde *f.* housefly • (lit.): shit-fly.

example: Il y a trop de **mouches à merde** chez ma tante!

translation: There are too many **houseflies** at my aunt's house!

as spoken: Y a trop d'**mouches à merde** chez ma tante!

oui ou merde *exp.* yes or no • (lit.): yes or shit.

example: Est-ce que tu m'accompagnes? **Oui ou merde**?

translation: Are you coming with me? **Yes or no**?

as spoken: Tu m'accompagnes? **Oui ou merde**?

petit merdeux *m.*/**petite merdeuse** *f.* a little twerp • (lit.): a little shit.

example: Ce **petit merdeux** me suit partout!

translation: That **little shit** follows me everywhere!

as spoken: Ce **p'tit merdeux**, y m'suit partout!

prendre pour de la petite merde (ne pas se) *exp.* to be arrogant, to think one's shit doesn't stink • (lit.): not to take oneself for a little shit.

example: Je ne peux pas supporter cette fille. Elle **se prend pas pour de la petite merde**.

translation: I can't stand that girl. She **thinks her shit doesn't stink**.

as spoken: J'peux pas supporter c'te fille. È s'prend pas pour d'la p'tite merde.

NOTE: This is a stronger version of the expression *ne pas se prendre pour de la petite bière,* literally "not to take oneself for a little beer."

VARIATION: **prendre pour de la merde (ne pas se)** *exp.* • (lit.): not to take oneself for shit.

semer la merde *exp.* to cause confusion, to kick up shit.

example: Tu as invité Raymond à nous rejoindre?! Mais il **sème la merde**, lui!

translation: You invited Raymond to join us? But he **causes nothing but shit**!

as spoken: T'as invité Raymond à nous rejoindre?! Mais y **sème la merde**, lui!

sentir la merde *exp.* • **1.** to stink to high heaven • **2.** to smell fishy • (lit.): to smell of shit.

example (1): Ça **sent la merde** dans cette poissonnerie!

translation: It **stinks to high heaven** in this fish market!

as spoken: Ça **sent la merde** dans c'te poissonnerie!

example (2): Depuis que nous avons engagé Cécile, la caisse est toujours à court d'argent. Ça **sent la merde**!

translation: Ever since we hired Cecilia, the cash register is always short of money. That **smells fishy**.

as spoken: Depuis qu'on a engagé Cécile, la caisse, elle est toujours à court d'argent. Ça **sent la merde**!

système démerde *m.* operation "get out of deep shit."

example: Quel problème! Il est temps d'employer le **système démerde**.

translation: What a problem! It's time to implement **operation get out of shit**.

as spoken: Quel problème! Il est temps d'employer l'**système démerde**.

traîner quelqu'un dans la merde *exp.* • **1.** to drag someone through a lot of shit • **2.** to slander someone's reputation.

example (1): Mon patron m'a **traîné dans la merde** pendant deux ans. J'en ai assez!

translation: My boss **dragged me through a lot of shit** for two years. I've had it!

as spoken: Mon patron, y m'a **traîné dans la merde** pendant deux ans. J'en ai assez!

example (2): Nous avons parlé à Cécile des problèmes de caisse, sur quoi elle s'est mise en colère et nous a accusés de la **traîner dans la merde**! Tu te rends comptes?

translation: We spoke to Cécile about the cash register problems, at which point she got mad and accused us of **slandering her**! Can you believe it?

as spoken: On a parlé à Cécile des problèmes de caisse, sur quoi è s'est mise en colère et nous a accusés d'la **traîner dans la merde**! Tu te rends comptes?

LEÇON HUIT - The Many Uses of "Chier"

Henri avait la chiasse pendant tout le film!

(trans.): *Henry was scared shitless during the entire film!*
(lit.): *Henri had the shits during the entire film!*

Leçon Huit

Christine: Il est **chiant**, ce prof. Ce **chieur**, il nous a foutu une **chiée** de devoirs à faire ce weekend. Quelle **chierie**! Bon. **Il n'y a pas à chier**: Il **ne se fait pas chier**, lui.

Michelle: *Un de ces quatre,*[1] il va me **faire chier** une fois de trop et ça va **chier dur**! Je te préviens. Je vais l'**envoyer chier**.

Christine: Bonne idée. Je **me fais chier** dans sa classe et j'*en ai marre* [2] de regarder **sa gueule à chier dessus**.

Michelle: Comme tu dis. Il a une gueule qui **me fait chier dans les frocs**!

Christine: Moi, aussi. Il me **donne la chiasse**, lui!

Translation in English

Henry was scared shitless during the entire movie!

Christine: This professor's **annoying**. That **asshole** gave us a **shitload** of homework to do this weekend. What a **pain in the ass**! Well. **There's no two ways about it**: That guy **has some nerve.**

Michelle: *One of these days,* he's going **to bug the shit out of me** once too often and **the shit's gonna hit the fan**! I'm warning you. I'm gonna tell him **to fuck off**.

Christine: Good idea. I'm **bored shitless** in his class and *I've had it* with looking at **his ugly face**.

Michelle: You know it. He has a face **that scares the shit out of me**!

Christine: Same here. The guy **scares the shit out of me**.

Dialogue in slang as it would be spoken

Henri, il avait la chiasse pendant tout l'film!

Christine: Il est **chiant**, c'prof. Ce **chieur**, y nous a foutu une **chiée** de d'voirs à faire c'weekend. Quelle **chierie**! Bon. **Y a pas à chier**: Y **s'fait pas chier**, lui.

Michelle: *Un d'ces quatre*, y va m'**faire chier** une fois de trop et ça va **chier dur**! J'te préviens. J'vais l'**envoyer chier**.

Christine: Bonne idée. Je **m'fais chier** dans sa classe et j'*en ai marre* de regarder **sa gueule à chier d'ssus**.

Michelle: Comme tu dis. Il a une gueule qui **m'fait chier dans les frocs**!

Christine: Moi aussi. Y m'donne la **chiasse**, lui!

Vocabulary

chiasse (avoir la) _exp._ to be scared shitless • (lit.): to have the shits (or "diarrhea").

> example: J'ai eu la **chiasse** quand j'ai vu l'avalanche.

> translation: I was **scared shitless** when I saw the avalanche.

> as spoken: [no change]

chiant(e) (être) _adj._ to be annoying as shit.

> example: Oh, mais tu es **chiant**! Laisse-moi tranquille!

> translation: Oh, you're **annoying as shit**! Leave me alone!

> as spoken: Oh, mais t'es **chiant**! Laisse-moi tranquille!

chier (se faire) _exp._ to be bored shitless • (lit.): to make oneself shit (from boredom).

> example: Je **me fais chier** à cette soirée. On s'en va?

> translation: I'm **bored shitless** at this party. Wanna get out of here?

> as spoken: J'**me fais chier** à c'te soirée. On s'en va?

chiée _f._ a lot, a shitload.

> example: J'ai une **chiée** de devoirs à faire ce soir.

> translation: I have a **shitload** of homework to do tonight.

> as spoken: J'ai une **chiée** de d'voirs à faire c'soir.

chierie *f.* a pain in the ass (said of a situation or thing).

      example: Mon père m'a demandé de peindre l'extérieur de la maison. Quelle **chierie**!

    translation: My father asked me to paint the outside of the house. What a **pain in the ass**!

    as spoken: Mon père, <u>y</u> m'a <u>d</u>'mandé <u>d</u>'pein<u>d</u>' l'extérieur <u>d</u>'la maison. Quelle **chierie**!

chier dans les frocs *exp.* to be scared shitless • (lit.): to shit in one's pants.

      example: En voyant s'approcher la tornade, j'ai **chié dans mes frocs**.

    translation: When I saw the tornado approaching, I was **scared shitless**.

    as spoken: [no change]

    NOTE: **frocs** *m.pl.* pants.

chier dur *exp.* said of a situation that's going to get worse, the shit's going to hit the fan • (lit.): to shit hard.

      example: Quand ta mère verra ce que tu as fait de sa cuisine, ça va **chier dur**.

    translation: When your mother sees what you did to her kitchen, the **shit's going to hit the fan**.

    as spoken: Quand ta mère verra <u>c</u>'que <u>t</u>'as fait <u>d</u>'sa cuisine, ça va **chier dur**.

chieur, euse *n.* despicable person, asshole • (lit.): shitter.

      example: Ce **chieur** de patron vient de baisser mon salaire!

    translation: That **asshole** of a boss just lowered my salary!

    as spoken: Ce **chieur** <u>d</u>'patron, <u>y</u> vient <u>d</u>'baisser mon salaire!

chier quelqu'un (faire) *exp.* to make someone angry as shit • (lit.): to make someone shit.

>   example: Ça **me fait chier** quand tu empruntes mes affaires sans me demander!

>   translation: It **bugs the shit out of me** when you borrow my things without asking.

>   as spoken: Ça **m'fait chier** quand t'empruntes mes affaires sans me d'mander!

envoyer chier quelqu'un *exp.* to tell someone to fuck off • (lit.): to send someone to go shit.

>   example: Quand il m'a accusé d'avoir menti, je **l'ai envoyé chier**!

>   translation: When he accused me of lying, I **told him to fuck himself**!

>   as spoken: Quand y m'a accusé d'avoir menti, j'**l'ai envoyé chier**!

faire chier (ne pas se) *exp.* • **1.** to have nerve • **2.** to have a good time (lit.): not to make oneself shit.

>   example (1):   Marc s'est invité à mon dîner. Il **ne se fait pas chier**, c'est sûr!

>   translation: Marc invited himself to my dinner party. He **really has some nerve**, that's for sure.

>   as spoken: Marc, y s'est invité à mon dîner. Y ~ **s'fait pas chier**, c'est sûr!

>   example (2):   Je **ne me fais pas chier** ici!

>   translation: I'm **having a great time** here!

>   as spoken: Je ~ **m'fais pas chier** ici!

>   **NOTE:**   Using a negative to express something positive, as seen in example (2), is extremely popular in French. For example, to signify that something tastes good would commonly be said as: *C'est pas mauvais, ça!* rather then *C'est bon, ça!*

gueule à chier dessus (avoir une) *exp.* to be as ugly as shit •
(lit.): to have a face to shit on.

> example: Laurent veut être acteur mais à mon avis, il a une
> **gueule à chier dessus**.

> translation: Laurent wants to be an actor but in my opinion, he's **as
> ugly as shit**.

> as spoken: Laurent, y̲ veut êt̲r̲'acteur mais à mon avis, il a une
> **gueule à chier d̲'ssus**.

il n'y a pas à chier *exp.* there's no two ways about it • (lit.): there's no
shitting.

> example: **Il n'y a pas à chier**. Elle l'épouse pour son argent.

> translation: **There's no two ways about it**. She's marrying him
> for his money.

> as spoken: ~ **Y'a pas à chier**. È̲ l'épouse pour son argent.

A CLOSER LOOK:
The Many Uses of "Chier"

The verb *chier*, literally meaning "to shit," lends itself to a variety of different
shapes; it can be used as a verb, a noun, an adjective, and as the milestone in
a number of popular expressions. Even if your journey to France is for a short
period of time, you are sure to encounter one of the forms of *chier* shortly after
your arrival, especially if you visit a family with younger members.

c'est chié *exp.* that's fantastic.
> example: Tu as gagné dix mille
> francs? **C'est chié**, ça!

> translation: You won ten
> thousand francs? **That's
> fantastic**!

as spoken: T'as gagné dix mille francs? **C'est chié**, ça!

ça ne chie pas exp. it doesn't matter a fucking bit.

example: Si tu manques ton avion, **ça ne chie pas**. Tu en prendras un autre demain.

translation: If you miss your plane, **it doesn't matter a fucking bit**. You'll just take another one tomorrow.

as spoken: Si tu manques ton avion, **ça ~ chie pas**. T'en prendras un aut' demain.

ça va chier exp. the shit's going to hit the fan.

example: Si le patron découvre que tu étais en retard pour la troisième fois cette semaine, **ça va chier**!

translation: If the boss discovers that you were late for the third time this week, **the shit's gonna hit the fan**.

as spoken: Si l'patron, y découv' que t'étais en r'tard pour la troisième fois cette s'maine, **ça va chier**!

VARIATION -1: **ça va chier dur** exp. • (lit.): it's going to shit hard.

VARIATION -2: **ça va chier sec** exp. • (lit.): it's going to shit dry.

VARIATION -3: **ça va chier des bulles** exp. • (lit.): it's going to shit bubbles.

VARIATION -4: **ça va chier des flammes** exp. • (lit.): it's going to shit flames.

chiant(e) (être) adj. • **1.** to be annoying as all hell • **2.** to be as boring as shit.

example (1): Oh, il est **chiant**, ce professeur. Il nous donne toujours des devoirs à faire pendant nos vacances.

translation: Oh, this teacher is **annoying as all hell**. He always gives us homework to do over our vacation.

as spoken: Oh, il est **chiant**, c'prof~. Y nous donne toujours des d'voirs à faire pendant nos vacances.

example (2): Ce cours de mathématiques est **chiant**!

translation: This math class is **boring as shit**!

as spoken: Ce cours de maths, il est **chiant**!

chiasse (avoir la) exp. • **1.** to have the runs • **2.** to be scared shitless • (lit.): to have the shits.

example (1): Je pense que j'ai mangé quelque chose de malsain. Deux heures après mon déjeuner, j'ai eu **la chiasse**.

translation: I think I ate something bad. Two hours after eating lunch, I **got the shits**.

as spoken: J'pense que j'ai mangé quèque chose d'malsain. Deux heures après mon dèj, j'ai eu **la chiasse**.

example (2): J'ai eu **la chiasse** quand l'avion a commencé à ballotter.

translation: I was **scared shitless** when the airplane started pitching back and forth.

as spoken: J'ai eu **la chiasse** quand l'avion, il a commencé à ballotter.

chiasser v. to be scared shitless • (lit.): to have diarrhea.

example: Quand j'ai vu l'ours, j'ai **chiassé**!

translation: When I saw the bear, I **was scared shitless**!

as spoken: [no change]

chiasseur, euse n. scardey-cat • (lit.): shitter, one who gets scared shitless.

example: Robert a peur d'entrer dans cette maison parce qu'il pense que c'est hanté. Quel **chiasseur**!

translation: Robert is scared to go into that house because he think it's haunted. What a **scardey-cat**!

as spoken: Robert, il a peur d'entrer dans c'te maison pasqu'y pense que c'est hanté. Quel **chiasseur**!

VARIATION: chiasseux, euse n.

chiée (une) f. a shitload.

example: Elle a **une chiée** d'enfants, celle-là.

translation: That lady's got **a shitload** of kids.

as spoken: [no change]

chier (être à) exp. to be extremely boring.

example: Ce film est **à chier**!

translation: This film is **boring as shit**!

as spoken: Ce film, il est **à chier**!

chier (faire) v. to bug the shit out of someone • (lit.): to make someone shit.

example: Tu ne vas pas l'inviter à notre soirée! Il **me fait chier**, lui!

translation: You're not going to invite him to our party! He **bugs the shit out of me**!

as spoken: Tu ~ vas pas l'inviter à not' soirée! Y **m'fait chier**, lui!

chier (se faire) *exp.* to be bored shitless • (lit.): to make oneself shit.

example: Je **me fais chier** à cette soirée!

translation: I'm **bored shitless** at this party!

as spoken: J'**me fais chier** à c'te soirée!

chier dans la colle *exp.* to exaggerate, to shit (someone) • (lit.): to shit in the glue.

example: Tu as vu un gars qui faisait trois mètres?! Tu **chies dans la colle**, non?

translation: You saw a guy who was three meters (about ten feet) tall? You're **shitting me**, aren't you?

as spoken: T'as vu un gars qui faisait trois mètres?! Tu **chies dans la colle**, non?

NOTE: **gars** *m.* guy, "dude."

SYNONYM -1: **chier dans la confiture** *exp.* • (lit.): to shit in the jam.

SYNONYM -2: **chier dans le pot** *exp.* • (lit.): to shit in the pot.

chier dans les bottes de quelqu'un *exp.* to play a dirty trick on someone • (lit.): to shit in someone's boots.

example: Je ne parle plus à Christophe. Il a **chié dans mes bottes**!

translation: I'm not speaking to Christopher anymore. He **played a shitty trick on me**.

as spoken: J'parle pu à Christophe. Il a **chié dans mes bottes**!

chier dans ses frocs/son froc *exp.* to be scared shitless • (lit.): to shit in one's pants.

example: J'ai **chié dans mes frocs** quand le tremblement de terre a commencé.

translation: I **was scared shitless** when the earthquake hit.

as spoken: J'ai **chié dans mes frocs** quand il a commencé, l'tremblement d'terre,

NOTE: **froc** *m.* pants / **frocs** *m.pl.* clothes.

chier la honte (ne pas) *exp.* to have nerve • (lit.): not to shit shame.

example: En rencontrant mes amis riches, Louis leur a demandé de lui prêter de l'argent. Il **ne chie pas la honte**, ce type!

translation: Upon meeting my rich friends, Louis asked them

to lend him some money. He **has some nerve**, that guy!

as spoken: En rencontrant mes amis riches, Louis, y leur a d'mandé d'lui prêter d'l'argent. Y **chie la honte**, c'type!

> **NOTE:** **type** m. (*very popular*) guy, "dude" / **typesse** f. girl, "chick."

chier pour son matricule
exp. to be in for it, to be sorry • (lit.): to shit for one's I.D. number.

example: Si tu prends la voiture de ton père sans permission, **ça va chier pour ton matricule**!

translation: If you take your father's car without permission, **you're gonna be sorry**!

as spoken: Si tu prends la voiture d'ton père sans permission, **ça va chier pour ton matricule**!

chier v. to shit, crap.
example: Le chien a **chié** sur le nouveau tapis!

translation: The dog **crapped** on the new rug!

as spoken: Le chien, il a **chié** sur l'nouveau tapis!

chierie f. a pain in the ass.
example: Quelle **chierie** ces devoirs!

translation: This homework in a **pain in the ass**!

as spoken: Quelle **chierie** ces d'voirs!

chieur, euse d'encre n.
paper pusher, desk jockey • (lit.): shitter of ink.

example: Mon père est vice président de sa compagnie mais il a commencé comme **chieur d'encre**.

translation: My father is vice president of his company but he started out as a **paper pusher**.

as spoken: Mon père, il est vice président d'sa compagnie mais il a commencé comme **chieur d'encre**.

chieur, euse n. annoying
person • (lit.): shitter.

example: Jean-Paul m'a téléphoné quatre fois en une heure pour discuter de Clarisse. Quel **chieur**!

translation: Jean-Paul called me four times in one hour to talk about Clarisse. What a **pain in the butt**!

as spoken: Jean-Paul, y m'a téléphoné quat' fois en une heure pour discuter d'Clarisse. Quel **chieur**!

chiottes (les) *f.pl. (extremely popular)* the bathroom, the "shit house."

example: Je dois aller aux **chiottes**. Je reviens.

translation: I have to go to the **shithouse**. I'll be right back.

as spoken: J'dois aller aux **chiottes**. Je r'viens.

drôle à chier (être) *exp.* •
1. to be extremely funny in a sarcastic way • **2.** said of something not funny at all.

example (1): Pierrot a glissé sur une peau de banane et a déchiré son froc. C'était **drôle à chier**!

translation: Pierrot slid on a banana peel and tore his pants. It was **hilarious**!

as spoken: Pierrot, il a glissé sur une peau d'banane et a déchiré son froc. C'était **drôle à chier**!

example (2): L'enterrement était **drôle à chier**.

translation: The burial was **wasn't funny at all**.

as spoken: L'enterrement, il était **drôle à chier**.

envoyer chier *exp.* to tell (someone) to fuck off • (lit.): to send (someone) shitting.

example: J'en ai assez de lui. Je vais **l'envoyer chier**!

translation: I've had it with him. I'm gonna **tell him to fuck off**!

as spoken: J'en ai assez d'lui. J'vais **l'envoyer chier**!

SYNONYM: envoyer paître *exp.* • (lit.): to send out to pasture.

gueule à chier dessus (avoir une) *exp.* to be butt ugly • (lit.): to have a face to shit on.

example: Suzanne veut devenir actrice?! Mais elle **a une gueule à chier dessus**!

translation: Susan wants to become an actress?! But she's **butt ugly**!

as spoken: Suzanne, è veut dev'nir actrice?! Mais elle **a une gueule à chier d'ssus**!

NOTE: gueule *f. (derogatory)* • **1.** face • **2.** mouth • (lit.): the mouth of an animal.

il n'y a pas à chier *exp.* there's no two ways about it.

example: **Il n'y a pas à chier**, c'est la plus grande maison que j'ai jamais vue, ça.

translation: **There's no two ways about it**. That's the biggest house I've ever seen.

as spoken: ~ **Y a pas à chier**, c'est la plus grande maison qu'j'ai jamais vue, ça.

triste à chier (être) *exp.* to
be extremely sad and tragic.

example: La mère de Robert est
sénile. C'est **triste à chier**.

translation: Robert's mother is
senile. It's **so sad**.

as spoken: La mère de Robert,
elle est sénile. C'est **triste à
chier**.

va te faire chier *exp. (very
popular)* get fucked.

example: Je ne peux pas croire
que tu m'as menti. **Va te
faire chier**!

translation: I can't believe you
lied to me. **Go get fucked**!

as spoken: J'peux pas croire
qu'tu m'as menti. **Va t'faire
chier**!

LEÇON NEUF - The Many Uses of "Con"

Ce chauffeur-là, c'est le roi des cons!

(trans.): That driver is the biggest jerk!
(lit.): That driver is the king of the jerks!

Leçon Neuf

Marc: Tiens! Voilà Guy. Quel **con**, ce type. Je ne sais pas pourquoi cette **connasse** de patronne l'a engagé. Il ne fait que **déconner** toute la journée.

Thierry: J'*en ai assez de* [1] ses **conneries**, moi aussi. On est allé prendre un café ensemble et il n'a pas arrêté de *draguer* [2] la serveuse. Mais ça *sautait aux yeux* [3] qu'elle s'intéressait pas du tout à lui. Ah, le **pauvre con**! C'était gênant de le voir **faire le con** comme ça. Il faut le dire. C'est le **roi des cons**.

Marc: Oh, il est **con comme la lune**. Et tu devrais rencontrer sa femme — une vraie **connarde**, celle-là!

Leçon Neuf

Translation in English

That driver is the biggest jerk!

Marc: Hey! There's Guy. What a **jerk** he is. I don't know why this **idiot** of a boss hired him. He does nothing but **goof off** all day.

Thierry: *I've had it with* his **bullshit**, too. We went to get coffee together and he didn't stop *hitting on* the waitress. And it was *obvious* she wasn't interested in him at all. Man, that **poor fucker**! It was uncomfortable seeing him **make a jerk out of himself** like that. I have to say it. He's the **king of the jerks**.

Marc: Oh, he's **a total jerk**. And you should meet his wife — a real **idiot**!

Dialogue in slang as it would be spoken

Ce chauffeur-là, c'est l'roi des cons!

Marc: Tiens! V'là Guy. Quel **con**, c'type. J'sais pas pourquoi c'te **connasse** de patronne, è l'a engagé. Y fait que **déconner** toute la journée.

Thierry: *J'en ai assez d'*ses **conn'ries**, moi aussi. On est allé prendr'un café ensemble et il a pas arrêté d'*draguer* la serveuse. Mais ça *sautait aux yeux* qu'è s'intéressait pas du tout à lui. Ah, l'**pauv' con**. C'était gênant d'le voir **faire le con** comme ça. Faut le dire. C'est l'**roi des cons**.

Marc: Oh, il est **con comme la lune**. Et tu devrais rencontrer sa femme — une vraie **connarde**, celle-là!

Vocabulary

FOOTNOTES FROM THE DIALOGUE

(1) _avoir assez de (en)_:

exp. to have had it with (something or someone) • _J'en ai assez de ses mensonges!_; I've had it with his/her lies!

(2) _draguer_:

v. (_extremely popular_) to flirt, to cruise, to hit on.

(3) _sauter aux yeux_:

exp. to be obvious • (lit.): to jump to the eyes.

---

con m. • **1.** idiot, jerk • **2.** a despicable term meaning "asshole."

example (1): Guy a échoué à tous ces cours à l'école. Quel **con**!

translation: Guy failed all of his courses at school. What an **idiot**!

as spoken: Guy, i̲l a échoué à tous ces cours à l'école. Quel **con**!

example (2): Paul m'a dénoncé au patron. Quel **con**!

translation: Paul reported me to the boss. What an **asshole**!

as spoken: Paul, y̲ m'a dénoncé au patron. Quel **con**!

con comme la lune (être) exp. to be as nutty as a fruitcake • (lit.): to be as crazy as the moon.

example: Mon oncle est **con comme la lune**. Il parle à des personnes imaginaires tout le temps.

translation: My uncle is **as nutty as a fruitcake**. He talks to imaginary people all the time.

as spoken: Mon oncle, i̲l est **con comme la lune**. Y̲ parle à des personnes imaginaires tout l̲'temps.

con (faire le) *exp.* to act like a jerk.

> example: Chaque fois que René est près d'une jolie fille, il **fait le con**.

> translation: Every time René is near a pretty girl, he **acts like a jerk**.

> as spoken: Chaque fois que René est près d'une jolie fille, y̲ **fait l'con**.

connard(e) *n.* jerk, idiot.

> example: Quel **connard**, Jean. Il a mis du sel dans son café en pensant que c'était du sucre.

> translation: What an **idiot** Jean is. He put salt in his coffee thinking it was sugar.

> as spoken: Quel **connard**, Jean. Il a mis du sel dans son café en pensant qu̲'c'était du sucre.

connasse *f.* a despicable term for a woman meaning "cunt."

> example: Cette **connasse** de Sandra a essayé de me faire mettre à la porte!

> translation: That **cunt** Sandra tried to get me fired!

> as spoken: C̲'te **connasse** de Sandra, e̲l̲l̲e̲ a essayé d̲'me faire mett̲r̲'à la porte!

connerie *f.* • **1.** foolishness • **2.** dirty trick.

> example (1):   Arrête tes **conneries**! Nous sommes en public!

> translation: Stop your **foolishness**! We're in public!

> as spoken: Arrête tes **conn'ries**! O̲n̲ e̲s̲t̲ en public!

> example (2):   Je ne parle plus à Marc. La semaine dernière il m'a fait une **connerie** inexcusable.

> translation: I'm not speaking to Marc anymore. Last week he played an unforgiveable **dirty trick** on me.

> as spoken: J̲'parle p̲u̲ à Marc. La s̲'maine dernière y̲ m'a fait une **conn'rie** inexcusable.

déconner *v.* • **1.** to goof off • **2.** to talk nonsense, to lose it • **3.** to function erratically (said of a machine).

      example (1):   Arrête de **déconner**. On a du travail à faire.

      translation: Stop **goofing off**. We have work to do.

      as spoken: [no change]

      example (2):   Oh, mais qu'est-ce que tu racontes? Tu **déconnes**!

      translation: Oh, what are you talking about? You're talking absolute **nonsense**!

      as spoken: Oh, mais qu'est-<u>c</u>'que tu racontes? Tu **déconnes**!

      example (3):   Je crois qu'il est temps d'acheter un nouvel ordinateur. Celui-ci **déconne** trop.

      translation: I think it's time to buy a new computer. This one **acts goofy** all the time.

      as spoken: J'crois qu'il est temps d'ach'ter un nouvel ordinateur. Celui-ci, <u>y</u> **déconne** trop.

pauvre con *m.* poor or pathetic guy.

      example: Oh, le **pauvre con**. Il à été mis à la porte deux jours avant Noël.

      translation: Oh, the **poor guy**. He was fired two days before Christmas.

      as spoken: Oh, l'**pauv'** con. Il a été mis à la porte deux jours avant Noël.

roi des cons *exp.* the king of jerks • (lit.): [same].

      example: Pourquoi as-tu invité Albert à nous joindre? C'est le **roi des cons**!

      translation: Why did you invite Albert to join us? He's the **king of jerks**!

      as spoken: Pourquoi <u>t</u>'as invité Albert à nous joindre? C'est l'**roi des cons**!

A CLOSER LOOK:
The Many Uses of "Con"

The term *con* is one of the most widely used words in the French repertory since it has so many meanings. It is important to note that the original connotation of *con* was extremely strong and vulgar, meaning "vagina," or more closely, "cunt." Over the years, it has lost its original meaning and is now used by everyone in a variety of expressions.

con • **1.** *adj.* stupid, silly • **2.** *m.* jerk, bastard, asshole.

example (1): Le film que j'ai vu hier soir était tout à fait **con**.

translation: The movie I saw last night was totally **stupid**.

as spoken: Le film que j'ai vu hier soir, <u>il</u> était tout à fait **con**.

example (2): Ce **con** m'a dénoncé au patron parce que je suis arrivé au boulot avec dix minutes de retard.

translation: That **asshole** reported me to the boss because I arrived ten minutes late.

as spoken: Ce **con**, <u>y</u> m'a dénoncé au patron <u>pasque</u> <u>j'</u>suis arrivé au boulot avec dix minutes de <u>r'</u>tard.

example (3): Quel bande de **cons**!

translation: What a bunch of **idiots**!

as spoken: [no change]

NOTE: **espèce de con** is a common expression meaning "what a huge idiot, or literally, "species of an idiot."

VARIATION: **conneau** *m.*

con (à la) *adj.* stupid.

example: Comme président, il est abominable. Il a des idées **à la con**.

translation: He's a horrible present. His ideas are **stupid**.

as spoken: [no change]

con comme la lune (être) *exp.* to be as dumb as an ox • (lit.): to be as crazy as the moon.

example: Christophe a été augmenté?! Mais il est **con comme la lune**, lui!

translation: Christopher was promoted?! But he's **as dumb as an ox**!

as spoken: Christophe, <u>il</u> a été augmenté?! Mais il est **con comme la lune**, lui!

NOTE: In this expression, *lune* (meaning "moon") is the root word for the English word "lunatic."

SYNONYM -1: **con comme ses pieds (être)** *exp.* • (lit.): to be as crazy as one's feet.

SYNONYM -2: **con comme un balai (être)** *exp.* • (lit.): to be as crazy as a broom.

SYNONYM -3: **con comme un panier (être)** *exp.* • (lit.): to be as crazy as a basket.

con (faire le) *exp.* to act like an idiot.

example: Hier soir, Albert a **fait le con** devant tous mes amis. Il a descendu quatre verres de vin et a fini par danser sur la table!

translation: Last night, Albert **acted like an idiot** in front of all my friends. He downed four glasses of wine and ended up dancing on the table!

as spoken: Hier soir, Albert, i̱l a **fait l'con** ḏ'vant tous mes amis. Il a descendu quaṯ' verres de vin et a fini par danser sur la table!

con fini (un) *m.* a total asshole.

example: Il a triché, Antoine. C'est un **con fini**, lui!

translation: Antoine cheated. He's a **total asshole**!

as spoken: Il a triché, Antoine. C̱'t'un **con fini**, lui!

connard(e) *n.* jerk, asshole.

example: Oh, ce **connard**-là! Il conduit dans la mauvaise file!

translation: Woah, that **jerk**! He's driving in the wrong lane!

as spoken: Oh, c̱'**connard**-là! Y̱ conduit dans la mauvaise file!

connasse *f.* bitch.

example: As-tu rencontré la femme du patron? Elle est très arrogante. Quelle **connasse**!

translation: Did you meet the boss's wife? She's really arrogant. What a **bitch**!

as spoken: Ṯ'as rencontré la femme du patron? Elle est très arrogante. Quelle **connasse**!

conne *f.* (said of women) • **1.** idiot, jerk • **2.** bitch.

example (1): Josette a oublié de venir me chercher à l'aéroport. Quelle **conne**!

translation: Josette forgot to pick me up at the airport. What an **idiot**!

as spoken: Josette, e̱lle a oublié de v̱'nir m̱'chercher à l'aéroport. Quelle **conne**!

example (2): Je ne peux pas supporter cette marchande. C'est une vraie **conne**.

translation: I can't stand that saleswoman. She's a real **bitch**.

as spoken: J'peux pas supporter c'te marchande. C't'une vraie **conne**.

NOTE: The difference between **1.** and **2.** simply depends on the context.

connerie f. • **1.** foolishness • **2.** dirty trick.

example (1): Arrête tes **conneries**! Nous sommes en public!

translation: Stop your **foolishness**! We're in public!

as spoken: Arrête tes **conn'ries**! On est en public!

example (2): Je ne parle plus à Marc. La semaine dernière il m'a fait une **connerie** inexcusable.

translation: I'm not speaking to Marc anymore. Last week he played an unforgiveable **dirty trick** on me.

as spoken: J'parle pu à Marc. La s'maine dernière y m'a fait une **conn'rie** inexcusable.

déconner v. • **1.** to goof around, to lose it • **2.** to function erratically (said of a machine) • (lit.): originally this meant "to pull out" when con was used to mean "cunt."

example (1): Arrête de **déconner**. C'est une situation sérieuse.

translation: Stop **goofing around**. This is a serious situation.

as spoken: Arrête de **déconner**. C't'une situation sérieuse.

example (1): Cette télévision **déconne** et je viens de l'acheter!

translation: Cette television is **acting weird** and I just bought it!

as spoken: C'te télé~, è **déconne** et j'viens d'l'ach'ter!

drôlement con (être) exp. to be really silly and fun.

example: Le film que j'ai vu hier soir était **drôlement con**. Tu devrais aller le voir!

translation: The movie I saw last night was **really silly and fun**. You should go see it!

as spoken: Le film que j'ai vu hier soir, il était **drôlement con**. Tu devrais aller l'voir!

du con *exp.* used to call someone; "hey, you moron!"

example: Hé, **du con**! Tu as pris mon livre par accident!

translation: Hey, **you**! You took my book by mistake!

as spoken: Hé, **du con**! T'as pris mon li<u>v</u>' par accident!

pas si con *exp.* not such a bad idea • (lit.): not to stupid.

example: "Tu veux aller faire un pique-nique aujourd'hui?" "**Pas si con**. Il fait très beau dehors."

translation: "Do you want to go on a picnic today?" "**That's not such a bad idea**. The weather is beautiful outside."

as spoken: "Tu veux aller faire un pique-nique aujourd'hui?" "**Pas si con**. <u>Y</u> fait très beau dehors."

pauvre con *m.* poor guy, foolish bastard, loser.

example: Le **pauvre con**. Grégoire a perdu toute sa fortune aux courses.

translation: **Poor guy**. Greg lost his entire fortune at the races.

as spoken: Le **pau<u>v</u>' con**. Grégoire, <u>il</u> a perdu toute sa fortune aux courses.

petit con *m.* (*commonly pronounced: ti-con*) small-minded idiot • (lit.): little idiot.

example: Ah, le **petit con**. Ça fait trois fois qu'il a versé un verre de jus de tomate sur la robe de sa femme.

translation: Oh, the **little idiot**. It's been three times already that he's spilled tomato juice on his wife's dress.

as spoken: Ah, l'**tit con**. Ça fait trois fois qu'il a versé un verre <u>d</u>'jus <u>d</u>'tomate sur la robe <u>d</u>'sa femme.

roi des cons (le) *exp.* a complete idiot or jerk • (lit.): the king of the idiots/jerks.

example: C'est la cinquième fois cette semaine que Michel a enfermé ses clés dans la voiture. Je te jure, c'est **le roi des cons**.

translation: This is the fifth time this week that Michel locked his keys in the car. I swear to you, he's the **biggest idiot**.

as spoken: C'est la cinquième fois cette <u>s</u>'maine que Michel, <u>il</u> a enfermé ses clés dans la voiture. <u>J</u>'te jure, c'est **l'roi des cons**.

LEÇON DIX - The Many Uses of "Foutre"

Il s'en fout plein la lampe toute la journée.

(trans.): He eats like a pig all day.
(lit.): He stuffs his belly full all day.

Leçon Dix

Adrienne: Moi, j'**en fous un coup** au boulot même quand je suis **mal foutu** tandis que Michel, il **ne fout pas une rame**. Il **s'en fout plein la lampe** au travail toute la journée. Et son bureau est un **foutoir**. Et lui, il est toujours **foutu comme l'as de pique**!

Marcel: Mais qu'est-ce que ça **peut te foutre**?

Adrienne: Normalement, je **m'en fous comme de l'an quarante** mais on doit *bosser* (1) ensemble! Chaque fois que je lui donne du boulot à **foutre**, il **fout tout en l'air**. Il est **foutrement** con, lui! Il n'est pas **foutu de** terminer son boulot, c'est tout! Et c'est un **je-m'en-foutiste**!

Marcel: Peut-être qu'il a besoin que tu lui **foutes un coup de main** de temps en temps.

Adrienne: **Rien à foutre**! La seule chose que je veux lui **foutre** est un coup de pied! Et je ne suis pas le seul qui veux l'**envoyer se faire foutre**. Tout le monde **se fout de sa gueule**.

Marcel: Mais pourquoi le patron, il ne lui dit pas de **foutre le camp**?

Adrienne: Il ne peut pas le **foutre à la porte**… c'est son *beauf*. (2)

Marcel: En ce cas-là, tu es **foutu**, *mon vieux*. (3)

Translation in English

He eats like a pig all day

Adrienne: I **work my butt off** at work even when I'm **sick**, whereas Michel **doesn't do jack shit**. He **pigs out** at work all day. And his desk is a **fucking clutter**. And as for him, he's always a **fucking mess**!

Marcel: Why should you **give a fuck**?

Adrienne: Normally, I **couldn't give a shit** but we have *to work* together! Every time I give him work **to do**, he **screws it all up**. The guy's **totally** stupid! He's not **capable** of completing his work, that's all! And **he doesn't give a damn about anything**!

Marcel: Maybe he needs you to **give him a hand** from time to time.

Adrienne: **No fucking way**! The only thing I want **to give him** is a swift kick! And I'm not the only one who wants to **tell him to fuck off**. Everyone **makes fun of him**.

Marcel: So why doesn't the boss tell him **to get the fuck out**?

Adrienne: He can't **fire him**… it's his *brother-in-law*.

Marcel: In that case, you're **fucked**, *my friend*.

Dialogue in slang as it would be spoken

Y s'en fout plein la lampe toute la journée

Adrienne: Moi, j'**en fous un coup** au boulot même quand j'suis **mal foutu** tandis qu'Michel, y **fout pas une rame**. Y **s'en fout plein la lampe** au travail toute la journée. Et son bureau, c't'un **foutoir**. Et lui, il est toujours **foutu comme l'as de pique**!

Marcel: Mais qu'est-c'que ça **peut t'foutre**?

Adrienne: Normalement, j'**m'en fous comme d'l'an quarante** mais on doit *bosser* ensemble! Chaque fois que j'lui donne du boulot à **foutre**, y **fout tout en l'air**. Il est **foutrement** con, lui! Il est pas **foutu de** terminer son boulot, c'est tout! Et c't'un **j'-m'en-foutiste**!

Marcel: P't-êt' qu'il a besoin qu'tu lui **foutes un coup d'main** d'temps en temps.

Adrienne: **Rien à foutre**! La seule chose que j'veux lui **foutre**, c't'un coup d'pied! Et j'suis pas l'seul qui veux l'**envoyer s'faire foutre**. Tout l'monde **s'fout d'sa gueule**.

Marcel: Mais pourquoi le patron, y lui dit pas d'**fout' le camp**?

Adrienne: Y peut pas l'**foutre à la porte**… c'est son *beauf.*

Marcel: En c'cas-là, t'es **foutu**, *mon vieux.*

Vocabulary

```
┌─────────────────────────────────────────────────────┐
│              FOOTNOTES FROM THE DIALOGUE              │
│                                                       │
│  (1) bosser:                                          │
│       v. (very popular) to work.                      │
│  (2) beauf:                                           │
│       m. a common abbreviation of: beau-frère meaning │
│       "brother-in-law."                               │
│  (3) mon vieux / ma vieille:                          │
│       m. my ol' chum, my ol' pal • (lit.): my old one.│
└─────────────────────────────────────────────────────┘
```

envoyer quelqu'un se faire foutre *exp.* to tell someone to go fuck him/herself • (lit.): to send someone to go fuck him/herself.

> example: Il a refusé de me laisser tranquille alors je **l'ai envoyé se faire foutre**.

> translation: He wouldn't leave me alone, so I **told him to fuck off**.

> as spoken: Il a r'fusé d'me laisser tranquille alors j'**l'ai envoyé s'faire foutre**.

foutoir *m.* a disorderly mess.

> example: Mais regarde ta chambre! C'est un **foutoir**! Va la ranger tout de suite!

> translation: Just look at your bedroom! It's a **disaster area**! Go clean it up right now!

> as spoken: Mais r'garde ta chambre! C't'un **foutoir**! Va la ranger tout d'suite!

foutre *v.* • **1.** to give • **2.** to put

> example (1): Le mauvais temps m'a **foutu** la crève.

> translation: The bad weather **gave** me a cold.

> as spoken: Le mauvais temps, y m'a **foutu** la crève.

> example (2): En entrant, elle a **foutu** ses affaires sur la table.

> translation: Upon entering, she **put** her belongings on the table.

> as spoken: En entrant, elle a **foutu** ses affaires sur la table.

foutre à quelqu'un (pouvoir) *exp.* to be someone's business.

    example: Qu'est-ce que ça **peut me foutre**?

    translation: What does that **have to do with me**?

    as spoken: Qu'est-<u>c</u>'que ça **peut <u>m</u>'foutre**?

foutre comme de l'an quarante (s'en) *exp.* not to give a damn
- (lit.): not to give a damn as much as one would about the year forty.

    example: Si Marie ne veut pas m'inviter à sa soirée, je **m'en fous comme de l'an quarante**.

    translation: If Marie doesn't want to invite me to her party, I **couldn't give a damn**.

    as spoken: Si Marie, <u>è</u> ~ veut pas m'inviter à sa soirée, <u>j</u>'**m'en fous comme** <u>d</u>'l'an quarante.

    VARIATION -1: **foutre comme de sa première chemise (s'en)** *exp.* • (lit.): not to give a damn as much as one would about one's first shirt.

    VARIATION -2: **foutre comme de sa première chaussette (s'en)** *exp.* • (lit.): not to give a damn as much as one would about one's first sock.

foutre de la gueule de quelqu'un (se) *exp.* to make fun of someone • (lit.): to make fun of someone's face (or "person").

    example: Pourquoi est-ce que tu ris? Tu **te fous de ma gueule** ou quoi?

    translation: What are you laughing? Are you **making fun of me** or what?

    as spoken: Pourquoi tu ris? Tu <u>**t'fous**</u> <u>**d'ma gueule**</u> ou quoi?

    NOTE: **gueule** *f.* derogatory for "mouth" or "face" when applied to a person, since it's literal translation is "the mouth of an animal."

foutre le camp *exp.* to beat it, to get the fuck out.

> example: **Fous le camp**!
>
> translation: **Leave me the fuck alone**!
>
> as spoken: **Fous l'camp**!

foutre plein la lampe (s'en) *exp.* to stuff one's face • (lit.): to stuff one's belly (or *lampe*, meaning "lamp") full.

> example: Je m'en suis **foutu plein la lampe** chez ma mère. Elle est cuisinère extra!
>
> translation: I **stuffed my face** at my mom's. She's a great cook!
>
> as spoken: J'm'en suis **foutu plein la lampe** chez ma mère. C't'une cuisinère extra!

foutre quelqu'un à la porte *exp.* to fire someone • (lit.): to throw someone to the door.

> example: Le patron m'a dit qu'il va me **foutre à la porte** si je continue à boire.
>
> translation: The boss said he's going **to fire me** if I continue to drink.
>
> as spoken: Le patron, y m'a dit qu'y va m'**foutr'à la porte** si j'continue à boire.

foutre quelque chose en l'air *exp.* to fuck something up • (lit.): to fuck something into the air.

> example: Je n'ai pas de chance. Le client était à deux doigts de signer le contract mais j'ai tout **foutu en l'air** quand je l'ai insulté par accident.
>
> translation: I don't have any luck. The client was on the verge of signing the contract but I **fucked everything up** when I insulted him by accident.
>
> as spoken: J'ai pas d'chance. Le client, il était à deux doigts d'signer l'contract mais j'ai tout **foutu en l'air** quand j'l'ai insulté par accident.

NOTE -1: **à deux doigts (être)** *exp.* to be on the verge (of doing something) • (lit.): to be two fingers away.

NOTE -2: **foutre quelqu'un en l'air** *exp.* to kill or "waste" someone.

foutre un coup (en) *exp.* to work hard.

example: Je suis épuisé. J'**en ai foutu un coup** au boulot aujourd'hui.

translation: I'm exhausted. I **worked my butt off** at work today.

as spoken: J'suis épuisé. J'**en ai foutu un coup** au boulot aujourd'hui.

foutre un coup de main *exp.* to give someone a hand.

example: Cette caisse est trop lourde pour moi. Tu peux me **foutre un coup de main**?

translation: This box is too heavy for me. Can you **give me a hand**?

as spoken: C'te caisse, elle est trop lourde pour moi. Tu peux m'**foutr'un coup d'main**?

foutre une rame (ne pas) *exp.* not to do a fucking thing • (lit.): not to do an oar's worth of work (in other words, not to pull one's oar while everyone else is rowing).

example: Robert **ne fout pas une rame** au boulot.

translation: Robert **doesn't do a fucking thing** at work.

as spoken: Robert, y ~ **fout pas une rame** au boulot.

je-m'en-foutiste *m.* said of someone who is apathetic • (lit.): an "I-don't-give-a-damner."

example: Il n'est jamais enthousiaste. C'est un vrai **je-m'en-foutiste**.

translation: He's never enthusiastic. He's a real **apathetic person**.

as spoken: Il ~ est jamais enthousiaste. C't'un vrai **j'-m'en-foutiste**.

foutrement *adv.* extremely • (lit.): fucking.

> example: Paule est **foutrement** bizarre!
>
> translation: Paula is **fucking** weird!
>
> as spoken: Paule, <u>elle</u> est **foutrement** bizarre!

foutu(e) (être) *adj.* to be in big trouble, to be done for • (lit.): to be fucked.

> example: Dépêche-toi! Si tu n'as pas de devoirs à rendre au professeur, tu es **foutu**!
>
> translation: Hurry! If you don't have any homework to turn into the teacher, you're **ass is grass**!
>
> as spoken: Dépêche-toi! Si <u>t'</u>as pas <u>d'd'</u>voirs à rendr<u>'</u>au prof~, <u>t'</u>es **foutu**!

foutu(e) comme l'as de pique (être) *exp.* to be dressed badly, to be slobbed out.

> example: Mais tu ne peux pas aller chez mes parents habillé comme ça. Tu es **foutu comme l'as de pique**, voyons!
>
> translation: You can't go to my parents' house dressed like that. You're **slobbed out**, for crying out loud!
>
> as spoken: Mais tu ~ peux pas aller chez mes parents habillé comme ça. <u>T'</u>es **foutu comme l'as de pique**, voyons!
>
> **NOTE:**   The usage of *voyons* is extremely popular in French. Although its literally meaning is "let's see," it is commonly used to mean "for crying out loud."

foutu(e) de faire quelque chose (être) *exp.* • **1.** to be capable of doing something • **2.** to be bound to do something.

> example (1):   Georges n'est pas **foutu de faire** du ski. Il est trop gros.
>
> translation: Georges isn't **capable of** skiing. He's too fat.
>
> as spoken: Georges, <u>il</u> ~ est pas **foutu <u>d'</u>faire** du ski. Il est trop gros.

example (2): Mes parents sont **foutus d'**arriver avant que je range la maison!

translation: My parents are **bound to** arrive before I clean up the house!

as spoken: Mes parents, y sont **foutus <u>d'</u>**arriver avant <u>qu'</u>je range la maison!

mal foutu(e) (être) *adj.* to be sick, to be under the weather.

example: Ça me plaîrait énormément d'aller au cinéma avec vous mais je suis **mal foutu** ce soir. Je crois que j'ai besoin de sommeil.

translation: I'd love to go to the movies with you guys but I'm **under the weather** tonight. I think I need some sleep.

as spoken: Ça <u>m'</u>plaîrait énormément d'aller au ciné~ avec vous mais <u>j'</u>suis **mal foutu** <u>c'</u>soir. <u>J'</u>crois <u>qu'</u>j'ai <u>b'</u>soin <u>d'</u>sommeil.

rien à foutre *exp.* no way, nothing doing • (lit.): nothing to fuck.

example: Tu veux que j'aille chercher Christophe à l'aéroport?! **Rien à foutre**! La dernière fois, ça m'a mis deux heures avec les embouteillages et en plus, il ne m'a même pas remercié!

translation: You want me to go pick up Christopher at the airport?! **No fuckin' way**! The last time, it took me two hours with all the traffic and not only that, he didn't even thank me!

as spoken: Tu veux <u>qu'</u>j'aille chercher Christophe à l'aéroport?! **Rien à foutre**! La dernière fois, ça m'a mis deux heures avec les embouteillages et en plus, <u>y</u> ~ m'a même pas <u>r'</u>mercié!

A CLOSER LOOK (1):
The Many Uses of "Foutre"

It's hard to get through an entire day in France without hearing this term pop up in some form over and over again. It is important to note that although the original connotation of *foutre* was "to fuck," through time it has lost its original meaning and is now commonly used throughout France in a array of idioms and expressions.

You may find it interesting to note that the English version, "to fuck," took the opposite route from *foutre*. Where the strong meaning of *foutre* became more and more mild through the years, the verb "to fuck" became stronger and stronger. Hundreds of years ago it simply meant "to seed (a crop)." Later it was used as initials posted below a woman in the stockades accused of adultery, at which time "F.U.C.K." was used to mean "For Unlawful Carnal Knowledge."

argent foutu *exp.* money down the drain.

example: Tu vas jouer au lotto? Mais c'est de l'**argent foutu**, ça!

translation: Are you going to play the lotto? That's just **money down the drain**!

as spoken: Tu vas jouer au lotto? Mais c'est d'l'**argent foutu**, ça!

bien foutu(e) (être) to be well built (said of someone's body).

example: Regarde ce bodybuilder! Il est **bien foutu**, lui!

translation: Look at that bodybuilder! He's really **built**!

as spoken: Regarde c'bodybuilder! Il est **bien foutu**, lui!

NOTE: The term *bodybuilder* is an Americanism pronounced *bodi-bildeur*.

Ça la fout mal *exp.* it's a very awkward situation.

example: Louise est arrivée en shorts au bal de la Marquise de Rangnangnan. **Ça la fout mal**!

translation: Louise arrived in shorts to the Marquise of Rangnangnan's ball. **It was really awkward**!

as spoken: Louise, elle est arrivée en shorts au bal d'la Marquise de Rangnangnan. **Ça la fout mal**!

café boullu, café foutu

exp. "if you boil coffee, it's ruined."

example: Quand tu réchauffes le café, attention de ne pas le faire bouillir. **Café boullu, café foutu**!

translation: When you reheat the coffee, make sure not to boil it. **When you boil coffee, it's ruined**!

as spoken: Quand tu réchauffes le café, attention d'ne pas l'faire bouillir. **Café boullu, café foutu**!

NOTE: The past participle of *bouillir* is actually *bouilli*. However, in this expression, the past participle is humorously transformed in order to rhyme with *foutu,* the past participle of the verb *foutre,*" meaning "ruined" (in this case).

envoyer quelqu'un se faire foutre *exp.* to tell someone to go fuck off.

example: S'il continue à t'énerver, tu n'as qu'à **l'envoyer se faire foutre**!

translation: If he keeps bugging you, all you have to do is to **tell him to fuck off**.

as spoken: S'y continue à t'énerver, t'as qu'à **l'envoyer s'faire foutre**!

foutaise *f.* hogwash, bullshit.

example: C'est de la **foutaise** de prétendre qu'ils sont encore ensemble. Ils sont prêts à divorcer.

translation: It's **bullshit** to claim that they're still together. They're ready to get divorced.

as spoken: C'est d'la **foutaise** de prétend' qu'y sont encore ensemble. Y sont prêts à divorcer.

NOTE: The verb *prétendre* is a common *faux ami* ("false friend") in French. Although it would certainly be reasonable that a native speaker of English would assume that *prétendre* has the same meaning in French, this is not the case: *prétendre* = to claim; *faire semblant* = to pretend.

foutoir *m.* a fucking mess.

example: Quel **foutoir**, cette cuisine! Va la ranger tout de suite!

translation: What a **fucking mess** this kitchen is! Go clean it up right now!

as spoken: Quel **foutoir**, c'te cuisine! Va la ranger tout d'suite!

foutre *v.* • **1.** to do • **2.** to put with force, to throw • (lit.): to fuck.

example (1): Qu'est-ce que tu **fous** ici?

translation: What are you **doing** here?

as spoken: Tu **fous** quoi ici? [or] Quequ'tu **fous** ici?

example (2): En rentrant, Emile a **foutu** ses clés sur la table.

translation: Upon coming home, Emile **threw** his keys on the table.

as spoken: En rentrant, Emile, il a **foutu** ses clés sur la table.

foutre (ne rien) *v.* not to do a damn thing.

example: Tu **ne fous rien** toute la journée tandis que moi, je me décarcasse pour nettoyer cette maison avant que les invités arrivent!

translation: You **don't do a damn thing** all day whereas I'm working my butt off to get this house clean before the guests arrive!

as spoken: Tu ~ **fous rien** toute la journée tandis que moi, j'me décarcasse pour nettoyer c'te maison avant qu'les invités arrivent!

foutre (s'en) *v.* not to give a damn.

example: "Claire est fâchée avec toi."
"**Je m'en fous**! Elle est toujours fâchée avec quelqu'un."

translation: "Claire is angry with you."
"**I don't give a damn**! She is always angry with someone.

as spoken: "Claire, elle est fâchée avec toi."
"**J'm'en fous**! Elle est toujours fâchée avec quelqu'un."

VARIATION -1: **foutre comme de sa première chausette (s'en)** *exp.* • (lit.): not to give a damn about something as much as one's first sock.

VARIATION -2: **foutre comme de sa première chemise (s'en)** *exp.* • (lit.): not to give a damn about something as much as one's first shirt.

VARIATION -3: **foutre comme de l'an quarante (s'en)** *exp.* • (lit.): not to give a damn about something as much as the year forty.

foutre de la gueule de quelqu'un (se) *exp.* to make fun of someone.

example: Pourquoi est-ce tu ris? Tu **te fous de ma gueule** ou quoi?

translation: Why are you laughing? Are you **making fun of me** or what?

as spoken: Pourquoi tu ris? Tu **t'fous d'ma gueule** ou quoi?

foutre de quelqu'un (se) *exp.* • **1.** to make fun of someone • **2.** to rip someone off.

example (1): Tu **te fous de moi**?

translation: Are you **making fun of me**?

as spoken: Tu **t'fous d'moi**?

example (2): Le mec qui t'a vendu cette voiture **s'est foutu de toi**.

translation: The guy who sold you this car **ripped you off**.

as spoken: Le mec qui t'a vendu c'te voiture, y **s'est foutu d'toi**.

NOTE: **mec** *m.* (*very popular*) guy, "dude."

foutre dedans (se) *exp.* to blow it, to stick one's foot in it.

example: Le professeur a su que j'ai triché à l'examen. Cette fois-ci, je me suis vraiment **foutu dedans**.

translation: The teacher found out that I cheated on the test. This time, I really **blew it**.

as spoken: Le **prof**, **il** a su que j'ai triché à l'**exam**. Cette fois-ci, je **m'**suis vraiment **foutu dedans**.

NOTE: Although the verb *savoir* literally means "to know," when used in the past tense, its connotation becomes "to have found out."

foutre en l'air *exp.* • **1.** to ruin • **2.** to kill • **3.** to beat up severely.

example (1): La pluie a **foutu** tous nos projets **en l'air**.

translation: The rain **ruined** all of our plans.

as spoken: La pluie, **ça** a **foutu** tous nos projets **en l'air**.

example (2): Le marchand s'est fait **foutre en l'air** par le voleur.

translation: The salesman got **killed** by the thief.

as spoken: Le marchand, **y** s'est fait **foutre en l'air** par **l'**voleur.

example (3): J'ai un œil au beurre noir parce que je me suis disputé avec mon frère et il a finit par me **foutre en l'air**!

translation: I have a black eye because I had a fight with my brother and he ended up **beating the crap out of me**!

as spoken: J'ai un œil au beurre noir pasque je m'suis disputé avec mon frère et il a finit par m'**foutre en l'air**!

foutre et s'en contre-foutre (s'en) *exp.* not to give a damn whatsoever.

example: Je **m'en fous et m'en contre-fous** de ce qu'il dit.

translation: I **don't give a damn whatsoever** what he says.

as spoken: J'**m'en fous et m'en contre-fous** de c'qu'y dit.

foutre la paix à quelqu'un *exp.* to leave someone alone • (lit.): to give someone peace.

example: Tu m'énerves! **Fous-moi la paix**!

translation: You're bugging me! **Beat it**!

as spoken: [no change]

SYNONYM: foutre le camp, *p. 199.*

foutre la trouille à quelqu'un *exp.* to scare the crap out of someone • (lit.): to give extreme fear to someone.

example: Ça m'a **foutu la trouille** quand j'ai fait ma présentation devant les cadres.

translation: It **scared the crap out of me** when I did my presentation in front of the executives.

as spoken: Ça m'a **foutu la trouille** quand j'ai fait ma présentation d'vant les cadres.

foutre le camp *exp.* to beat it.

example: **Fous le camp**!

translation: **Beat it**!

as spoken: **Fous l'camp**!

SYNONYM: foutre la paix à quelqu'un, *p. 199.*

foutre par terre (se) *exp.* • **1.** to fall flat on one's face • **2.** to embarrass oneself.

example (1): Je me suis **foutu par terre** en sortant du supermarché.

translation: I **fell down** while leaving the supermarket.

as spoken: Je m'suis **foutu par terre** en sortant du supermarché.

example (2): Sa présentation à la classe était mal faite et il s'est **foutu par terre**.

translation: His presentation to the class was poorly done and he **totally embarrassed himself**.

as spoken: Sa présentation à la classe, elle était mal faite et y s'est **foutu par terre**.

foutre plein la lampe

(s'en) *exp.* to stuff one's face • (lit.): to fill up one's stomach.

example: Je **m'en suis foutu plein la lampe** à la soirée.

translation: I **stuffed my face** at the party.

as spoken: J'**m'en suis foutu plein la lampe** à la soirée.

NOTE: **lampe** *f.* stomach • (lit.): lamp.

foutre quelqu'un à la

porte *exp.* to fire someone.

example: Apres avoir volé de l'argent du boulot, Daniel s'est fait **foutre à la porte**.

translation: After having stolen money from work, Daniel got himeself **canned**.

as spoken: Apres avoir volé d'l'argent du boulot, Daniel, y s'est fait **foutr'à la porte**.

NOTE: **boulot** *m.* (*very popular*) work, job.

foutre sur la gueule (se)

exp. to beat each other up • (lit.): to throw each other on each other's mouth.

example: Hervé et Pierre ont commencé à disputer et ont fini par **se foutre sur la gueule**!

translation: Hervé and Pierre started disputing and ended up **beating each other up**!

as spoken: Hervé et Pierre, y z'ont commencé à disputer et ont fini par **s'fout' sur la gueule**!

foutre un coup de pied à

quelqu'un *exp.* to kick someone.

example: Quand je me suis accroupi, mon petit frère m'a **foutu un coup de pied**!

translation: When I bent down, my little brother **kicked me**!

as spoken: Quand je m'suis accroupi, mon p'tit frère, y m'a **foutu un coup d'pied**!

foutre un coup *exp.* • 1. to

traumatize, to give someone an emotional jolt • **2.** to give someone a sudden _____.

example (1): La mort de sa mère lui a **foutu un coup**. Il ne s'en est jamais remis.

translation: His mother's death **traumatized him**. He never got over it.

as spoken: La mort d'sa mère, ça lui a **foutu un coup**. Y ~ s'en est jamais r'mis.

example (2): Cela lui a **foutu un coup de** vieux de travailler dans une grande compagnie.

translation: Working in a big company **made him age suddenly**.

as spoken: Cela lui a **foutu un coup d'** vieux d'travailler dans une grande compagnie.

foutre une baffe à quelqu'un exp. to give someone a slap in the face • (lit.): to throw a slap at someone.

example: Quand il l'a insultée, elle lui a **foutu une baffe**!

translation: When he insulted her, she **gave him a slap in the face**.

as spoken: Quand il l'a insultée, è lui a **foutu une baffe**!

SYNONYM -1: **foutre un gnon à quelqu'un** exp. • (lit.): to throw a hit to someone.

SYNONYM -2: **foutre une prune à quelqu'un** exp. to hit someone • (lit.): to throw a plum to someone.

NOTE: The noun *prune* is a common *faux ami* ("false friend") in French. Although it would certainly be reasonable that a native speaker of English

would assume that *prune* has the same meaning in French, this is not the case:

prune = plum;
pruneau = prune.

foutu(e) (être) adj. • **1.** to be ruined • **2.** to be done for.

example (1): J'ai fait tomber la télévision. Maintenant, elle est **foutue**.

translation: I dropped the TV. Now it's **wrecked**.

as spoken: J'ai fait tomber la télé. Maintenant, elle est **foutue**.

example (2): Si le patron te voit dans ce bar, tu es **foutu**!

translation: If the boss sees you in this bar, you're **cooked**!

as spoken: Si l'patron te voit dans c'bar, t'es **foutu**!

foutrement adv. very, totally.

example: Bernard est **foutrement** bizarre!

translation: Bernard is **totally** bizarre!

as spoken: Bernard, il est **foutrement** bizarre!

VARIATION -1: **foutument** adv.

VARIATION -2: **fichtrement** adv. a milder variation of: *foutument*.

foutu(e) comme l'as de pique *exp.* to be poorly dressed.

example: Tu ne peux pas entrer dans ce restaurant comme ça. Tu es **foutu comme l'as de pique**.

translation: You can't go into that restaurant like that. You're **dressed like a slob**.

as spoken: Tu ~ peux pas entrer dans c'resto comme ça. T'es **foutu comme l'as de pique**.

foutu(e) de faire quelque chose (être) *exp.* • **1.** to be capable of doing something • **2.** to be bound to do something.

example (1): Je ne suis pas **foutu de faire** du ski. C'est trop dur pour moi.

translation: I'm not **capable** of skiing. It's too hard for me.

as spoken: J'suis pas **foutu d'faire** du ski. C'est trop dur pour moi.

example (2): Antoine est **foutu** d'arriver en retard.

translation: Antoine is **bound** to arrive late.

as spoken: Antoine, il est **foutu** d'arriver en retard.

je-m'en-foutisme *n.* apathy.

example: Le **je-m'en-foutisme** regne chez les adolescents d'aujourd'hui.

translation: **Apathy** reigns among the adolescents of today.

as spoken: Le **j'm'en-foutisme**, ça regne chez les ados d'aujourd'hui.

NOTE: The preposition *chez* is commonly used in reference to a personality trait and could be translated as "within." Therefore, *"chez lui"* could be translated as either "at his house" or "within him" depending on the context. Example: *L'agression est un comportement courant chez les singes;* Agression is a common behavior among monkeys.

mal foutu(e) (être) *adj.* to be sick.

example: Je ne peux pas aller à l'école ce matin. Je suis **mal foutu** aujourd'hui.

translation: I can't go to school this morning. I'm **really sick** today.

as spoken: J'peux pas aller à l'école c'matin. J'suis **mal foutu** aujourd'hui.

Qu'est-ce que ça peut me foutre? *exp.* What's it got to do with me?

example: "Je dois te parler de ce qui est arrivé hier." "**Qu'est-ce que ça peut me foutre**?"

translation: "I have to talk to you about what happened yesterday." **"What's it got to do with me?"**

as spoken: "J'dois t'parler de c'qui est arrivé hier." **"Qu'est-c'que ça peut m'foutre?"**

SYNONYM: **Qu'est-ce que j'en ai à foutre?** *exp.* •

(lit.): What do I have to do with that?

va te faire foutre *exp.* fuck off.

example: Laisse-moi tranquille! **Va te faire foutre!**

translation: Leave me alone! **Fuck off!**

as spoken: Laisse-moi tranquille! **Va t'faire foutre!**

A CLOSER LOOK (2):
Being Obscene Unintentionally

When I first arrived in Paris as a fifteen-year-old, I was enthusiastically welcomed by my relatives, who were anxious to hear my reputedly flawless French. In a matter of only a few minutes, somehow I accidentally managed to call my uncle a bastard, tell my aunt that I was in great heat for her, and finally inform the entire family that I was pregnant!

In French, there are a few ways to be obscene unintentionally:

1. Often if you don't know how to say a word in French, you may opt to use the English word with a French accent hoping that it will be correct. Although this can certainly be true at times, there are other instances where this can only lead to great embarrassment.

2. Mispronouncing a word slightly can often give the word an entirely new and shocking meaning.

3. Translating literally word-for-word from English into French, as you will see in the following chart.

CORRECT USAGE		INCORRECT USAGE
beaucoup		**beau cul**
Merci, beaucoup! Thanks alot!		*Merci, beau cul!* Thanks, hot ass!
bêtes		**pets**
Vous avez des bêtes? Do you have any pets?		*Vous avez des pets?* Do you have any farts?
betterave		**beet (bite)**
Passez-moi les betteraves. Pass me the beets.		*Passez-moi les bites.* Pass me the dicks.
donner un baiser		**baiser**
Son mari lui a donné un baiser avant de partir. Her husband gave her a kiss before leaving.		*Son mari l'a baisé avant de partir.* Her husband fucked her before leaving.
j'ai chaud	*not*	**je suis chaud**
J'ai chaud aujourd'hui! I'm hot today!		*Je suis chaud aujourd'hui!* I'm really in heat today!
J'ai mal au cou		**J'ai mal au cul**
Quand je regarde trop la télé, j'ai mal au cou. When I watch too much much T.V., I get a neck-ache.		*Quand je regarde trop la télé, j'ai mal au cul.* When I watch too much much T.V., I get an ass-ache.
Je n'ai plus faim		**Je suis plein(e)**
Ça suffit, merci. Je n'ai plus faim. No more, thanks. I'm satisfied.		*Ça suffit, merci. Je suis plein(e).* No more, thanks. I'm pregnant.
Je me réjouis		**Je jouis**
Je me réjouis de te revoir! I'm so delighted to see you again!		*Je jouis de te revoir!* I'm having an orgasm seeing you again!

CORRECT USAGE		INCORRECT USAGE
Je suis contre		**Je suis con**
La libération des femmes, vous êtes pour ou contre? Women's rights, are you pro or con?		*La libération des femmes, vous êtes pour ou con?* Women's rights, are you pro or a total jerk?
oie		**gousse**
On va manger de l'oie pour Noël. We're going to eat goose for Christmas.	***not***	*On va manger de la gousse pour Noël.* We're going to eat some lesbian (dyke) for Christmas.
répéter		**repéter**
Tu peux répéter ça, s'il te plaît? Can you repeat that, please?		*Tu peux repéter ça, s'il te plaît?* Can you fart that again, please?
salut		**salaud**
M. DuBois! Salut! Mr. Du Bois! Hello, there!		*M. DuBois! Salaud!* Mr. DuBois! You bastard!

RULE: Never eat with one hand in your lap!

In France, it is considered very rude and downright obscene to rest one hand in your lap while eating at the table, since it is assumed that you must be doing something naughty to yourself or to your neighbor!

Glossary

à tout casser *adv.* at the most, at the outside • (lit.): to break everything.

example: Sa mère doit avoir trente ans **à tout casser**!

translation: His mother must be thirty years old **at the outside**!

as spoken: Sa mère, **è** doit avoir trente ans **à tout casser**!

ALSO: **à tout casser** *adv.* total, complete.

example: Eric est un idiot **à tout casser**!

translation: Eric is a **total** idiot!

as spoken: Eric, **c't'**un idiot **à tout casser**!

abruti *m.* idiot, jerk, nerd.

example: Quel **abruti**! Jean se promène en shorts alors qu'il pleut dehors!

translation: What a **jerk**! Jean is walking around in shorts and it's raining outside!

as spoken: Quel **abruti**! Jean, **y** **s'**promène en shorts alors qu'**y** pleut dehors!

alléger les bourses (s') *exp.* to have sex, to "get off" • (lit.): to lighten one's purse.

example: Guillaume **s'allège les bourses** avec les prostituées!

translation: William **gets off** with prostitutes!

as spoken: Guillaume, y **s'allège les bourses** avec les prostituées!

NOTE: **bourses** *f.pl.* testicles • (lit.): purses.

andouille *f.* idiot, jerk, nerd.

example: Quelle **andouille**, ce Patrice! Au restaurant, il a renversé tout un verre de jus de tomate sur Michelle et elle portait une nouvelle robe blanche!

translation: What a **nerd** Patrice is. At the restaurant, he spilled an entire glass of tomato juice on Michelle and she was wearing a new white dress!

as spoken: Quelle **andouille**, c'Patrice! Au <u>resto</u>, il a renversé tout un verre d'jus d'tomate sur Michelle et **è** portait une nouvelle robe blanche!

anglais (avoir ses) *exp.* to be on one's period, to be "on the rag" • (lit.): to have one's English.

example: Geneviève ne peut pas nager aujourd'hui parce qu'elle **a ses anglais**.

translation: Geneviève can't go swimming today because she's **on the rag**.

as spoken: Geneviève, è ~ peut pas nager aujourd'hui pasqu'elle **a ses anglais**.

avorton *m. (applies to a man)* runt • (lit.): leftover from an *avortement* meaning "abortion."

example: Georges m'a dit qu'il veut devenir mannequin! Mais il rêve, ce petit **avorton**!

translation: George told me that he wants to become a model! That little **runt** is dreaming!

as spoken: Georges, y m'a dit qu'y veut dev'nir mann'quin! Mais y rêve, ce p'tit **avorton**!

bandeuse *f.* a "hot number," sexy woman • (lit.): one who causes men to *bander* meaning "to have an erection."

example: Carole est connue pour être une **bandeuse** et couche avec un différent gars chaque nuit!

translation: Carole is known for being a **nymphomaniac** et goes to bed with a different guy every night!

as spoken: Carole, elle est connue pour êtr'une **bandeuse** et couche avec un différent gars chaque nuit!

barbaque *f.* inferior meat.

example: Tu as goûté la **barbaque** que Jacqueline a servi hier soir? C'était horrible!

translation: Did you taste the **shoe leather** that Jacqueline served last night? It was horrible!

as spoken: T'as goûté la **barbaque** qu'elle a servi hier soir, Jacqueline? C't'ait horrible!

bécoter (se) *v.* to kiss, "to neck" • (lit.): to "beak" (since this comes from the masculine noun *bec* meaning "the beak of a bird").

example: J'ai vu Henri et Madeleine **se bécoter** derrière la maison!

translation: I saw Henri and Madeleine **making out** behind the house!

as spoken: J'ai vu Henri et Madeleine **s'bécoter** derrière la maison!

NOTE: **bécot** *m.* a kiss.

SYNONYM -1: **bisou** *m.*

SYNONYM -2: **bise** *f.*

bien roulée (être) *adj. (said of a woman)* to be voluptuous, to have a great body • (lit.): to be well-rounded.

example: Elle est **bien roulée** pour son âge!

translation: She's got a **great figure** for her age!

as spoken: [no change]

SYNONYM: **bien balancée (être)** *adj.* • (lit.): to be well-balanced.

bisenesseuse f. a prostitute, "working girl" • (lit.): a "businesswoman."

example: Ce quartier a beaucoup changé. Maintenant, c'est plein de **bisenesseuses**.

translation: This neighborhood has changed a lot. Now it's full of **working girls**.

as spoken: Ce quartier, i̱l a beaucoup changé. Maintenant, c'est plein ḏ'**bisenesseuses**.

bordel interj. an interjection used in anger or disbelief; "holy shit" • (lit.): brothel.

example: Oh, **bordel**! J'ai brûlé le dîner!

translation: Oh, **holy shit**! I burned the dinner!

as spoken: Oh, **bordel**! J'ai brûlé ḻ'dîner!

boucler son égout exp. to shut one's mouth • (lit.): to shut one's sewer.

example: Si tu vas continuer à me critiquer, tu peux **boucler ton égout**.

translation: If you're going to keep on criticizing me, you can **shut your trap**.

as spoken: Si tu vas continuer à m̱'critiquer, tu peux **boucler ton égout**.

boudin m. ugly and fat woman • (lit.): blood sausage.

example: Sophie m'a dit qu'elle veut devenir mannequin. A mon avis, ça ne se réalisera jamais. C'est un **boudin**, celle-là!

translation: Sophie told me she wants to become a model. In my opinion, it'll never happen. She's a **fat pig**!

as spoken: Sophie, è m'a dit qu'è veut dev̱'nir manṉ'quin. A mon avis, ça ~ s̱'réalis̱'ra jamais. C̱'t'un **boudin**, celle-là!

bouffe f. food, "grub," "chow."

example: J'ai faim. Tu as de la **bouffe** chez toi?

translation: I'm hungry. You got any **chow** at your house?

as spoken: J'ai faim. Ṯ'as ḏ'la **bouffe** chez toi?

NOTE: **bouffer** v. (extremely popular) to eat.

bourge m. a shortened version of the term "bourgeois(e)," yuppie scum.

example: Laisse-moi tranquille, sale **bourge**!

translation: Leave me alone, you **yuppie scum**!

as spoken: [no change]

NOTE: Since France is rather class conscious, insulting a person's status in society or telling a person that he/she comes from a lower class is considered very offensive.

boxon m. • **1.** whorehouse • **2.** a complete mess, chaos.

example (1): Je vois toujours des drôles de mecs et des nanas super sexy entrer chez les voisins d'à côté. Je commence à avoir l'impression que leur maison est un **boxon**!

translation: I always see strange men and sexy girls go into the neighbor's house next door. I'm starting to get the feeling that their home is a **whorehouse**!

as spoken: J'vois toujours des drôles d'mecs et des nanas super sexy entrer chez les voisins d'à côté. J'commence à avoir l'impression qu'leur maison, c't'un **boxon**!

example (2): Va ranger ta chambre! Quel **boxon**!

translation: Go clean up your room! What a **pigsty**!

as spoken: [no change]

branler (s'en) *v. (very popular)* not to give a damn • (lit.): to shake oneself of it.

example: Je **m'en branle** de ce que tu penses!

translation: I don't **give a damn** what you think!

as spoken: J'**m'en branle** de c'que tu penses!

NOTE: **branler (se)** *v.* to masturbate • (lit.): to shake oneself.

capote *f.* condom, "rubber."

example: De nos jours, il faut absolument porter une **capote** pour participer dans des rapports sexuels.

translation: Nowadays, it's absolutely necessary to wear a **rubber** when participating in sexual relations.

as spoken: De nos jours, ~ faut absolument porter une **capote** pour participer dans des rapports sexuels.

caqueter *v.* to blab on and on • (lit.): to cackle.

example: Arthur parle sans arrêt. Il a **caqueté** pendant toute une heure de la même histoire!

translation: Arthur talks nonstop. He **blabbed on and on** for an entire hour about the same story!

as spoken: Arthur, y parle sans arrêt. Il a **caqueté** pendant toute une heure d'la même histoire!

casquette en peau de fesses (avoir la) *exp.* to be totally bald • (lit.): to have a cap made out of butt skin.

example: Ça fait dix ans que je n'ai pas vu Guillaume. Il a toujours eu de beaux cheveux, lui. C'est pour ça que j'étais stupéfait de voir qu'il a une **casquette en peau de fesses** maintenant!

translation: It's been ten years since I've seen Guillaume. He's always had such beautiful hair. That's why I was shocked to see that he's **totally bald** now!

as spoken: Ça fait dix ans qu'j'ai pas vu Guillaume. Il a toujours eu d'beaux ch'veux, lui. C'est pour ça qu'j'étais stupéfait d'voir qu'il a une **casquette en peau d'fesses** maintenant!

casser les couilles à quelqu'un *exp.* to annoy someone greatly, to bug the shit out of someone • (lit.): to break someone's testicles or "balls."

example: J'espère que tu n'as pas invité Claude à nous rejoindre. Il **me casse les couilles**, celui-là!

translation: I hope you didn't invite Claude to join us. He **bugs the shit out of me**!

as spoken: J'espère qu't'as pas invité Claude à nous r'joindre. Y **m'casse les couilles**, çui-là!

NOTE: This expression can also be softened by replacing *les couilles* with *les*: Il me les casse, lui!; • (lit.): He breaks mine!

casser les oreilles à quelqu'un *exp.* to talk someone's ear off • (lit.): to break someone's ears.

example: Voilà Thérèse! Je dois me cacher. Si elle me voit, elle va **me casser les oreilles** comme d'habitude!

translation: There's Theresa! I have to hide. If she sees me, she'll **talk my ear off** as usual.

as spoken: V'là Thérèse! J'dois m'cacher. Si è m'voit, è va **m'casser les oreilles** comme d'habitude!

casser les pieds à quelqu'un *exp.* to bug the daylights out of someone • (lit.): to break someone's feet.

example: Tu commences à **me casser les pieds** avec tes questions interminables!

translation: You're starting **to bug the daylights out of me** with your interminable questions!

as spoken: Tu commences à **m'casser les pieds** avec tes questions interminables!

NOTE -1: This expression is a mild version of the popular expression, *casser les couilles à quelqu'un* meaning "to piss someone off" or literally "to break someone's balls." This expression is also commonly shortened to: *Tu me les casses!* where *"les"* replaces *"couilles."*

NOTE -2: **casse-pieds** *m.* an annoying person • (lit.): foot-breaker.

NOTE: This is a mild version of the popular slang term, *casse-couilles* meaning "a pain-in-the-ass" or literally a "ball-breaker."

chaud de la pince (être) *exp. (only applies to men)* to be oversexed • (lit.): to have a hot claw.

example: Même à son âge, il est toujours **chaud de la pince**.

translation: Even at his age, he's still **oversexed**.

as spoken: Même à son âge, il est toujours **chaud d'la pince**.

chiant(e) (être) *adj.* to be annoying as shit.

example: Oh, mais tu es **chiant**! Laisse-moi tranquille!

translation: Oh, you're **annoying as shit**! Leave me alone!

as spoken: Oh, mais t'es **chiant**! Laisse-moi tranquille!

chiasse (avoir la) *exp.* to be scared shitless • (lit.): to have the shits (or "diarrhea").

example: J'ai eu la **chiasse** quand j'ai vu l'avalanche.

translation: I was **scared shitless** when I saw the avalanche.

as spoken: [no change]

chiée *f.* a lot, a shitload.

example: J'ai une **chiée** de devoirs à faire ce soir.

translation: I have a **shitload** of homework to do tonight.

as spoken: J'ai une **chiée** de d'voirs à faire c'soir.

chier (se faire) *exp.* to be bored shitless • (lit.): to make oneself shit (from boredom).

example: Je **me fais chier** à cette soirée. On s'en va?

translation: I'm **bored shitless** at this party. Wanna get out of here?

as spoken: J'**me fais chier** à c'te soirée. On s'en va?

chier dans les frocs *exp.* to be scared shitless • (lit.): to shit in one's pants.

example: En voyant s'approcher la tornade, j'ai **chié dans mes frocs**.

translation: When I saw the tornado approaching, I was **scared shitless**.

as spoken: [no change]

NOTE: **frocs** *m.pl.* pants.

chier dur *exp.* said of a situation that's going to get worse, the shit's going to hit the fan • (lit.): to shit hard.

example: Quand ta mère verra ce que tu as fait de sa cuisine, ça va **chier dur**.

translation: When your mother sees what you did to her kitchen, the **shit's going to hit the fan**.

as spoken: Quand ta mère verra c'que t'as fait d'sa cuisine, ça va **chier dur**.

chier quelqu'un (faire) *exp.* to make someone angry as shit • (lit.): to make someone shit.

example: Ça **me fait chier** quand tu empruntes mes affaires sans me demander!

translation: It **bugs the shit out of me** when you borrow my things without asking.

as spoken: Ça **m'**fait chier quand t'empruntes mes affaires sansy me d'mander!

chier *v.* to shit, to crap.

example: Ah, non! Ces oiseaux de malheur ont **chié** sur ma nouvelle voiture!

translation: Oh, no! These darn birds **crapped** on my new car!

as spoken: Ah, non! Ces oiseaux d'malheur, y z'ont **chié** sur ma nouvelle voiture!

chierie f. a pain in the ass (said of a situation or thing).

example: Mon père m'a demandé de peindre l'extérieur de la maison. Quelle **chierie**!

translation: My father asked me to paint the outside of the house. What a **pain in the ass**!

as spoken: Mon père, y m'a d'mandé d'peind' l'extérieur d'la maison. Quelle **chierie**!

chieur, euse n. despicable person, asshole • (lit.): shitter.

example: Ce **chieur** de patron vient de baisser mon salaire!

translation: That **asshole** of a boss just lowered my salary!

as spoken: Ce **chieur** d'patron, y vient d'baisser mon salaire!

chiottes f.pl. (extremely popular) the bathroom, the "shit house."

example: Je dois aller aux **chiottes** avant de partir.

translation: I have to go to the **shit house** before we leave.

as spoken: J'dois aller aux **chiottes** avant d'partir.

cloque (être en) exp. to be knocked up • (lit.): to be in blister (to look as if one is wrapped up in a big blister).

example: Tu as entendu les nouvelles? Irène est **en cloque** et elle n'a que seize ans!

translation: Did you hear the news? Irene is **knocked up** and she's only sixteen years old!

as spoken: T'as entendu les nouvelles? Irène, elle est **en cloque** et elle ~ a qu'seize ans!

cocotter v. to have an overpowering odor.

example: Ça **cocotte** dans cette parfumerie!

translation: It **stinks** in this perfume shop!

as spoken: Ça **cocotte** dans c'te parfum'rie!

SYNONYM: **schlinguer** v.

con (faire le) exp. to act like a jerk.

example: Chaque fois que René est près d'une jolie fille, il **fait le con**.

translation: Every time René is near a pretty girl, he **acts like a jerk**.

as spoken: Chaque fois que René est près d'une jolie fille, y **fait l'**con.

con comme la lune (être) exp. to be as nutty as a fruitcake • (lit.): to be as crazy as the moon.

example: Mon oncle est **con comme la lune**. Il parle à des personnes imaginaires tout le temps.

translation: My uncle is **as nutty as a fruitcake**. He talks to imaginary people all the time.

as spoken: Mon oncle, il est **con comme la lune**. Y parle à des personnes imaginaires tout l'temps.

con m. • **1.** idiot, jerk • **2.** a despicable term meaning "asshole."

example (1): Guy a échoué à tous ces cours à l'école. Quel **con**!

translation: Guy failed all of his courses at school. What an **idiot**!

as spoken: Guy, il a échoué à tous ces cours à l'école. Quel **con**!

example (2): Paul m'a dénoncé au patron. Quel **con**!

translation: Paul reported me to the boss. What an **asshole**!

as spoken: Paul, y m'a dénoncé au patron. Quel **con**!

conducteur du dimanche m. Sunday driver • (lit.): same.

example: Oh, ce **conducteur du dimanche** conduit trop lentement!

translation: Oh, this **Sunday driver** is driving too slowly!

as spoken: Oh, c'**conducteur du dimanche**, y conduit trop lent~!

NOTE: You may have noticed that in the previous *as spoken* paragraph, *lentement* was changed to *lent*. It is very common in French to change adverbs to adjectives.

connard(e) n. jerk, idiot.

example: Quel **connard**, Jean. Il a mis du sel dans son café en pensant que c'était du sucre.

translation: What an **idiot** Jean is. He put salt in his coffee thinking it was sugar.

as spoken: Quel **connard**, Jean. Il a mis du sel dans son café en pensant qu'c'était du sucre.

connasse f. a very crude insult originally meaning "cunt."

example: Cette **connasse** de Sandra a essayé de me faire mettre à la porte!

translation: That **cunt** Sandra tried to get me fired!

as spoken: C'te **connasse** de Sandra, elle a essayé d'me faire mettr'à la porte!

NOTE: This comes from the masculine noun *con* originally meaning "cunt."

connerie f. • **1.** foolishness • **2.** dirty trick.

example (1): Arrête tes **conneries**! Nous sommes en public!

translation: Stop your **foolishness**! We're in public!

as spoken: Arrête tes **conn'**ries! On est en public!

example (2): Je ne parle plus à Marc. La semaine dernière il m'a fait une **connerie** inexcusable.

translation: I'm not speaking to Marc anymore. Last week he played an unforgiveable **dirty trick** on me.

as spoken: J'parle pu à Marc. La s'maine dernière y m'a fait une **conn'rie** inexcusable.

constipé de l'entre-jambe (être) *exp.* said of a man who can not "get it up" • (lit.): to be constipated in the "in-between" leg.

example: Quand j'ai eu ma première rencontre, j'étais tellement nerveux que j'étais **constipé de l'entre-jambe**.

translation: When I had my first encounter, I was so nervous that I **couldn't get it up**.

as spoken: Quand j'ai eu ma première rencontre, j'étais tellement nerveux qu'j'étais **constipé d'l'entre-jambe**.

couillon *m.* jerk.

example: Quel **couillon**, ce mec!

translation: What a **jerk** this guy is!

as spoken: Quel **couillon**, c'mec!

NOTE: **mec** *m. (extremely popular)* guy, "dude."

couillonnades *f.pl.* nonsense, "bullshit."

example: Ne crois rien à ce qu'il te dit. Tout ce qu'il balance ne sont que des **couillonnades**.

translation: Don't believe anything he tells you. Everything that comes out of his mouth is nothing but **bullshit**.

as spoken: ~ Crois rien à c'qu'y te dit. Tout c'qu'y balance ~ sont qu'des **couillonnades**.

NOTE: **balancer** *v.* to jabber, to chatter on about something • (lit.): to throw.

coup de foudre *m.* love at first sight • (lit.): thunder clap.

example: Quand j'ai vu ta maman pour la première fois, c'était le **coup de foudre**!

translation: When I saw your mother for the first time, it was **love at first sight**!

as spoken: Quand j'ai vu ta maman pour la première fois, c'était l'**coup d'foudre**!

crados (être) *adj. (pronounced: "crados" with the "s" articulated)* to be filthy.

example: Enlève tes chaussures avant d'entrer dans la maison. Elles sont **crados**!

translation: Take off your shoes before coming into the house. They're **filthy**!

as spoken: Enlève tes chaussures avant d'entrer dans la maison. È sont **crados**!

craignos (être) *adj.* to be scary (from the verb *craindre* meaning "to have fear").

example: Tu as entendu parler de l'avion de ligne qui est tombé du ciel en panne? C'est **craignos**, ça!

translation: Did you hear about the commercial plane that conked out and crashed? That's **scary**.

as spoken: T'as entendu parler d'l'avion d'ligne qu'est tombé du ciel en panne? C'est **craignos**, ça!

crâneur, euse *n.* show-off.

example: Sophie parle toujours de sa fortune. C'est une vraie **crâneuse**, celle-là.

translation: Sophie always talks about her fortune. That girl's a real **show-off**.

as spoken: Sophie, è parle toujours d'sa fortune. C't'une vraie **crâneuse**, celle-là.

NOTE: **crâner** *v.* to show off.

SYNONYM: **frimeur, euse** *n.*

NOTE: **frimer** *v.* to show off.

crétin *m.* jerk • (lit.): cretin.

example: Ce **crétin** de Robert m'a demandé de sortir avec lui demain soir.

translation: That **jerk** Robert asked me to go out with him tomorrow night.

as spoken: Ce **crétin** d'Robert, y m'a d'mandé d'sortir avec lui d'main soir.

cuisse légère (avoir la) *exp.* said of a loose girl, "to have light ankles" • (lit.): to have the light thigh.

example: Tous les gars draguent Véronique parce qu'elle a **la cuisse légère**.

translation: All the guys flirt with Veronica because she **has light ankles**.

as spoken: Tous les gars, y draguent Véronique pasqu'elle a **la cuisse légère**.

NOTE: **draguer** *v. (extremely popular)* to flirt, to cruise (for sexual encounters).

dalle (avoir la) *exp. (very mild)* to be hungry.

example: J'ai **la dalle**, moi. Tu veux aller prendre à manger?

translation: I'm **hungry**. Do you want to get something to eat?

as spoken: J'ai **la dalle**, moi. Tu veux aller prendr'à manger?

SYNONYM: **fringale (avoir la)** *exp. (very mild)*.

dans la merde (être) *exp.* to be in a bad predicament, to be up shit creek • (lit.): to be in shit.

example: Le patron m'a dit que je suis **dans la merde** si j'arrive encore en retard au boulot.

translation: The boss told me that I'm **up shit creek** if I arrive to work late again.

as spoken: Le patron, y m'a dit qu'j'suis **dans la merde** si j'arrive encore en r'tard au boulot.

déconner *v.* • **1.** to goof off • **2.** to talk nonsense, to lose it • **3.** to function erratically (said of a machine).

example (1): Arrête de **déconner**. On a du travail à faire.

translation: Stop **goofing off**. We have work to do.

as spoken: [no change]

example (2): Oh, mais qu'est-ce que tu racontes? Tu **déconnes**!

translation: Oh, what are you talking about? You're talking absolute **nonsense**!

as spoken: Oh, mais qu'est-c'que tu racontes? Tu **déconnes**!

example (3): Je crois qu'il est temps d'acheter un nouvel ordinateur. Celui-ci **déconne** trop.

translation: I think it's time to buy a new computer. This one **acts goofy** all the time.

as spoken: J'crois qu'il est temps d'ach'ter un nouvel ordinateur. Celui-ci, y **déconne** trop.

décrotter (se) *v.* to clean oneself • (lit.): to "uncrap" oneself.

example: On doit quitter la maison d'ici cinq minutes! Va **te décrotter** tout de suite!

translation: We have to leave the house in five minutes! Go **clean yourself up** right now!

as spoken: On doit quitter la maison d'ici cin' minutes! Va **t'décrotter** tout d'suite!

NOTE: **crotte** *f.* turd, crap.

dégueuler ses tripes *exp.* to barf one's guts out • (lit.): to "unmouth" one's guts.

example: Le bateau n'a pas arrêté de balotter de long en large. J'ai **dégueulé mes tripes** pendant tout le voyage.

translation: The boat didn't stop tossing back and forth. I **barfed my guts out** during the entire trip.

as spoken: Le bateau, il ~ a pas arrêté d'balotter d'long en large. J'ai **dégueulé mes tripes** pendant tout l'voyage.

NOTE: **gueule** *f.* derogatory for "mouth" or "face" when applied to a person, since its literal translation is "the mouth of an animal."

démerder (se) *v.* to get out of a fix, to get out of a shitty situation • (lit.): to "unshit" oneself.

example: J'ai promis à Gisèle que j'irais à sa soirée mais je viens de savoir que mon ancien petit ami, que je ne peux pas supporter, va y être aussi! Je ne veux plus y aller! Comment je vais **me démerder**?

translation: I promised Gisèle that I'd go to her party, but I just found out that my old boyfriend, who I can't stand, is going to be there, too! How am I going **to get out of this**?

as spoken: J'ai promis à Gisèle que j'irais à sa soirée mais j'viens d'savoir qu'mon ancien p'tit ami, que j'peux pas supporter, va y êtr'aussi! J'veux pu y aller! Comment j'vais **m'**démerder?

NOTE: When the verb *savoir* is used in the previous manner, its connotation changes from "to know" to "to find out."

démon de midi (avoir le)
    exp. to have a midlife crisis, to be a dirty old(er) man or woman •
    (lit.): to have the devil strike at high noon (i.e. in the middle of one's life).

example: A l'âge de cinquante ans, M. DuBois sort tous les soirs avec différentes nanas. Je suppose qu'il **a le démon de midi**.

translation: At age fifty, Mr. DuBois goes out every night with all sorts of girls. I guess he **has the midlife hornies**!

as spoken: A l'âge de cinquante ans, M. DuBois, y sort tous les soirs avec différentes nanas. Je suppose qu'il **a l'démon d'midi**.

écrases-merde *f.pl.* shoes, "shit-kickers" •
    (lit.): shit-smashers.

example: Mais, tu ne vas pas porter ces **écrases-merde**-là! On va à un restaurant de luxe!

translation: You're not going to wear those **shit-kickers**! We're going to a fancy restaurant!

as spoken: Mais, tu ~ vas pas porter ces **écrases-merde**-là! On va à un resto d'luxe!

emmerdant(e) (être) *adj.* to be annoying as hell.

example: Elle est **emmerdante**, celle-là. Elle me pose des questions sans arrêt.

translation: She's as **annoying as hell**. She asks me questions nonstop.

as spoken: Elle est **emmerdante**, celle-là. È m'pose des questions sans arrêt.

emmerdements *m.pl.* a big problems.

example: J'ai un tas d'**emmerdements** au boulot aujourd'hui. Pour commencer, mon assistant a donné sa démission.

translation: I have a pile of **problems** at work today. For starters, my assistant quit.

as spoken: J'ai un tas d'**emmerdements** au boulot aujourd'hui. Pour commencer, mon assistant, i̲l a donné sa démission.

emmerder (s') *v.* to be bored to death, to be bored shitless.

example: Je **m'emmerde** dans cette classe de philosophie!

translation: I'm **bored shitless** in this philosophy class!

as spoken: J̲'**m'emmerde** dans c'te classe de philo~!

emmerder quelqu'un *v.* •
1. to annoy someone, to bug the shit out of someone • **2.** to tell someone to fuck off.

example (1): Il **m'emmerde** avec toutes ses questions.

translation: He **bugs the shit out of me** with all of his questions.

as spoken: Y̲ **m'emmerde** avec toutes ses questions.

example (2): Voilà Marguerite! Je **l'emmerde**! Elle a couché avec mon petit ami!

translation: There's Marguerite! She can go **fuck off**! She went to bed with my boyfriend!

as spoken: V̲'là Marguerite! J̲'**l'emmerde**! Elle a couché avec mon p̲'tit ami!

emmerdeur, euse *n.* a pain in the ass (said of a person).

example: Quel **emmerdeur**, ce professeur. Il nous a donné un tas de devoirs à faire ce weekend.

translation: What a **pain in the ass** this professor is. He gave us a pile of homework to do over the weekend.

as spoken: Quel **emmerdeur**, c'prof~. Y̲ nous a donné un tas de d̲'voirs à faire c̲'weekend.

en l'air (foutre quelqu'un) *exp.* to kill someone • (lit.): to throw someone up in the air.

example: Elle a **foutu en l'air** son mari quand elle l'a trouvé au lit avec une autre femme.

translation: She **wasted** her husband when she found him in bed with another woman.

as spoken: Elle a **foutu en l'air** son mari quand è l'a trouvé au lit avec une aut̲' femme.

envoyer chier quelqu'un *exp.* to tell someone to fuck off • (lit.): to send someone to go shit.

example: Quand il m'a accusé d'avoir menti, je **l'ai envoyé chier**!

translation: When he accused me of lying, I **told him to fuck himself**!

as spoken: Quand y m'a accusé d'avoir menti, j'**l'ai envoyé chier**!

envoyer quelqu'un se faire foutre *exp.* to tell someone to go fuck him/herself • (lit.): to send someone to go fuck him/herself.

example: Il a refusé de me laisser tranquille alors je **l'ai envoyé se faire foutre**.

translation: He wouldn't leave me alone, so I **told him to fuck off**.

as spoken: Il a r'fusé d'me laisser tranquille alors j'**l'ai envoyé s'**faire foutre.

espèce d'ordure *f.* lowlife scum • (lit.): species of trash.

example: **Espèce d'ordure**! Tu as ruiné mon tricot!

translation: **You lowlife scum**! You ruined my sweater!

as spoken: **Espèce d'ordure**! T'as ruiné mon tricot!

étron *m.* turd.

example: C'est dégoutant! Il y a des **étrons** de chiens sur tout le trottoir!

translation: This is disgusting! There are dog **turds** all over the sidewalk!

as spoken: C'est dégoutant! Y a des **étrons** d'chiens sur tout l'trottoir!

F

faillot *m.* brown-noser, one who sucks up • (lit.): bean.

example: Georges est un sacré **faillot**. C'est pour ça que le patron lui donne toujours des augmentations.

translation: George is a real **brown-noser**. That's why the boss always gives him raises.

as spoken: C't'un sacré **faillot**, Georges. C'est pour ça que l'patron, y lui donne toujours des augmentations.

SYNONYM: **lèche-bottes** *n.* • (lit.): boot-licker.

faire chier (ne pas se) *exp.*
• **1.** to have nerve • **2.** to have a good time (lit.): not to make oneself shit.

example (1): Marc s'est invité à mon dîner. Il **ne se fait pas chier**, c'est sûr!

translation: Marc invited himself to my dinner party. He **really has some nerve**, that's for sure.

as spoken: Marc, y s'est invité à mon dîner. Y ~ **s'**fait pas chier, c'est sûr!

example (2): Je **ne me fais pas chier** ici!

translation: I'm **having a great time** here!

as spoken: Je ~ **m'**fais pas chier ici!

NOTE: Using a negative to expressive something positive is extremely popular in French. For example, to express that something tastes good would commonly be said as: *C'est pas mauvais, ça!* rather then *C'est bon, ça!*

faire des mamours à quelqu'un *exp.* to be kissy-kissy with someone, to be all lovey-dovey with someone, to caress someone.

example: Ils **se font des mamours** en public. Ça m'énerve, ça!

translation: They're **all touchy-feely with each other** in public. I can't stand that!

as spoken: Y **s'font des mamours** en public. Ça m'énerve, ça!

SYNONYM -1: **faire des papouilles à quelqu'un** *exp.* to touch someone all over • (lit.): to make sexual touches to someone.

SYNONYM -2: **peloter** *v.* to grope, to neck • (lit.): to ball up together like a ball of wool.

NOTE: **pelotage** *m.* groping, necking.

example: On a fait une partie de **pelotage** pendant trois heures hier soir!

translation: We engaged in a **makeout session** for three hours last night!

as spoken: On a fait une partie d'**pelotage** pendant trois heures hier soir!

faire marcher quelqu'un *exp.* to lead someone on • (lit.): to make someone walk.

example: Tu me **fais marcher** depuis deux mois et hier j'ai appris que tu es marié!

translation: You've been **leading me on** for two months and yesterday I found out that you're married!

as spoken: Tu m'**fais marcher** depuis deux mois et hier j'ai appris qu't'es marié!

feignasse *f.* a lazy person, a lazy bum.

example: Tu vas demander à Léon de te donner un coup de main? Bonne chance! C'est une **feignasse** de premier ordre!

translation: You're going to ask Leon to give you a hand? Good luck! He's a big-time **lazy bum**!

as spoken: Tu vas d'mander à Léon de te donner un coup d'main? Bonne chance! C't'une **feignasse** de premier ordre!

NOTE -1: This comes from the noun *feignant(e)* meaning "lazy."

NOTE -2: Also spelled: **faignasse**.

fiche le camp *exp.* to leave, "to beat it" • (lit.): to make the camp.

example: Tu m'énerves! **Fiche le camp**!

translation: You're bugging me! **Beat it**!

as spoken: [no change]

VARIATION: **foutre le camp**
exp. (a stronger variation of: *fiche le camp*).

flasher (faire) *v.* to turn on sexually • (lit.): to startle with a flash of light.

example: Diane n'est pas très belle mais elle **fait flasher** les mecs sans effort.

translation: Diane isn't very pretty but she **turns on** guys without any effort.

as spoken: Diane, <u>elle</u> ~ est pas très belle mais <u>è</u> **fait flasher** les mecs sans effort.

flirter *v.* (*Americanism*) to flirt.

example: Georges a **flirté** avec moi toute la soirée.

translation: George **flirted** with me all night.

as spoken: Georges, il a **flirté** avec moi toute la soirée.

foutoir *m.* a disorderly mess.

example: Mais regarde ta chambre! C'est un **foutoir**! Va la ranger tout de suite!

translation: Just look at your bedroom! It's a **disaster area**! Go clean it up right now!

as spoken: Mais <u>r'</u>garde ta chambre! <u>C't'</u>un **foutoir**! Va la ranger tout <u>d'</u>suite!

foutre *v.* • **1.** to give • **2.** to put • **3.** to do.

example (1): Le mauvais temps m'a **foutu** la crève.

translation: The bad weather **gave** me a cold.

as spoken: Le mauvais temps, <u>y</u> m'a **foutu** la crève.

example (2): En entrant, elle a **foutu** ses affaires sur la table.

translation: Upon entering, she **put** her belongings on the table.

as spoken: En entrant, elle a **foutu** ses affaires sur la table.

example (3): Qu'est-ce que vous **foutez**, vous deux? Arrêtez ça tout de suite!

translation: What **the hell are you two doing**? Stop that right now!

as spoken: Vous **foutez** quoi, vous deux? Arrêtez ça tout <u>d'</u>suite!

foutre à quelqu'un (pouvoir) *exp.* to be someone's business.

example: Qu'est-ce que ça **peut me foutre**?

translation: What does that **have to do with me**?

as spoken: Qu'est-<u>c'</u>que ça **peut m'**foutre?

foutre comme de l'an quarante (s'en) *exp.* not to give a damn • (lit.): not to give a damn as much as one would about the year forty.

example: Si Marie ne veut pas m'inviter à sa soirée, je **m'en fous comme de l'an quarante**.

translation: If Marie doesn't want to invite me to her party, I **couldn't give a damn**.

as spoken: Si Marie, è ~ veut pas m'inviter à sa soirée, j'**m'en fous comme de l'an quarante**.

VARIATION -1: **foutre comme de sa première chemise (s'en)** *exp.* • (lit.): not to give a damn as much as one would about one's first shirt.

VARIATION -2: **foutre comme de sa premère chaussette (s'en)** *exp.* • (lit.): not to give a damn as much as one would about one's first sock.

foutre de la gueule de quelqu'un (se) *exp.* to make fun of someone • (lit.): to make fun of someone's face (or "person").

example: Pourquoi est-ce que tu ris? Tu **te fous de ma gueule** ou quoi?

translation: Why are you laughing? Are you **making fun of me** or what?

as spoken: Pourquoi tu ris? Tu **t'**fous d'ma gueule ou quoi?

NOTE: **gueule** *f.* derogatory for "mouth" or "face" when applied to a person since it's literal translation is "the mouth of an animal."

foutre le camp *exp.* to beat it, to get the fuck out.

example: **Fous le camp**!

translation: **Leave me the fuck alone**!

as spoken: **Fous l'**camp!

foutre plein la lampe (s'en) *exp.* to stuff one's face • (lit.): to stuff one's belly (or *lampe,* meaning "lamp") full.

example: Je m'en suis **foutu plein la lampe** chez ma mère. Elle est cuisinère extra!

translation: I **stuffed my face** at my mom's. She's a great cook!

as spoken: J'm'en suis **foutu plein la lampe** chez ma mère. C't'une cuisinère extra!

foutre quelqu'un à la porte *exp.* to fire someone • (lit.): to throw someone to the door.

example: Le patron m'a dit qu'il va me **foutre à la porte** si je continue à boire.

translation: The boss said he's going **to fire me** if I continue to drink.

as spoken: Le patron, y m'a dit qu'y va m'**foutr'**à la porte si j'continue à boire.

foutre quelque chose en l'air *exp.* to fuck something up • (lit.): to fuck something into the air.

example: Je n'ai pas de chance. Le client était à deux doigts de signer le contract mais j'ai tout **foutu en l'air** quand je l'ai insulté par accident.

translation: I don't have any luck. The client was on the verge of signing the contract but I **fucked everything up** when I insulted him by accident.

as spoken: J'ai pas d'chance. Le client, il était à deux doigts d'signer l'contract mais j'ai tout **foutu en l'air** quand j'l'ai insulté par accident.

NOTE -1: **à deux doigts (être)** *exp.* to be on the verge (of doing something) • (lit.): to be two fingers away.

NOTE -2: **foutre quelqu'un en l'air** *exp.* to kill or "waste" someone.

foutre un coup (en) *exp.* to work hard.

example: Je suis épuisé. J'**en ai foutu un coup** au boulot aujourd'hui.

translation: I'm exhausted. I **worked my butt off** at work today.

as spoken: J'suis épuisé. J'**en ai foutu un coup** au boulot aujourd'hui.

foutre un coup de main
exp. to give someone a hand.

example: Cette caisse est trop lourde pour moi. Tu peux me **foutre un coup de main**?

translation: This box is too heavy for me. Can you **gimme a hand**?

as spoken: C'te caisse, elle est trop lourde pour moi. Tu peux m'**foutr'**un coup d'main?

foutre une rame (ne pas)
exp. not to do a fucking thing • (lit.): not to do an oar's worth of work (in other words, not to pull one's oar while everyone else is rowing).

example: Robert **ne fout pas une rame** au boulot.

translation: Robert **doesn't do a fucking thing** at work.

as spoken: Robert, y ~ **fout pas une rame** au boulot.

foutrement *adv.* extremely • (lit.): fucking.

example: Paule est **foutrement** bizarre!

translation: Paula is **fucking** weird!

as spoken: Paule, elle est **foutrement** bizarre!

foutu(e) (être) *adj.* to be in big trouble, to be done for • (lit.): to be fucked.

example: Dépêche-toi! Si tu n'as pas de devoirs à rendre au professeur, tu es **foutu**!

translation: Hurry! If you don't have any homework to turn into the teacher, you're **fucked**!

as spoken: Dépêche-toi! Si t'as pas d'd'voirs à rendr'au prof~, t'es **foutu**!

foutu(e) comme l'as de pique (être) *exp.* to be dressed badly, to be slobbed out.

example: Mais tu ne peux pas aller chez mes parents habillé comme ça. Tu es **foutu comme l'as de pique**, voyons!

translation: You can't go to my parents' house dressed like that. You're **slobbed out**, for crying out loud!

as spoken: Mais tu ~ peux pas aller chez mes parents habillé comme ça. T'es **foutu comme l'as de pique**, voyons!

NOTE: The usage of *voyons* is extremely popular in French. Although its literally meaning is "let's see," it is commonly used to mean "for crying out loud."

foutu(e) de faire quelque chose (être) *exp.* • **1.** to be capable of doing something • **2.** to be bound to do something.

example (1): Georges n'est pas **foutu de faire** du ski. Il est trop gros.

translation: Georges isn't **capable of** skiing. He's too fat.

as spoken: Georges, il ~ est pas **foutu d'**faire du ski. Il est trop gros.

example (2): Elle est **foutue de** partir avant que j'arrive.

translation: She's **bound to** leave before I arrive.

as spoken: Elle est **foutue d'**partir avant qu'j'arrive.

fumier *m.* a disparaging remark applied to either a man or a woman • (lit.): manure.

example: Il a volé ma voiture, le **fumier**!

translation: That **bastard** stole my car!

as spoken: [no change]

garce *f.* bitch.

example: Tu as rencontré la nouvelle voisine? C'est une vieille **garce**. Elle m'a dénoncé à la police pour avoir joué du piano à 8 heures du soir parce que ça l'a dérangé!

translation: Did you meet the new neighbor? She's an old **bitch**. She reported me to the police for playing the piano at 8 o'clock at night because it disturbed her!

as spoken: T'as rencontré la nouvelle voisine? C't'une vieille **garce**. È m'a dénoncé à la police pour avoir joué du piano à 8 heures du soir pasque ça l'a dérangé!

gerber *v.* to vomit, to "barf."

example: Je suis très malade. J'ai **gerbé** toute la matinée.

translation: I'm very sick. I **barfed** all morning.

as spoken: J'suis très malade. J'ai **gerbé** toute la matinée.

gerbos (être) *adj.* to be gross • (lit.): to be enough to make one vomit.

example: Suzanne est cuisinière horrible. Son dîner d'hier était **gerbos**!

translation: Suzanne is a horrible cook. Her dinner last night was **gross**!

as spoken: Suzanne, <u>elle</u> est cuisinière horrible. Son dîner d'hier, <u>il</u> était **gerbos**!

NOTE: **gerber** *v.* to throw up, to "barf."

grosse brioche *f.* fat stomach, paunch, gut • (lit.): fat brioche.

example: Tu veux encore une tranche de tarte? Attention. Tu ne veux pas avoir une **grosse brioche** comme celle de Marcel!

translation: You want another piece of pie? Be careful. You don't want to get a **gut** like Marcel's!

as spoken: Tu veux encore une tranche de tarte? Attention. Tu ~ veux pas avoir une **grosse brioche** comme celle de Marcel!

gueule à chier dessus (avoir une) *exp.* to be as ugly as shit • (lit.): to have a face to shit on.

example: Laurent veut être acteur mais à mon avis, il a une **gueule à chier dessus**.

translation: Laurent wants to be an actor but in my opinion, he's **as ugly as shit**.

as spoken: Laurent, <u>y</u> veut êtr'acteur mais à mon avis, il a une **gueule à chier <u>d'</u>**ssus.

il n'y a pas à chier *exp.* there's no two ways about it • (lit.): there's no shitting.

example: **Il n'y a pas à chier**. Elle l'épouse pour son argent.

translation: **There's no two ways about it**. She's marrying him for his money.

as spoken: ~ **Y'a pas à chier**. È l'épouse pour son argent.

jacasser *v.* to talk a lot, to blab.

example: Henri a **jacassé** pendant toute une heure de ses vacances.

translation: Henry **went on and on** for an entire hour about his vacation.

as spoken: Henri, <u>il</u> a **jacassé** pendant toute une heure <u>d'</u>ses vacances.

Je vous ai/t'ai demandé l'heure? *exp.* a contemptuous statement meaning "Was I talking to you?" • (lit.): I asked you the time?

example: **Je t'ai demandé l'heure**? Ta gueule!

translation: **Was I talking to you?** Shut up!

as spoken: **J't'ai d'mandé l'heure**? Ta gueule!

je-m'en-foutiste *m.* said of someone who is apathetic • (lit.): an "I-don't-give-a-damner."

example: Il n'est jamais enthousiaste. C'est un vrai **je-m'en- foutiste**.

translation: He's never enthusiastic. He's a real **apathetic person**.

as spoken: Il ~ est jamais enthousiaste. C't'un vrai **j'**-m'en-foutiste.

jeté(e) (être) *adj.* to be crazy • (lit.): to be thrown.

example: Ça sent le gaz ici. Oh hé! Mais ne craque pas cette allumette! Tu es **jeté** ou quoi?!

translation: It smells like gas here. Hey! Don't strike that match! What are you, **nuts**?!

as spoken: Ça sent l'gaz ici. Oh hé! Mais ~ craque pas c't'allumette! T'es **sh't'é** ou quoi?!

journal de cul *m.* a dirty magazine • (lit.): a newspaper of butt.

example: Je crois que mon frère cache des **journaux de cul** sous son matelas.

translation: I think my brother hides **dirty magazines** under his mattress.

as spoken: J'crois qu'mon frère, y cache des **journaux d'cul** sous son mat'las.

NOTE: It is important to note that although the term *cul* literally means "ass," it does not carry the same degree of vulgarity as it does in English, and is therefore used much for frequently.

lèche-bottes *m. (applies to either a man or a woman)* someone who flatters a boss in order to get in his/her good graces; "ass kisser" • (lit.): boot-licker.

example: Laurent est un vrai **lèche-bottes**. C'est pour ça que le patron l'adore!

as spoken: Laurent, c't'un vrai **lèche-bottes**. C'est pour ça qu'le patron l'adore!

translation: Laurent is a real **butt kisser**. That's why the boss loves him.

NOTE -1: **lèche-bottes (faire du)** *exp. (figurative)* to kiss someone's butt.

NOTE -2: The stronger form of *lèche-bottes* is *lèche-cul* meaning "ass-licker."

lèche-cul *m.* "kiss-ass" • (lit.): ass-licker.

example: David a acheté au patron un gros cadeau pour son anniversaire. Quel **lèche-cul**, lui!

translation: David bought the boss a big present for his birthday. What an **ass-licker**!

as spoken: David, il a ach't́é au patron un gros cadeau pour son anniversaire. Quel **lèche-cul**, lui!

mac m. short for *maquereau* meaning "pimp" • (lit.): mackerel.

example: Tu as vu comment il est habillé, celui-là. Je parie que c'est un **mac**.

translation: Did you see how he's dressed? I bet he's a **pimp**.

as spoken: T'as vu comment il est habillé, cui-là. J'parie que c't'un **mac**.

NOTE: **maquerelle** f. Madam (of a brothel).

mal baisée f. an extremely vulgar insult for a woman implying that she is extremely frigid and sexually undesirable • (lit.): bad fuck.

example: **Mal baisée**! J'en ai ras le bol de vos insultes!

translation: **You pathetic fuck**! I've had it with your insults!

as spoken: **Mal baisée**! J'en ai ras l'bol de vos insultes!

NOTE: **ras le bol (en avoir)** *exp. (very mild)* to have had it, to be fed up • (lit.): to have had it to the brim of the bowl.

mal foutu(e) (être) adj. to be sick, to be under the weather.

example: Ça me plaîrait énormément d'aller au cinéma avec vous mais je suis **mal foutu** ce soir. Je crois que j'ai besoin de sommeil.

translation: I'd love to go to the movies with you guys but I'm **under the weather** tonight. I think I need some sleep.

as spoken: Ça m'plaîrait énormément d'aller au ciné~ avec vous mais j'suis **mal foutu** c'soir. J'crois qu'j'ai b'soin d'sommeil.

mâter v. to look, to "check out."

example: Tu as **mâté** la robe qu'elle porte, Sylvie? C'est horrible!

translation: Did you **get a load of** the dress Sylvie is wearing? It's horrible!

as spoken: T'as **mâté** la robe qu'è porte, Sylvie? C'est horrible!

merde interj. shit (used to signify disbelief, surprise, or anger — same as in English) • (lit.): shit.

example: Oh, **merde**! J'ai cassé mes lunettes!

translation: Oh, **shit**! I broke my glasses!

as spoken: [no change]

merde (l'avoir à la) *exp.* to
  be in a terrible mood • (lit.): to
  have it (one's personality) like
  shit.

  example: On dirait que tu **l'as à
  la merde**. Qu'est-ce qu'il y a?
  Ton interview ne s'est pas bien
  passé?

  translation: You look like you're
  in a shitty mood. What's
  wrong? Your interview didn't go
  well?

  as spoken: On dirait q<u>u</u>'tu **l'as à
  la merde**. Qu'est-<u>c</u>'qu'il y a?
  Ton interview, <u>il</u> ~ s'est pas bien
  passé?

**merde dans les yeux
  (avoir de la)** *exp.* an
  insulting expression meaning "to
  be blind as a bat" • (lit.): to have
  shit in the eyes.

  example: Hé! Vous venez de me
  bousculer. Mais vous **avez de
  la merde dans les yeux**?

  translation: Hey! You just
  bumped me. What, do you
  have shit in your eyes?

  as spoken: Hé! Vous <u>v</u>'nez <u>d</u>'me
  bousculer, Mais vous **avez <u>d</u>'**la
  merde dans les yeux?

merdeux, euse *n.* a despicable
  person, a little "shit" • (lit.): shitty
  person.

  example: Comment est-ce que tu
  arrives à supporter ce petit
  merdeux de François? Il est
  carrément méchant.

  translation: How do you manage
  to tolerate that little **shit**
  François? He's plain mean.

  as spoken: Comment <u>t</u>'arrives à
  supporter <u>c'p</u>'tit **merdeux**
  <u>d'</u>François? Il est carrément
  méchant.

merdier *m.* a predicament, a
  "shitload" of trouble.

  example: Je suis dans un sacré
  merdier. J'ai pris la voiture de
  mon père sans permission et je
  l'ai démolie dans un accident!

  translation: I'm in a real **fix**. I
  took my father's car without
  permission and I wrecked it in
  an accident!

  as spoken: <u>J'</u>suis dans un sacré
  merdier. J'ai pris la voiture
  <u>d'</u>mon père sans permission et
  <u>j'</u>l'ai démolie dans un accident!

merdique (être) *adj.* shitty.

  example: J'en ai marre de ce
  boulot **merdique**!

  translation: I'm fed up with this
  shitty job!

  as spoken: J'en ai marre <u>d'</u>ce
  boulot **merdique**!

**mettre le grappin sur
  quelqu'un** *exp.* to put the
  bite on someone • (lit.): to put
  the grab on someone.

  example: Quand Marc a vu
  passer Josette, il s'est tellement
  amouraché d'elle qu'il lui a **mis
  le grappin dessus** tout de
  suite!

  translation: When Mark saw
  Josette pass by, he was so
  infatuated with her that he **put
  the bite on her** right away!

as spoken: Quand Marc, il a vu passer Josette, y s'ést tellement amouraché d'elle qu'y lui a **mis l'grappin d'ssus** tout d'suite!

NOTE: **amouracher de quelqu'un (s')** *exp.* to be infatuated with someone (from the noun *amour* meaning "love").

miché *m.* prostitute's client, "john."

example: Afin de combattre le problème de la prostitution dans le quartier, la police a commencé à arrêter tous les **michés**.

translation: In order to fight the prostitution problem in this neighbor- hood, the police have started to arrest all the **johns**.

as spoken: Afin d'combatt' le problème d'la prostitution dans l'quartier, la police, elle a commencé à arrêter tous les **michés**.

mitrailleuse *f.* a very talkative woman, blabbermouth • (lit.): machine gun.

example: Evelyne parle sans arrêt. C'est une sacrée **mitrailleuse**, cella-là.

translation: Evelyn talks nonstop. She's a friggin' **blabbermouth**.

as spoken: Evelyne, è parle sans arrêt. C't'une sacrée **mitrailleuse**, cella-là.

moche *adj.* ugly.

example: Hélène était très **moche** quand elle était petite. Maintenant, elle est devenue une très belle fille.

translation: Helen was very **ugly** when she was little. Now she's become a beautiful girl.

as spoken: Hélène, elle était très **moche** quand elle était p'tite. Maintenant, elle est d'venue une très belle fille.

molarder *v.* to spit, to hock "loogies."

example: Il est interdit de **molarder** dans le métro.

translation: It's forbidden to **spit** in the subway.

as spoken: Il est interdit d'**molarder** dans l'métro.

mordu(e) de quelqu'un (être) *adj.* to have a crush on someone • (lit.): to be bitten by someone.

example: Tu as vu la nouvelle étudiante dans notre cours de biologie? Je suis **mordu d'elle**!

translation: Did you see the new student in our biology class? I have such a **crush on her**!

as spoken: T'as vu la nouvelle étudiante dans not' cours de bio~? J'suis **mordu d'elle**!

morfaler (se) *v.* to pig out.

example: Je me sens malade. Je **me suis morfalé** trop de desserts!

translation: I feel sick. I **pigged out** on too many desserts.

as spoken: Je m'sens malade. Je **m'suis morfalé** trop d'desserts!

oui ou merde *exp.* yes or no •
(lit.): yes or shit.

example: Tu vas me rendre mon
argent? Oui ou **merde**.

translation: Are you going to give
me back my money? Yes or **no**.

as spoken: Tu vas m'rend' mon
argent? Oui ou **merde**.

paillasson *m.* an easy lay •
(lit.): a doormat.

example: Tu es sorti avec
Margot? On dit que c'est un
paillasson, celle-là!

translation: You went out with
Margot? They they she's a real
easy lay!

as spoken: T'es sorti avec
Margot? On dit qu'c't'un
paillasson, celle-là!

**SYNONYM: cuisse légère
(avoir la)** *exp.* said of
someone who is an easy lay •
(lit.): to have a light thigh (since
they're always up in the air).

patapouf *m. (applies to either a
man or a woman)* fatso, tub of
lard.

example: Je dois me mettre au
régime après mes vacances.
Sinon, je vais devenir un gros
patapouf.

translation: I have to put myself
on a diet after my vacation.
Otherwise, I'm going to become
a **tub of lard.**

as spoken: J'dois m'mettr'au
régime après mes vacances.
Sinon, j'vais dev'nir un gros
patapouf.

pauvre con *m.* a popular
expression meaning "poor jerk"
or "poor fucker."

example: Ah, le **pauvre con**. Il
a perdu sa maison dans une
grande incendie.

translation: Oh, the **poor
fucker**. He lost his home in a
big fire.

as spoken: Ah, l'**pauv'** con. Il a
perdu sa maison dans une
grande incendie.

**pervers sur les bords
(être)** *exp.* to be kinky •
(lit.): to be perverted around the
edges.

example: Je suis sorti avec Léon
hier soir et j'ai découvert qu'il
est un peu **pervers sur les
bords**.

translation: I went out with Léon
last night and I found out that
he's a little **kinky**.

as spoken: J'suis sorti avec Léon
hier soir et j'ai découvert qu'il
est un peu **pervers sur les
bords**.

péteur *m.* one who farts a lot •
(lit.): farter (from the verb *péter*
meaning "to fart").

example: Si tu ne manges rien
que des fibres, tu vas devenir un
péteur de premier ordre!

translation: If you eat nothing but
fiber, you're doing to turn into
one heck of a **farter**!

as spoken: Si tu ~ manges rien
que des fibres, tu vas dev_nir un
péteur de premier ordre!

phénomène *m.* a strange
person • (lit.): a phenomenon.

example: Roger, c'est un vrai
phénomène. Il ne porte que
du noir tous les jours.

translation: Roger is a **strange
guy**. He dresses in black every
day.

as spoken: Roger, c̲'t'un
vrai
. Y̲ porte que du noir tous les
jou̲rs.

pied (faire du) *exp.* to play
footsie • (lit.): to make (with the)
foot.

example: Le dîner d'affaires était
horrible! Quand nous étions tous
à table, le client a commencé a
me **faire du pied**!

translation: The business dinner
was horrible! When we were all
at the table, the client started
playing footsie with me!

as spoken: Le dîner d'affaires, il
était horrible! Quand nous
étions tous à table, le client, i̲l a
commencé a m'**faire du pied**!

**piffrer quelqu'un (ne pas
pouvoir)** *exp.* to be unable to
stand someone • (lit.): to be
unable to smell someone (from
the slang word *pif* meaning
"nose" or "schnoz").

example: Tu as invité Marie à la
soirée? Mais je **ne peux pas la
piffrer**, celle-là!

translation: You invited Marie to
the party? But I **can't stand
her**!

as spoken: T'as invité Marie à la
soirée? Mais j'**peux pas la
piffrer**, celle-là!

SYNONYM: **blairer
quelqu'un (ne pas
pouvoir)** *exp.* (from the slang
word *blair* also meaning "nose"
or "schnoz").

pipe *f.* blow job • (lit.): pipe.

example: Marcel m'a dlt que
Lucienne lui a fait une **pipe**
dans la voiture!

translation: Marcel told me that
Lucienne gave him a **blow job**
in the car!

as spoken: Marcel, y̲ m'a dit
qu'Lucienne, è̲ lui a fait une
pipe dans la voiture!

NOTE: **faire une pipe** *exp.* to
give a blow job.

pisse *f.* urine • (lit.): piss.

example: Tu as un chat? Ça sent
la **pisse** dans le salon.

translation: Do you have a cat? It
smells like **piss** in the living
room.

as spoken: T̲'as un chat? Ça sent
la **pisse** dans l̲'salon.

pisser *v.* to urinate • (lit.): to piss.

example: Quand j'ai soulevé le bébé, il a commencé à **pisser**.

translation: When I lifted the baby, he started **pissing**.

as spoken: Quand j'ai soul'vé l'bébé, il a commencé à **pisser**.

plaquer *v.* to jilt, to dump • (lit.): [none].

example: Après quatorze ans de mariage, Laurent a **plaqué** sa femme.

translation: After fourteen years of marriage, Laurent **dumped** his wife.

as spoken: Après quatorze ans d'mariage, Laurent, il a **plaqué** sa femme.

> **VARIATION:** **plaquouser** *v.*
> **SYNONYM:** **laisser choir** *exp.*
> • (lit.): to let (someone) drop.

pleurer son colosse (faire) *exp.* to urinate, to take a leak • (lit.): to make one's colossal one cry.

example: Après tous les verres d'eau que j'ai descendu, je dois **faire pleurer mon colosse**.

translation: After all the glasses of water I downed, I need to **take a leak**.

as spoken: Après tous les verres d'eau qu'j'ai descendu, j'dois **faire pleurer mon colosse**.

porté(e) sur la bagatelle (être) *exp.* to be oversexed, to have sex on the brain • (lit.): to be carried on the frivolity.

example: Grégoire sort avec une différente nana chaque soir. Il est vraiment **porté sur la bagatelle**, celui-là.

translation: Gregory goes out with a different girl every night. He's really **got sex on the brain**.

as spoken: Grégoire, y sort avec une différente nana chaque soir. Il est vraiment **porté sur la bagatelle**, cui-là.

porté(e) sur la chose (être) *exp.* to be obsessed with sex • (lit.): to be carried on the thing.

example: Tous ces journaux de cul sont à toi? Mais tu es **porté sur la chose** ou quoi?!

translation: All these dirty magazines are yours? Do you have **sex on the brain** or what?!

as spoken: Tous ces journaux d'cul, y sont à toi? Mais t'es **porté sur la chose** ou quoi?!

poser un lapin à quelqu'un *exp.* to stand someone up (on a date or meeting) • (lit.): to pose a rabbit to someone.

example: Ça fait une heure que je l'attends. Il m'a **posé un lapin** pour la dernière fois!

translation: I've been waiting for him for an hour. He's **stood me up** for the last time!

as spoken: Ça fait une heure qu'j'l'attends. Y m'a **posé un lapin** pour la dernière fois!

pouffiasse *f.* a fat woman or girl.

example: Si tu continues à manger comme ça, tu vas devenir **pouffiasse**.

translation: If you keep eating like that, you're going to turn into a **fatso**.

as spoken: Si tu continues à manger comme ça, tu vas dev'nir **pouffiasse**.

pouliche *f.* woman, "chick" • (lit.): filly.

example: Tu connais cette **pouliche**-là? Je la trouve super jolie!

translation: Do you know that **chick**? I think she's totally beautiful!

as spoken: Tu connais c'te **pouliche**-là? J'la trouve super jolie!

prendre au berceau (les) *exp.* to rob the cradle • (lit.): to take them from the cradle.

example: Hier soir j'ai vu Jean-Claude avec une très jeune fille. Evidemment il aime **les prendre au berceau**!

translation: Last night I saw Jean-Claude with a very young girl. Evidently he likes **to rob the cradle**!

as spoken: Hier soir j'ai vu Jean-Claude avec une très jeune fille. Evidemment il aime **les prendr'au berceau**!

prendre pour de la petite merde (ne pas se) *exp.* to think highly of oneself, to think one's shit doesn't stink • (lit.): not to take oneself for a little shit.

example: Cécile est très arrogante. Elle **ne se prend pas pour de la petite merde**.

translation: Cecily is very arrogant. She **thinks her shit doesn't stink**.

as spoken: Cécile est très arrogante. È **s'**prend pas pour d'la p'tite merde.

NOTE: The mild form of this expression is: *prendre pour de la petite bière (ne pas se)* literally meaning "not to take oneself for a little beer."

propre-sur-soi (être) *exp.* to be squeaky-clean (said of a person) • (lit.): to be clean on oneself.

example: Je vois que tu as pris une douche. Voilà ce qui s'appelle **propre-sur-soi**!

translation: I see you took a shower. Now that's what I call **squeaky-clean**!

as spoken: J'vois qu' t'as pris une douche. V'là c'qui s'appelle **propre-sur-soi**!

puceau/pucelle *n.* virgin.

example: A l'âge de quarante ans, Jeanne est toujours **pucelle**.

translation: At forty years of age, Jeanne is still a **virgin**.

as spoken: A l'âge de quarante ans, Jeanne, <u>elle</u> est toujours **pucelle**.

puer la merde *exp.* • **1.** to stink to high heaven • **2.** to smell fishy (said of something dishonest or shady) (lit.): to stink like shit.

example (1): Nous sommes près des égouts? Ça **pue la merde** ici.

translation: Are we near a sewer? It **stinks like shit** here.

as spoken: On <u>est</u>près des égouts? Ça **pue la merde** ici.

example (2): <u>C'</u>te voiture t'a coûté un malheureux mille francs?! Ça **pue la merde**. Ça peut être une voiture volée, ça!

translation: That car cost you a measly one thousand francs?! That **smells fishy**. It could be a stolen car!

as spoken: Cette voiture, <u>è</u> t'a coûté un malheureux mille francs?! Ça **pue la merde**. Ça peut êtr<u>'</u>une voiture volée, ca!

putain *f.* used as an interjection to denote surprise or anger • (lit.): whore.

example: Oh, **putain**! Elle est jolie, cette nana!

translation: Oh, **holy shit**! That girl is beautiful!

as spoken: Oh, **putain**! Elle est jolie, c'te nana!

NOTE: **nana** *f. (extremely popular)* girl, "chick."

pute *f.* prostitute, whore.

example: Edouard a une nouvelle petite amie et tout le monde sait qu'elle est **pute** sauf lui!

translation: Edward a a new girlfriend and everyone knows she's a **prostitute** except for him!

as spoken: Edouard, <u>il</u> a une nouvelle <u>p'</u>tite amie et tout <u>l'</u>monde sait qu'elle est **pute** sauf lui!

SYNONYM: **putain** *f.*

ramasser la chtouille *exp.* to catch a venereal disease, to catch the "clap."

example: La première fois que j'ai eu des rapports sexuels, j'ai **ramassé la chtouille**.

translation: The first time I had sex, I **got the clap**.

as spoken: La première fois qu<u>'</u>j'ai eu des rapports sexuels, j'ai **ramassé la chtouille**.

ras le cul (en avoir) *exp.* a harsh expression meaning "to be fed up" • (lit.): to have had it up to one's ass.

example: Maurice, il a encore menti? Oh, j'**en ai ras le cul**!

translation: Maurice lied again? Oh, I've **had it**!

as spoken: Maurice, <u>il</u> a encore menti? Oh, j'**en ai ras <u>l'</u>cul**!

rasoir (être) *adj.* to be boring
• (lit.): to be rasor.

example: Mon nouveau professeur de biologie est tout à fait **rasoir**. J'ai du mal à rester éveillé dans sa classe.

translation: My new biology teacher is totally **boring**. I have trouble staying awake in his class.

as spoken: Mon nouveau prof~ de bio~, il est tout à fait **rasoir**. J'ai du mal à rester éveillé dans sa classe.

rencart *m.* (from *rendez-vous*) date.

example: Je dois me dépêcher. J'ai un **rencart** avec Maurice dans une heure!

translation: I have to hurry. I have a **date** with Maurice is one hour!

as spoken: J'dois m'dépêcher. J'ai un **rencart** avec Maurice dans une heure!

> **NOTE -1:** Also spelled: *rencard*.
> **NOTE -2:** **rencarter** *v.* to have a date with someone.

renifler quelqu'un (ne pas pouvoir) *v.* to be unable to stand someone • (lit.): to be unable to sniff someone (since the mere smell of the person would be too much to bear).

example: Je ne vais pas inviter Suzanne à ma soirée. Je **ne peux pas la renifler**.

translation: I'm not going to invite Suzanne to my party. I **can't stand her**.

as spoken: J'vais pas inviter Suzanne à ma soirée. J'**peux pas la renifler**.

Retournez dans votre banlieue de merde! *exp.* an insulting meaning "Get the fuck out of here!" • (lit.): Go back to your suburb.

example: Arrêtez de gueuler et **retournez dans votre banlieue de merde**!

translation: Stop screaming and **get the fuck out of here**!

as spoken: Arrêtez d'gueuler et **retournez dans vot' banlieue d'merde**!

rien à foutre *exp.* no way, nothing doing • (lit.): nothing to fuck.

example: Tu veux que j'aille chercher Christophe à l'aéroport?! **Rien à foutre**! La dernière fois, ça m'a mis deux heures avec les embouteillages et en plus, il ne m'a même pas remercié!

translation: You want me to go pick up Christopher at the airport?! **No fuckin' way**! The last time, it took me two hours with all the traffic and not only that, he didn't even thank me!

as spoken: Tu veux qu'j'aille chercher Christophe à l'aéroport?! **Rien à foutre**! La dernière fois, ça m'a mis deux heures avec les embouteillages et en plus, y~ m'a même pas r'mercié!

roi des cons *exp.* the king of jerks • (lit.): [same].

example: Pourquoi as-tu invité Albert à nous joindre? C'est le **roi des cons**!

translation: Why did you invite Albert to join us? He's the **king of jerks**!

as spoken: Pourquoi t'as invité Albert à nous joindre? C'est l'**roi des cons**!

rouler une pelle *exp.* to deep-kiss with the tongue, to "French" kiss • (lit.): to roll a shovel.

example: Quand il m'a fait un baiser, il m'a **roulé une pelle**!

translation: When he kissed me, he **slipped me his tongue**!

as spoken: Quand y m'a fait un baiser, y m'a **roulé une pelle**!

SYNONYM: **rouler une escalope** *exp.* • (lit.): to roll a thin slice of meat.

saloperie *f.* • **1.** said of something nasty done to someone • **2.** piece of junk.

example (1): Je ne parle plus à Richard. Il m'a fait une **saloperie**.

translation: I'm not speaking to Richard anymore. He did **something really nasty** to me.

as spoken: J'parle pu à Richard. Y m'a fait une **salop'rie**.

example (2): Tu as vu la robe qu'elle porte, Nancy? Elle a payé deux cent dollars cette **saloperie**!

translation: Did you see the dress Nancy's wearing? She paid two hundred dollars for that **piece of junk**!

as spoken: T'as vu la robe qu'è porte, Nancy? Elle a payé deux cent dollars c'te **salop'rie**!

schlinguer *v.* to stink.

example: Je n'aime pas ce fromage parce que ça **schlingue**!

translation: I don't like this cheese because it **stinks**.

as spoken: J'aime pas c'fromage pasque ça **schlingue**!

SIDA *m.* an abbreviation for *Syndrome Immuno-Déficitaire Acquis* meaning "AIDS (Acquired Immune Deficiency Syndrome)."

example: Marie n'est pas du tout prudente. Un de ces jours, elle va sûrement finir par attraper le **SIDA**.

translation: Marie isn't careful at all. One of these days, she's definitely going to end up catching **AIDS**.

as spoken: Marie, elle est pas du tout prudente. Un d'ces jours, è va sûrement finir par attraper l'**SIDA**.

ta gueule *exp.* shut up •
(lit.): your mouth.

example: **Ta gueule**! Tu
commences à m'énerver!

translation: **Shut up**! You're
starting to annoy me!

as spoken: [no change]

tapin (faire le) *exp.* to work
the streets (said of a prostitute).

example: La pauvre. Elle **fait le
tapin** pour gagner sa vie.

translation: The poor thing. She
works the streets to earn
her living.

as spoken: La pauvre. **È fait
l'tapin** pour gagner sa vie.

tignasse *f.* hair.

example: Je vais me faire couper
la **tignasse**.

translation: I'm going to get my
hair cut.

as spoken: J'vais m'faire couper
la **tignasse**.

SYNONYM: **tifs** *m.pl.*

tombeur *m.* a womanizer,
seducer, "Don Juan" • (lit.): a
faller (i.e. girls fall before him or
under his charm).

example: Eric va se marier?!
Mais c'est un sacré **tombeur**,
celui-là! Ça m'étonnerait qu'il
soit content avec une seule fille
dans sa vie.

translation: Eric is getting
married?! But the guy's a real
womanizer! It'd really surprise
me if he were happy with just
one girl in his life.

as spoken: Eric, y va s'marier?!
Mais c't'un sacré **tombeur**,
çui-là! Ça m'étonn'rait qu'y soit
content avec une seule fille dans
sa vie.

SYNONYM: **dragueur** *m.*

NOTE: **draguer** *v.* to cruise
(for guys or girls), to flirt.

torche-cul *m.* toilet paper,
"ass-wipe" • (lit.): wipe-ass.

example: La dernière fois que je
suis allé faire du camping, j'avais
complètement oublié d'apporter
le **torche-cul**.

translation: The last time I went
camping, I totally forgot to bring
toilet paper.

as spoken: La dernière fois
qu'j'suis allé faire du camping,
j'avais complètement oublié
d'apporter l'**torche-cul**.

SYNONYM: **pécul** *m.* an
abbreviation of *papier-cul*
meaning "toilet paper" or
literally, "ass paper."

tremper (la) *exp.* to fornicate •
(lit.): to dip it in.

example: Tu as entendu les
nouvelles? Albert **la trempe**
avec une nana deux fois plus
âgée que lui.

translation: Did you hear the
news? Albert **is having sex**
with a woman twice as old as he
is.

as spoken: T'as entendu les nouvelles? Albert, y **la trempe** avec une nana deux fois plus âgée qu'lui.

NOTE: In this expression, *la* represents *la pine* meaning "penis."

trou *m.* place in general, "joint" • (lit.): hole.

example: Je refuse d'entrer dans ce **trou**. C'est plein de fumeurs!

translation: I refuse to go into that **joint**. It's full of smokers!

as spoken: Je r'fuse d'entrer dans c'**trou**. C'est plein d'fumeurs!

trouille (avoir la) *exp.* to be scared to death.

example: J'ai eu **la trouille** quand j'ai vu le voleur!

translation: I was **scared to death** when I saw the thief!

as spoken: J'ai eu **la trouille** quand j'ai vu l'voleur!

tuer les mouches à quinze pas *exp.* said of someone who has bad breath • (lit.): to kill flies fifteen feet away.

example: Oh, ce chien! Il **tue les mouches à quinze pas**, lui!

translation: Oh, this dog! He has **horrible breath**!

as spoken: Oh, c'chien! Y **tue les mouches à quinze pas**, lui!

valoir un pet de lapin (ne pas) *exp.* not to be worth a red cent • (lit.): not to be worth a rabbit's fart.

example: Tu as vu le collier que Nicole a porté à la soirée? Elle se vantait que son mari l'a payé une fortune mais ça sautait aux yeux que ça **ne valait pas un pet de lapin**!

translation: Did you the see that necklace Nicole wore to the party? She was bragging that her husband paid a fortune for it but it was obvious that it wasn't **worth shit**.

as spoken: T'as vu l'collier qu'Nicole a porté à la soirée? È s'vantait qu'son mari, y l'a payé une fortune mais ça sautait aux yeux qu'ça ~ **valait pas un pet d'lapin**!

NOTE: *sauter aux yeux* *exp.* to be obvious • (lit.): to jump to the eyes.

vieux bonze *m.* old man, an "old fart" • (lit.): old buddhist monk.

example: Carole est très jeune et très jolie. Je ne sais pas pourquoi elle sort avec un **vieux bonze** comme celui-là.

translation: Carole is very young and very pretty. I don't know why she goes out with an **old fart** like him.

as spoken: Carole, <u>elle</u> est très
jeune et très jolie. <u>C'hais</u> pas
pourquoi <u>è</u> sort avec un **vieux
bonze** comme <u>ç</u>'ui-là.

Zut alors! *interj.* Darn!

example: **Zut alors**! J'ai laissé
mes clés au restaurant!

translation: **Darn**! I left my keys at
the restaurant!

as spoken: **Zut alors**! J'ai laissé
mes clés au <u>resto</u>!

NOTE: *Zut* may also be used all by
itself. However, *alors* is commonly
used for extra emphasis.

PLEASE SEE ORDER FORM ON OTHER SIDE!

ORDER FORM

SLANGMAN PUBLISHING

12206 Hillslope Street
Studio City, CA 91604 • USA

INTERNATIONAL:
1-818-769-1914

TOLL FREE (US/Canada):
1-877-SLANGMAN
(1-877-752-6462)

Worldwide FAX:
1-413-647-1589

Get the latest news, preview chapters, and shop online at:

WWW.SLANGMAN.COM

SHIPPING

Domestic Orders
SURFACE MAIL
(delivery time 5-7 days).
Add $5 shipping/handling for the first item, $1 for each additional item.

RUSH SERVICE
available at extra charge. Please telephone us for details.

International Orders
OVERSEAS SURFACE
(delivery time 6-8 weeks).
Add $5 shipping/handling for the first item, $2 for each additional item.
Note that shipping to some countries may be more expensive. Please contact us for details.

OVERSEAS AIRMAIL
available at extra charge. Please phone for details.

PRODUCT	TYPE	PRICE	QTY	TOTAL
AMERICAN SLANG & IDIOMS				
STREET SPEAK 1:	book	$18.95		
Complete Course in American Slang & Idioms	cassette	$12.50		
STREET SPEAK 2:	book	$21.95		
Complete Course in American Slang & Idioms	cassette	$12.50		
STREET SPEAK 3:	book	$21.95		
Complete Course in American Slang & Idioms	cassette	$12.50		
SPANISH SLANG & IDIOMS				
STREET SPANISH 1:	book	$16.95		
The Best of Spanish Slang	cassette	$12.50		
STREET SPANISH 2:	book	$16.95		
The Best of Spanish Idioms	cassette	$12.50		
STREET SPANISH 3:	book	$16.95		
The Best of Naughty Spanish	cassette	$12.50		
STREET SPANISH DICTIONARY & THESAURUS	book	$16.95		
FRENCH SLANG & IDIOMS				
STREET FRENCH 1:	book	$16.95		
The Best of French Slang	cassette	$12.50		
STREET FRENCH 2:	book	$16.95		
The Best of French Idioms	cassette	$12.50		
STREET FRENCH 3:	book	$16.95		
The Best of Naughty French	cassette	$12.50		
STREET FRENCH DICTIONARY & THESAURUS	book	$16.95		
ITALIAN SLANG & IDIOMS				
STREET ITALIAN 1:	book	$16.95		
The Best of Italian Slang	cassette	$12.50		
STREET ITALIAN 2:	book	$16.95		
The Best of Naughty Italian	cassette	$12.50		

Total for Merchandise	
Sales Tax *(California Residents Only add current sales tax %)*	
Shipping *(See Left)*	
ORDER TOTAL	

prices subject to change

Name _____

(School/Company) _____

Street Address _____

City _____ State/Province _____ Postal Code _____

Country _____ Phone _____ Email _____

METHOD OF PAYMENT (CHECK ONE)

☐ Personal Check or Money Order *(Must be in U.S. funds and drawn on a U.S. bank.)*
☐ VISA   ☐ Master Card   ☐ Discover

Credit Card Number

Expiration Date

⬆ **Signature** *(important!)*